RELIGION AND SECURITY

RELIGION AND SECURITY
The New Nexus in International Relations

Edited by
Robert A. Seiple
and
Dennis R. Hoover

ROWMAN & LITTLEFIELD PUBLISHERS, INC.
Lanham • Boulder • New York • Toronto • Oxford

ROWMAN & LITTLEFIELD PUBLISHERS, INC.

Published in the United States of America
by Rowman & Littlefield Publishers, Inc.
A wholly owned subsidiary of The Rowman & Littlefield Publishing Group, Inc.
4501 Forbes Boulevard, Suite 200, Lanham, Maryland 20706
www.rowmanlittlefield.com

PO Box 317
Oxford
OX2 9RU, UK

British Library Cataloguing in Publication Information Available

Library of Congress Cataloging-in-Publication Data

Religion and security : the new nexus in international relations / edited by Robert
A. Seiple and Dennis R. Hoover.
    p. cm.
  Includes bibliographical references and index.
  ISBN 0-7425-3211-9 (alk. paper) — ISBN 0-7425-3212-7 (pbk. : alk. paper)
  1. Security, International—Religious aspects. 2. Religion and international
affairs. I. Seiple, Robert A., 1942– II. Hoover, Dennis.
  BL65.S375R45 2004
  201'.727—dc22
                          2004012243

Printed in the United States of America

♾™ The paper used in this publication meets the minimum requirements of American
National Standard for Information Sciences—Permanence of Paper for Printed Library
Materials, ANSI/NISO Z39.48-1992.

Contents

They have ffreely declared, that it is much on their hearts . . . to hold forth a livlie experiment, that a most flourishing civill state may stand and best bee maintained . . . with a full libertie in religious concernements; and that true pietye rightly grounded upon gospell principles, will give the best and greatest security to sovereignetye.

—Rhode Island Colonial Charter, 1663

Treat religious freedom as a security issue, not just a human rights issue.

—International Crisis Group, 2001

Foreword

A T THE OUTSET OF THE NEW MILLENNIUM, few would have predicted the dramatic change that lay ahead for the United States. In the blink of an eye, the sleeping giant was rudely awakened, and any opportunity for further hibernation was foreclosed for some time to come. The signs of change are far-reaching: small-town newspapers often resemble regional surveys of the Middle East, militant Islam and evacuation routes are subjects for discussion at town hall meetings, and working-class families debate the nuances of American foreign policy over dinner.

As the United States (and the West more generally) seeks to deal with this new world in which religion has become a major force on the international stage, it finds itself operating at a distinct disadvantage. While the specter of weapons of mass destruction married to religious extremism has rightfully become the overriding concern of most defense planners, policymakers and diplomats alike labor under tight constraints that are designed to keep matters of church and state separate and apart. If we as a nation are to navigate this new labyrinth with any degree of competence, we will need to reexamine

Douglas Johnston is founder and president of the International Center for Religion and Diplomacy in Washington, D.C. He has served as Deputy Assistant Secretary of the Navy, Director of Policy Planning and Management in the Office of the Secretary of Defense, founder and Director of Harvard University's Executive Program in National and International Security, and most recently, as Executive Vice President and COO of the Center for Strategic and International Studies. Among his publications are *Faith-Based Diplomacy: Trumping Realpolitik* (Oxford, 2003) and *Religion, the Missing Dimension of Statecraft* (Oxford, 1994).

these constraints and make the necessary concessionary adjustments. We also need to empower and bring to bear more effectively those assets we currently have at our disposal that are relevant to this new reality.

Before any of the above can happen, however, national security and foreign policy practitioners must begin to treat religion as a serious variable in the conduct of international relations. Our past disregard for religious considerations has left the United States ill-equipped to deal with religious differences in hostile settings (such as we are now confronting in Iraq) or with demagogues who manipulate religion for their own purposes, as did Slobodan Milosevic in Serbia. By way of contrast, the French, when bogged down militarily in the Algerian war for independence, often sent their military chaplains to negotiate with the Muslim insurgents. Thus, even those who gave birth to modern-day secularism understand the need to deal with religious imperatives.

To help address these blind spots, this book provides a much-needed call to arms. It also makes a persuasive case for why religious freedom—as one of the above imperatives—should be treated as a defining element of national security. Unless nation-states give full rein to religious expression, they risk falling victim to political unrest and instability. Further, or stated a bit differently, this book argues that religious freedom actively enhances a nation's security by offering inclusion in political life to elements that might otherwise be excluded. Finally, chief among the other telling points that this book raises, is the attention it calls to the often-overlooked potential of engaging religious leaders in efforts to avoid or abate conflict.

As for the earlier-mentioned concessionary adjustments, one possibility would involve creating a new position within the U.S. Foreign Service: a religion attaché who could be assigned to diplomatic missions in those countries where religion has particular salience. In addition to reporting on relevant religious movements, these attachés could help U.S. missions deal more effectively with complex religious issues that typically get short shrift because of other seemingly more pressing business. A cadre of thirty such attachés at an approximate annual cost of ten million dollars could cover the globe and greatly enhance our ability to anticipate new religious developments and their prospective impact on the conduct of international relations.

Among the assets we already have at our disposal that could be brought to bear in more helpful ways are the chaplain corps of the U.S. military services. Historically, the role of military chaplains has been one of addressing the spiritual needs of the men and women of the command to which they are attached. With additional training and expanded rules of engagement, however, they could significantly enhance their command's ability to deal with the religious dimension of military operations.

Through greater and more effective interaction with local religious communities and nongovernmental organizations, chaplains could develop an improved understanding of the religious and cultural nuances at play and help identify incipient threats to stability posed by religious frictions or ethnoreligious demagogues. At times, they might also be able to provide a reconciling influence in addressing misunderstandings or difficulties that may arise between the commands and local communities. Finally, they could provide informed and politically sensitive advice to their commanders on the religious and cultural implications of operational decisions that are about to be taken or that should be taken. In other words, in addition to their ongoing function of addressing human casualties after conflict has erupted, chaplains could and should be viewed as important tools for preventing its eruption in the first instance.

As the events of September 11, 2001, suggest and as this book confirms, the stakes are enormous and the need for action is urgent. No longer can we afford to underestimate religious concerns in the practice of international politics. No longer can we afford the luxury of uninformed foreign policy choices.

Douglas Johnston
April 2004

Introduction: Religion Gets Real

Dennis R. Hoover

J UST AS THERE ARE FEW ATHEISTS IN FOXHOLES, in the wake of the terrorist attacks of September 11, 2001, there are few scholars and practitioners of international relations who subscribe to secularization theory. Of course, the assumption of secularization theory—that as modernization advanced, the
salience of religion would recede—was being challenged from many disciplinary angles well before 9/11. Already in the 1980s it had become de rigueur in
articles and books about "culture wars" in American politics to make intro-
ductory remarks about the hapless record of the theory. By contrast, professional discourse about international politics, at least in the West, was somewhat slower to take religion seriously (this notwithstanding the splash made
by the "clash of civilizations" debate in the mid-1990s). But 9/11 was a great
leveler among observers of international affairs, specialists and spectators
alike. Most such observers came simultaneously to a simple, if not simplistic,
realization: "There are religious fanatics trying to kill us."

Thus jolted into a consensus that religion matters, it is perhaps no surprise
that in the ensuing discussion the nexus of religion and security has been approached mostly in negative terms. That is, security imperatives are, by necessity, at the top of the agenda, and the definitions and paradigms of security are
changing in ways that often implicate religion. Especially for Americans, the
word "security" used to connote very clear and tangible military images—here,
a tank; there, a war between armies; all of it overseas. Then 9/11 happened: educated suicidals, in the name of religion, attacked the United States in ways its
military could not defend against. Now the images are much different, but no

less palpable—here, a metal detector; there, the postal worker's rubber gloves; all of it within our borders.

The result has been a new urgency about understanding the ways that violent religious radicalism (often inaccurately described as religious "fundamentalism") can threaten security. And Exhibit A in our display case of security nightmares is, of course, Islamist radicalism. Prior to 9/11 most Westerners assumed this particular threat was mainly an issue of rogue states in the Middle East. Today no one doubts that religious nonstate actors like al Qaeda and its ilk are truly global players to be reckoned with as well. Nor does violence within and between other religious traditions seem quite as far off as it once did, be it Hindus in conflict with Muslims (India), Jews in conflict with Muslims (the West Bank), Christians in conflict with Jews and Muslims (Eastern Europe), or Christians in conflict with Christians (Northern Ireland).

Unfortunately, while there is now broad consensus that the security establishment needs a strategy for containing and reducing violent religious radicalism, there is less understanding of the multiple nuances, alternatives, and dilemmas involved. There has been, perhaps understandably, much anger in the West directed at societies that harbor religious radicals; we wonder why governments in these places cannot (or will not) crack down and keep their own house in order. But if we take the time to understand how religion really works, we can see how crackdowns employing only "hard power" methodologies can be counterproductive. Consider, for instance, Central Asia. In Afghanistan under the Taliban, we witnessed a religiously intolerant regime blow up world-treasured Buddhist monuments, pin yellow stars on Hindus, and provide sanctuary to other intolerant Islamic terrorist groups that eventually attacked the United States as well as other Central Asian countries. With no history of statehood, let alone pluralism, Central Asian governments responded to these terrorist attacks by repressing their citizens' right to worship. In Uzbekistan, for example, as Chris Seiple and Joshua White note in this volume, a reactionary dragnet has oppressed many pious but otherwise nonthreatening Muslims. In turn, this repression has ironically created the very environment that terrorists seek, one without mechanisms for political grievance as moderates become receptive to more radical means.

It is an oft-repeated cycle in our world, and in order to break it our analytical paradigms will need to go beyond naïve versions of secularization theory. But that is only a start. We will also need to think more holistically about both religion and security. Most importantly, we must not limit our examination of the nexus between religion and security to threat assessments: religion is not only part of the problem; it is part of the solution.

The product of a national conference convened in 2003 by the Institute for Global Engagement, this book takes as its point of departure the following thesis: nations that do not foster respect for religion will be vulnerable to a number of significant threats to stability and security. Conversely, nations that find a way to protect a principled, robust religious pluralism in civil society are the most likely to enjoy genuinely sustainable security. There is, put simply, a positive nexus between religion and security, and the international community ignores it at its considerable peril. The hard-nosed, security-conscious realists have not always had much in common with the human rights community, as the two typically regard each other with suspicion. The tragic irony is that, especially with respect to religious human rights, they are often two sides of the same coin.

This topic comes at a dramatic point in history as governments reconsider their role in the world and the security they provide for their citizens, and nongovernmental organizations reconsider their strategies of engagement. Only ten years ago, religious freedom was discussed in mostly domestic terms in the context of highly politicized and tired debates (like school prayer) in the culture war. Now we know we are in a real war, a war of mortars and minds that is simultaneously intranational, transnational—and religious.

While not ignoring tensions between religion and security, this volume's charge is foremost the exploration of positive nexus points, with a particular emphasis on resources within the Abrahamic faith traditions—Judaism, Christianity, and Islam—for recognizing and acting on such nexus points. The present war on terrorism has been described by some as a "civilization conflict" that both reflects and exacerbates security problems between these Abrahamic traditions. The challenge to diplomacy is great, but constructive responses will arise by facing religious differences, not papering over them. The distinguished contributors to this volume bring diverse perspectives and expertise to bear, yet they agree that ultimately, sustainable solutions to these problems will be achieved not in spite of faith-based engagement in international affairs but precisely because of it.

The call to "bring religion back in" to the study and praxis of international affairs is not entirely new. Indeed, Douglas Johnston and Cynthia Sampson's influential 1994 volume, *Religion, the Missing Dimension of Statecraft*, helped start a wave in the literature that has yet to crest. Unfortunately, however, many studies still err on the side of disciplinary insularity and theoretical esoterica. To be sure, specialization is entirely appropriate in some contexts; but religion in international politics is not one of them. Especially outside the West, where notions of compartmentalizing or privatizing faith are often entirely alien, religion's relevance operates at multiple levels; therefore, so must those who would study the role of religion in global public life. Focused interdisciplinary approaches are needed—approaches that find a common language for the professional discourses of international relations and religion.

Influenced by Johnston and Sampson's work, some international relations specialists have paid lip service to the need to bring faith-based voices directly into the conversation, but too few have found a way to actually do it. Likewise, faith-based communities have too often contributed only moral platitudes on the margins of international relations, rather than engaging the field in depth, thereby earning an actual place at the table. This volume expands the table by bringing together under a unified theme leading scholars and practitioners in security, diplomacy, conflict resolution, human rights, and theology. It differs from existing literature not only in its balanced exploration of religion and security, but also in its candid approach to the incorporation of faith-based voices from the Abrahamic faith traditions. The interaction of these traditions is very much at the center of many of today's pressing security issues.

Divided into four sections, *Religion and Security* is designed to address sequentially four integral thematic couplings: (1) religious violence and religious repression, (2) religious pluralism and political stability, (3) religious influences on military intervention and postconflict reconciliation, and (4) religious freedom and civil society. The chapters in section I, "Religion and (In)Security: The Twenty-first Century Challenge," describe the key problems and dilemmas of the religion-and-security nexus in contemporary international affairs. Here the risks of misunderstanding either the peril or the promise of religion's influence are compellingly detailed. The remaining sections of the book then address in turn different dimensions of the interdependence between the flourishing of religion and a healthy stability in political society. These chapters break new ground and challenge conventional wisdom about the ability of religion—including religion that is taken seriously, even literally—to have practical relevance in the effort to build sustainable security and to advance human dignity.

In chapter 1, Pauletta Otis surveys the contemporary state of analysis and discourse regarding religion as a factor in security threats and war. She argues that both the U.S. government and the faith-based community tend to address religious issues and actors "in an ad hoc, haphazard, and superficial way." Reviewing the ways in which transnational religion and globalization are changing the traditional assumptions of the Westphalian state system, Otis concludes that "a useful appraisal of the role of religion in warfare will not be limited to a simplistic cause-effect equation (vis-à-vis the motivations of individual combatants) but will add a nuanced approach to religion's contributory effects in dynamic relationship to other factors."

In chapter 2, Philip Jenkins discusses "The Politics of Persecuted Religious Minorities" and argues that "the experience of religious minorities under persecution constitutes a major, if under-explored, element of the explanation of why some processes of nation-building fail." He explains that persecution often creates an embittered minority that is subversive and receptive to the idea of religious violence. Under pressure, the persecuted community may come to see itself as an agent of divine retribution upon the persecutors, creating political unrest, refusing to contribute to national life, or even becoming obsessive about martyrdom.

In chapter 3, a case study of the "crucible of religion and security" that illustrates many of the themes discussed by Otis and Jenkins, Chris Seiple and Joshua White analyze Central Asia generally, and Uzbekistan in particular. Whereas prior to 9/11 many Americans would have had trouble locating the region on a map, the war in Afghanistan against the Taliban and al Qaeda has demonstrated that Central Asia is one of the most geopolitically important contexts of our time. Uzbekistan's experience trying to constrain Islamic militancy via a counterproductive crackdown also highlights the delicate balance of religious freedom and security.

Section II, "Perspectives on Pluralism: Making a World Safe for Diversity," begins with Manfred T. Brauch's chapter on Abrahamic pluralism in theological perspective. He argues that the diversity of the Abrahamic family will only offer authentic and stable security when all members—especially theologians from each branch of the family—find the courage to deal honestly with areas of common ground in scripture, thereby enabling the choice of "embrace" over "exclusion" in a way that does not sacrifice theological integrity. His primary example is the Abrahamic scriptural legacy of the prophet Isaiah, whose radical vision of blessing and reconciliation for the historic enemies Assyria, Israel, and Egypt was often deliberately mistranslated to suggest ethnoreligious exclusivity.

In chapter 5, Christopher A. Hall further explores themes of pluralism and stability from a specifically Christian perspective, while in chapter 6 Osman bin Bakar does the same from his position in the Islamic tradition. Hall argues against the view that holding and advocating ultimate Truth claims is necessarily incompatible with pluralism. Offering a "Christian dialogical perspective" on the virtues required in good "religious diplomacy," Hall argues: "Pretending differences do not exist, or worse that they don't really mean anything, will not result in consensus 'rules of the game' for pluralism; now more than ever, these norms of discourse are essential for linking religion positively to sustainable security." Bakar then describes an Islamic foundation for pluralism and religious freedom based on his analysis of Qur'anic injunctions such as "there is no compulsion in religion" and of traditions of Islamic discourse and diversity. He contends that true Islam requires not just grudging, temporary acceptance but genuine respect and peaceful coexistence.

Section III, "Into the Breach: Restoring Sustainable Security," offers chapters by Jean Bethke Elshtain and Marc Gopin. Each examines different ways in which faith-based perspectives can help shape a constructive response to the reality of violent conflict. Elshtain looks at the issue from the vantage point of imminent or ongoing conflict, while Gopin's analysis is focused mainly on postconflict responses. Elshtain explores the meaning of "justice" in situations when military intervention is needed to restore even rudimentary security. Her thesis is that security "can in fact be made more sustainable if military intervention is guided not by classic realpolitik nor by naïve humanitarianism but by a religiously grounded philosophy of *justice as equal regard.*" In chapter 8, "When the Fighting Stops: Healing Hearts with Spiritual Peacemaking," Gopin argues that while much theological effort is typically expended on the question of what makes for a "just war," regrettably little emphasis is placed on the spiritual dimensions of conflict resolution. Drawing on his extensive expertise as a scholar and practitioner of reconciliation, he argues that emotions and spirituality are a crucial aspect of making peace and security. "It is a matter not just of theory but of practical results," he writes.

The final section of the book unpacks the assertion that religious freedom is the linchpin of civil society, which in turn upholds stability. In chapter 9, Kevin J. Hasson looks at the philosophy and "public anthropology" of a civil society consensus on the value of religious freedom, despite profound differences between religious worldviews. The key, according to Hasson, is to recognize that an essential part of human nature—and of human dignity—is a built-in "thirst for the transcendent." Consequently he argues that "a state that accommodates the religious aspirations of its citizenry promotes stability and security for a very simple reason: such a state accurately recognizes who its citizens are."

In chapter 10, "Relational Realism," Harold H. Saunders advocates replacing the state-based realpolitik paradigm with a new, relational paradigm capable of appreciating the significance of civil society in negotiating contextually appropriate balances between religious freedom and security. He draws on his knowledge and experience of Tajikistan to illustrate the necessity of an intentional process of "sustained dialogue" in the real-world politics and diplomacy of religious freedom in difficult environments.

Finally, in the concluding chapter, "A Lively Experiment, A Most Flourishing Civil State," Robert A. Seiple contends that "just as the true test of a government's commitment to liberal democracy is tolerance for opposition parties, the true test of commitment to civil society is religious freedom." He uses diverse illustrations—from ancient Egypt to the colonial Rhode Island Charter to modern-day Mogadishu—to warn today's oppressors that violations of religious freedom in the name of "security" inevitably subvert real security. Integrating many of the themes emphasized throughout the volume, he argues that a mature civil society, with a cornerstone of religious freedom, is a guarantor of genuine security for all.

Collaborative in aims and methodologies, this volume is about helping to inculcate a new security culture that recognizes the complexity and interconnectedness of contemporary global problems, and the value of seeing "disparate" issues—like religious freedom and security—as two components woven of the same cloth. Positive nexus points between religion and security abound. But to recognize and act on them in such a time as this, we need fresh perspectives on all sides—geopolitically, militarily, theologically.

RELIGION AND (IN)SECURITY: THE TWENTY-FIRST CENTURY CHALLENGE

Religion and War in the Twenty-first Century

Pauletta Otis

THE TWENTY-FIRST CENTURY will be a time of religious violence and warfare. Indeed, as religious zealots and opportunists use the power inherent in religious ideology to escalate the forms, levels, and types of violence, there is potential for devastation and destruction previously unknown in human history. Although religion has long been recognized as one factor, among many, relevant to discussions of security and warmaking (for example, the *jus ad bellum* and *jus in bello* criteria of just war theory), it is now emerging (or rather, re-emerging) as the single most important political-ideological default mechanism in global conflict. Yet the Western world has had trouble coming to terms with this reality. Some scholars maintain that the West has often been self-blinded to the reality of global religious issues because it is beholden to an ahistorical vision of a "secular" state and therefore unable to provide a full explanation of contemporary warfare. Conversely, others contend that the Western world is only too aware of history—but it merely shudders at the tragic mistakes of past generations without taking proactive steps to learn from them.[1]

Pauletta Otis is professor of strategic studies at the Joint Military Intelligence College. Recently retired from the Colorado State University system where she was professor of international relations, she maintains an active speaking and publication agenda. She has lectured at the National War College, U.S. Marine Corps, U.S. State Department, Defense Intelligence Agency, and CENTCOM. Recent academic and professional publications include "The Academic in the Intelligence Community," in *Bringing Intelligence About* (DIA/Joint Military Intelligence College, 2003), and "Religious Terrorism and the Religious Terrorist" (*Journal of Defense Intelligence*, 2002).

For their part, leaders from each major religious tradition earnestly reiterate that the purpose of religion is love and peace, not killing. Nevertheless, each and every religion is, in important ways, an ideology that provides comprehensive ideals and principles that govern both life and death. Religions not only answer the question, "How should I live?" but also the question, "For what am I willing to kill and die?" Thus, what is true for the foreign policy establishment is no less true for faith-based communities. That is, they can no longer afford to compartmentalize their thinking about religion and conflict, but must seek sound principles based in systematic investigation and awareness of the spiritual dimension.

"A man with an idea is more powerful than 100 men with interests," said John Locke—and when ideas and interests combine, the chemistry can be lethal. It is this combination of religious ideology and group interests that is becoming an increasingly potent force in Africa, Asia, the Middle East, and even the Americas. As the world's hegemonic power, the United States has been involved in many of these conflicts, most notably in the Balkans, Somalia, Afghanistan, and Iraq. In each of these cases, religious factors were a significant part of the enemy's motivation, intent, capabilities, and goals. In addition, global terrorism is increasingly characterized by violence perpetuated by individuals and small groups with religious motivation—using nonconventional weapons, choosing symbolic targets, and judging success by obedience to God.[2]

As the United States becomes increasingly engaged on a global scale, a grim picture emerges of largely conventional forces of the single world superpower fighting various groups of global religious mujahideen in asymmetrical wars where the stakes include economic, political, and cultural power. Still, it would be too simple to resign world events to the inevitability of "doom and gloom." What is needed is the courage and commitment to press through the complexity and to develop balanced perspectives that work in concert with the faith aspects of belief systems rather than simplistically ignoring or condemning them. We are in a global competition for "hearts and minds"—our own and those of our "enemy."

In spite of the immediacy of this requirement, both the U.S. government and the faith-based community have been slow to address religious factors in conflict, war, and terrorism. Too often analysis proceeds in an ad hoc, haphazard, and superficial way. Although a number of conferences have been held and experts (and "instant experts") engaged, the generally low level of integrated knowledge and wisdom reflects the marginalized nature accorded to religion in the conventional discourse of international relations. Given the increasing visibility and importance of religious factors in contemporary conflict situations, this is no longer a preferred or viable option. Of course, no one would seriously suggest that religion is the only explanatory factor in warfare; religion relates to and overlaps with other explanatory variables—specifically economic and political factors. But, whether religion is treated as causal in ideological explanations, or as a contributing factor to other variables, it is an integral piece of the security puzzle and as such, deserves focused attention.

The Traditional U.S. Neglect of Religion in Security Analysis

Until very recently there has been reluctance on the part of the people of the United States to address religion in relationship to national security. There are four major reasons: (1) a preference for the "wall of separation" at both a legal and cultural level; (2) traditional realpolitik analysis; (3) the inherent level of risk in the topic (which makes some rigid institutions avoid the issue); and (4) the potential for political backfire given the sensitivities and sensibilities of the American public.[3]

The first reason is fundamental: in the United States, there has been a tradition in support of a "wall of separation" between religion and politics. For many, the separation of state and religion in politics, albeit not strictly a constitutional wall, has seemed to be an important conflict prevention mechanism.[4] The Framers of the Constitution, well versed in European history, were only too aware of the potential for religious conflict and chaos, and they hoped to set the new nation on a more enlightened path. Even during the Civil War and Spanish American War, the relationship between religion and war was not of the Old World "crusade" variety. Through most of the nation's history there seemed to be a circumspect acknowledgment that although the United States had "Christian" culture and values, institutionalized church-state establishments were inherently problematic. The world's experiences in the twentieth century have also weighed heavily on U.S. attitudes toward the religion-and-politics nexus. In World War I and World War II, there was an unsavory connection between religion and national fascism. The ugly reality was that religion, in this case the Christian religion, was used for demonic purposes. Subsequently religion, albeit universally found as part of culture and society, came to be seen as dangerous when linked to politics (or war) in any way. "Religion," however defined, became suspect and the rules regarding the separation of church and state contested and convoluted.[5]

Secondly, the theoretical approach used by Cold War military analysts was generally that of realpolitik. It was assumed that ideologies such as communism merely masked the reality of state power of countries such as the Soviet Union or China. Thus the study of war became the study of balance of power, replacing an earlier emphasis on the role of ideas with behavioral analysis and quantification of military power. Security analysts typically measured war-making capabilities on the basis of things that are "countable"; the bottom line was weapons systems and uniformed military. Although there were always those who included "strength and will," the scales balanced towards quantification of power.

In the past twenty years, however, the quest for "security" has replaced war aims, and the result has been a more nuanced approach to international power. National security is now seen as a complex arrangement of political, economic, social, and military factors. U.S. military power is hegemonic but it is recognized that even overwhelming military power can accomplish only limited security objectives. The nature of "the enemy," in warfare terms, has changed. Along with that change, the nature of conflict is understood differently; it is no longer conventional force-on-force, but low intensity conflict, asymmetric warfare, and urban warfare. The frame of reference is less about "victory" and more about "prevailing" in a globalized competitive environment.[6]

Thirdly, religion is a delicate and difficult subject. Knowing what the United States needs to know—and why—takes expertise, balance, and mature judgment, qualities not necessarily evenly distributed among U.S. government personnel. There is a significant risk both of misusing religious information and of neglecting religious information. A prevalent concern is that religious information could be used in a cynical manipulation of critical human values. And there is a related concern: individuals within the U.S. government have personal and private religious preferences. It is assumed, given the power of religious belief, that personal agendas might interfere with the task at hand and thereby lead to a corruption or misuse of information. Many worry that finding the "right" people to deal with the religious dimensions of foreign policy—people who are balanced and informed, with integrity and evenhandedness—would be difficult if not impossible.[7]

The fourth reason that the U.S. government has been reluctant to take on religious issues is the sensitivity and potential divisiveness of religious matters where they overlap politics. There is a wide divergence of views within the United States as to the role of religion, politics, and warfare. As such, anyone taking a visible or strong stand can be risking political or professional suicide. There is also a divergence of views in the rest of the world about what U.S. or international military forces should and should not pursue with the use of force. Some contend that military forces should be deployed to confront injustice whenever and wherever it is found—interventions in environmental catastrophes, operations to stem systematic abuses of human rights, preemptive strikes against "rogue" states, campaigns to eliminate tyrants, and so on. Others argue that military force should be used only in defense of territorial borders. Anything resembling agreement on engaging in conflicts that have a religious component would be ephemeral.

Heightening the potential for bitter controversy still further is the widespread tendency toward what we might call "theological overattribution" (i.e., the tendency to attribute all hostility to the theology of an unfamiliar religion.)[8] The singular focus on theology has tended to blind many to the complex relationships between religion, culture, politics, and war in global conflict environments. For example, Aum Shinrikyo is found in Australia, New Zealand, and Japan where there is a great divergence in political, cultural, and economic factors. Likewise, these factors are found in different configurations for Akali Dal in India, the Christian militia in the United States, the new and virulent form of Hindu nationalism in India, Hezbollah and Hamas in the eastern Mediterranean, and millenarian movements throughout Africa and the Pacific. The range of diversity and complexity seems overwhelming. All religions provide reason for living and dying within their respective theologies. But how this is applied varies in specific contextual arrangements. In reality the cultural application of religious principles indicates more about the nature of violence than of basic theology—but most find it easier to just blame an "alien" theology.[9]

There are, in short, many reasons why some have taken the old adage about polite dinner conversation—"never bring up religion or politics"—and applied it to international relations. But even with these cautionary notes, the United States is now a mature hegemonic power, so it is important to "take the risk" in a self-conscious and systematic manner. Faith leaders and foreign policy leaders alike have no alternative but to think these things through very carefully. We must interpret conflictual behaviors in their social, economic, and political context before making spurious judgments.

Security and "Religious" Conflict

Traditional U.S. reticence notwithstanding, the country is now the sole superpower faced with a world that seems increasingly plagued with religious conflict. If faith leaders and security professionals intend to contribute meaningfully to a positive nexus between religion and security, they must first understand the ways in which many contemporary global conflicts are—and are not—religious.

It is apparent that religion plays a critical role in human security, both in preventing and provoking various forms of conflict—from conventional state-vs.-state warfare to unconventional forms of political violence carried out by individuals or groups. More specifically, we must bear in mind that:[10]

- Religion is relevant to all conflict, as it concerns life and death, just war, and justice in war.

- Religious conflicts tend to have higher levels of intensity, severity, brutality, and lethality than other forms of war.
- Wars are longer in duration when religion is a major factor.
- Over half of all contemporary conflicts have a significant religious dimension.
- Religious leaders emerge as primary authority figures under conditions of state failure.
- Religious factors are invariably related to ethnic group identity, language, territory, politics, and economics.
- Religious factors are an essential component of effective conflict management and resolution.

Currently, religious factors play a role in conflicts on all continents and between all major religions.[11] The Hindu and Muslim strains are apparent in Gujarat. The Shi'a-Sunni divisions continue to factor in the Iraq conflict. The Lord's Revolutionary Army in Uganda pits Christians against Christians. In Sudan, the Muslims are said to repress and enslave Christians and animists. In Nigeria, the many ethnic groups have gradually polarized and redefined the ethnic-tribal conflict as basically religious. Aum Shinrikyo in Japan was responsible for the use of chemical weapons in a terrorist attack in a Tokyo subway. The conflict between Israel and Palestine is often held to be a religiously complicated war between Jews and Muslims. Lebanon pits groups identified as religious—Druze, Maronite, Catholic, and Shi'a—against one another. In Eastern Europe, various Christian groups—Orthodox, Catholic, Protestant—have evidenced levels of hatred and hostility not seen since the seventeenth century.[12]

Why now? Religion's emergence as a critical dimension of twenty-first-century warfare is a result of at least three principal dynamics: (1) the seeming failure of other ideologies and institutions; (2) the power of religion in providing ideological resources supporting social justice; and (3) the power of religion in providing an ideological basis for social coherence and comprehensiveness.

In the twentieth century, as the world's problems became more complex and more visible, the solutions available in the ideologies and corresponding programs of Marxism, communism, fascism, nationalism, and materialism became less able to explain injustice or provide programs to ameliorate suffering. Even capitalism and democracy have had significant problems explaining the mismatch between the ideal and the reality to peoples of the so-called Third World. Democracy has succeeded in some places, failed in others, but the important point today is that much of the world believes that democracy will not work *for them*. They believe it works only in the Western context and that it is dependent on exploitative world capitalism. Some also maintain that democracy (even a constitutional democracy) is merely the rule of the majority, and consequently not "moral and ethical." They contend that only the guidance and rules provided by a Supreme Being should structure the political affairs of man.

No one can disagree with the fact that the world remains horribly divided between rich and poor, haves and have-nots. The competing ideologies of the twentieth century that promised hope and a quick fix failed much of the world's population—hence the entrance of religion as "default" ideology, filling the vacuum.

As human attempts are deemed inadequate, recourse to the supernatural power seems to be the only available strategy to ensure both temporal and spiritual security. Religion provides both rationale and modality for fighting against injustice and provides hope when all else has been "tried and failed." This is more than a passive mechanism; religion is reemerging as a new, invigorated, and powerful force in global politics.[13]

Religion is an integrated, systematized set of beliefs, behaviors, values, institutions, modes of communication, and leadership. It institutionalizes transcendence and provides preferred patterns of behavior for human beings in relationship both to a supernatural power and to fellow humans. It is an ideology and a set of normative behaviors reflective of that ideology. Moreover, it derives from an external framework, linking individuals to the greater whole and providing formal institutions that help to define and organize that whole. It provides a meaningful worldview as well as the rules and standards of behavior that connect individual actions and goals to the worldview. It has the ability to legitimize actions and institutions.

Religion as the codification of individual and group behaviors mirroring religious ideology(ies) was institutionalized relatively early in Christian history. The church had responsibility for both secular and spiritual realms; religion was the central ordering social device, and legitimacy came from the church. This was challenged during the Reformation period, when the world saw the emergence of the sovereign state. Its authority became "official" at the Treaty of Westphalia, in 1648, after which the church and the state were to share power.[14]

The power of the state limited the authority of religious institutions; prerogatives of the church were limited by the state. This empowered both while keeping some of their respective, negative aspects at bay. The division of power and authority was essentially codified, and constitutions reflected a fear of the unlimited power of either. The Western world then tried to impose this arrangement on the rest of the world in the form of the "secular state" but with mixed success. Even in Europe and the Americas, where it has seemed more durable, this arrangement is now undergoing significant challenge as a result of globalization. And of course in many other regions around the world, religion and politics have never really been separated. Colonialism and nationalism, to this way of thinking, failed in large part because the Western world did not understand this basic religiocultural reality.

At the same time that assumptions about religion-state separation have come into question, scholarly assumptions concerning the centrality of the state and its monopoly control over the use of force are now also undergoing significant challenge. There are political challenges emanating from the human rights and environmental communities and challenges to military hegemony from both private military enterprises and global terrorists. The power generally attributed to states has been undermined and redistributed in terms of economics, politics, culture, and military capabilities, thereby reshaping and enlarging the definition of international security. Economic, social, and political viability is now dependent on international agreements variously connecting individuals, economies, and societies in networks of complex relationships. There is a growing sense that the state—conceptually and pragmatically—has at best fragmented and at worst failed, because it is no longer keeping pace with an increasingly fluid reality.

In some ways religion has effectively filled this void, uniting populations over state territorial borders and providing social cohesiveness not explainable by any other factor. The emerging cultural fault lines have clear religious boundaries. In short, analysts such as Samuel Huntington and Robert Kaplan are correct when they observe that the importance of ideas and identities (including religious ones) is rising at precisely the same time that political and security systems are becoming fragmented.[15]

For the United States, the writing is on the wall: although commonly acknowledged as the world's dominant superpower, it may be hegemonic only in terms of sheer catastrophic military capabilities. Human security and state power have been redefined in the new global environment.[16]

It is also important to note that even as religion is becoming more important it is becoming less "institutionalized" in the conventional sense. Decision-making authority is now devolving to the individual or small group. Individuals and groups contest the role of formal religion in favor of a more "democratic" religion. In this context, the individual is directly responsible to God rather than to "man-made" religious institutions. Individual transcendence and responsibility take the place of group worship and community involvement. Individuals are no longer responsible to a traditional institution (mosque, synagogue, temple, church) but are encouraged to think for themselves. This is a global phenomenon and examples abound in Africa, North and South America, Europe, South Asia, and the Middle East. In short, the rules that govern warfare are now challenged by individuals who see themselves responsible only to God.[17]

Individuals and groups on all continents and in all social strata have begun constructing a new religious politics based on the relationship between a transcendent being and themselves—bypassing or redefining traditional forms of state/church authority. The new reality is the emergence of particularistic do-it-yourself religion(s), in which some individuals use a peculiar form of logic to perpetuate violence in order to fulfill what they believe is God's will. Thus, the structure of violence and warfare in the modern world is not that of state against state. Rather, it is violence perpetuated by individuals on the global stage in pursuit of transcendent goals—albeit by earthly means.[18]

As Mark Juergensmeyer points out in his book, *Terror in the Mind of God*, the religious terrorist believes that there is a grave social injustice that offends God, that there is a single enemy responsible for the social injustice, that individuals are required to obey God, and that God will approve of actions taken on His behalf.[19] This is pointedly an individualistic premise as opposed to one supported by a traditional, institutionalized religious community. The implication is clear: a focus on mainstream religious beliefs and behaviors is not sufficient to explain current instances of religious violence in the emerging global context. This "democratization" of religion is occurring as part of globalization. It can be identified as emerging out of traditional, mainstream Christian, Jewish, Islamic, Hindu, Buddhist, and Sikh communities, but it is not a direct result of the respective theologies.

The United States must come to terms, then, with the new realities of religious warfare. Care must be taken in the language we use, for it is misleading and alarmist to suggest that contemporary "religious warfare" pits mainstream religions against one another. And there must be a rejection of hyperbole. For example, this is not a period in history where the entire "*umma*" of Islam is fighting the entire "*brotherhood*" of Christianity. Islam has one billion adherents; very few are engaged in any sort of conflict of any kind at any time. Christians are certainly not united in opposition to all Muslims. Not all Hindus hate all Muslims. Buddhists are not always pacifist.

Yet, it is clear that "religion," however defined, plays a role in all conflict and war. After all, one of the major functions of religion is to explain the meaning and value of life and the conditions under which it is justifiable to take life. Therefore, a clear analysis of religion in international security will have empirical and practical value when it keeps crucial distinctions in focus. A useful appraisal of the role of religion in warfare will not be limited to a simplistic cause-effect equation (vis-à-vis the motivations of individual combatants) but will add a nuanced approach to religion's contributory effects in dynamic relationship to other factors.

There are clear cases in which religion contributes to warfare but is not the primary explanatory factor. In Sri Lanka, the Hindu Tamil and Buddhist Sinhalese have had a tragic civil war that seems particularly intransigent. Religion is used as an identity marker, and some religious personages have exacerbated the polarization of the communities by use of incendiary language. Schools and places of worship have been variously destroyed or used as a basis for guerrilla operations. And yet, no one would say that the Sri Lankan conflict is basically about "religion" per se. Ireland is another case in point: the protagonists are separated by religious identity, leaders have been variously contributory to violence and to peace, religious institutions have been used by each as symbols of "the other," and international journalists refer to the parties as "Catholic" and "Protestant." Clearly religion plays a role, but neither side can really claim that the mandate for violence comes from scripture.

Likewise in Uganda, the Lord's Revolutionary Army uses and abuses children in religious rites and practices prior to sending them into battle for causes largely unrelated to religion. In the Sudan, the parties to the conflict are identified as Muslim and Christian, but neither the causes of nor the cures for the conflict will be found exclusively in their respective theologies. In 1991, Saddam Hussein seemingly became "religious" virtually overnight. Al Queda is trying to hijack Islam, but has been condemned by authoritative Islamic clergy. And, who would contend that the current situation in Palestine and Israel is simply based in the Talmud and Qur'an?

Religion is generally a negative contributory variable in conflict when used in conjunction with other factors. For example, religion can be used to rationalize terrorism primarily undertaken for political goals. It can be used to legitimize the use of weaponry designed to inflict maximum suffering, and it can be a mobilizing factor in genocide by defining the enemy in religious terms. Religion is a significant factor in suicide bombing and death squads, providing both a sense of mission and a promise of reward. Religion plays a role in ethnic violence because it typically is one of the major dimensions of group identification. In some societal contexts, it can undermine the state and thereby contribute to state failure when the leaders of the polity are not seen as "religious enough."[20]

Finally, religion should not be analyzed solely in terms of its potential negative effects but must also be studied with regard to its "assets."[21] Religion, more specifically, has power in relation to war and security as a direct result of its control of *resources, interpersonal relationships, communications,* and *expertise.*

The *resources* of religious leaders and institutions include control over goods and services, organizational capabilities, social networks that are community based (but may also be global in scope), and various types of charisma, agendas, and programs. The resources of a particular religion are a direct result of numbers, reputation, coherence, and willingness to mobilize for political/religious purposes.

Religion is also an important power broker in human *relationships*. It helps define the attributes of a good and trustworthy person, prescribes rules concerning how individuals are to transact social, political, and economic business, and identifies "friend" and "enemy" according to its criteria. When states fail, or particular political notables are delegitimatized, religious personages often help define who, when, and under what conditions a new political leader will emerge. Most importantly, religious leaders are also assumed to be in touch with the power of a Supreme Being and therefore to have special insight concerning social relations among God's children.

An additional asset of religion is that it provides for common means of *communication* and language among members of a group. Religious leaders communicate with authority, generally have written and spoken expertise, have access to media, and know significant music, poetry, and art forms of nonverbal, symbolic communication. Religious leaders and institutions are often deeply involved in the education of children and the training of future generations. Parents rely on religious educational and medical institutions when government fails to provide those resources. Historical languages often provide a sense of continuity and may be used to great effect in motivational or in symbolic communication. Religious leaders are also accustomed to keeping confidences or secrets, and are trusted for their discretion. Most importantly, religious leaders often have more grassroots credibility in failed or fragile states than political leaders. They therefore have power above and beyond the sheer strength of numbers or observable resources.

Lastly, religious actors usually have *expertise* that is greater than that of the general population. They have an in-depth knowledge of people, places, and communities. For instance, religious leaders sometimes know more about food, water, and health than others in the community because people in need turn to clergy first. And they typically have intimate knowledge of the sensitivities of their community, including the personal history of community leaders and their families. They move easily in the community and have access to areas off limits to others. Quite literally, they know where the bodies are buried.

Religion, then, is a kind of "force multiplier"—it has significant social-cultural power and is able to affect war and peace more than is commonly recognized. Both on "our" side and the "other" side, religious leaders have the capacity to engage the topic of security, and to use their inherent power to move towards a more peaceful world. But will they actually do it, and will security leaders meet them halfway?

Conclusion

Fortunately, notwithstanding the traditional U.S. aversion to the intermingling of religion and politics, there are now clear signs that the security establishment is interested in the religion-security nexus. Those responsible for U.S. national security are increasingly convinced that religion and war must be addressed in a new, comprehensive, and focused way. Not only did the events of September 11, 2001, provide a tragic, if clarion call, but the wars in Afghanistan and Iraq were telling instances of the consequences of "not knowing."

The White House and Congress have shown enthusiasm for supporting faith-based nongovernmental organizations in aspects of homeland security and peacekeeping operations. The Department of Defense now demonstrates a keen, if belated, interest in religious factors relevant to the Middle East. The Departments of State, Justice, and Homeland Security are engaged in learning about the "religious factor" as it applies to their responsibilities. There have been dozens of conferences in Washington, D.C., that provide a forum for dialogue between government sponsors and faith-based community representatives. Meanwhile, there has been an explosion of attention to topics of religion and warfare in the news media and scholarly journals. The caveat is that public and elite attention can be a two-edged sword. It is important to remain sober, thoughtful, and careful stewards of information and insight; an increase in the *quantity* of attention to religion and security does not necessarily translate into increased *quality*.

As military experts and faith-based scholars are increasingly realizing, religion is not only part of a complex problem, it is also part of a complex solution. Peace is about more than winning against an enemy or merely achieving the cessation of hostilities. Peace is not "made" only after fighting stops. In all stages along the time dimensions of war and peace, religion plays a crucial role. It is an important element in the process of decision-making that precedes hostilities, exerts influence on behavior during the most intense fighting, and is a resource for setting parameters for peace negotiations and reconciliation.

The relevance of this discussion is therefore not limited to protecting and defending the homeland, or even to global U.S. interests. Rather it extends to a genuinely sound analysis of the global politics of security. The complex configuration and interplay of economic, political, social, and religious factors as they relate to war and peace are of concern to all. The fear of ethnoreligious wars, the incomprehensibility of religiously motivated terrorism, the shadow of "clash of civilizations" scenarios—all are on the forefront of world consciousness, and provide motivation for taking the subject of religion very seriously. Put differently, none of the many pressing concerns on the global security agenda—hegemonic state power, pre-emptive strikes, torture (or "torture-lite"), refugees, use of nonlethal weapons by police and security forces, and so on—will be addressed adequately without the careful and prayerful contributions of faith communities. Regardless of country or creed, the dilemmas presented by such questions are challenging for everyone; they go to the heart of the relationship between religion and violence. The answers will require a serious and systematic approach, deep soul-searching, sound theological scholarship, and courageous truth-telling.

Notes

1. In *Religion, the Missing Dimension of Statecraft* (New York: Oxford University Press, 1994) and *Faith-Based Diplomacy: Trumping Realpolitik* (New York: Oxford University Press, 2002), Douglas Johnston makes the point that the religious factor is regularly overlooked in the analysis of both warmaking and peacemaking.

2. In his recent volume, *Terror in the Mind of God: The Global Rise of Religious Violence*, 3rd ed. (Berkeley, CA: University of California Press, 2003), Mark Juergensmeyer provides information and analysis of six terrorist groups. His work provides clear evidence of the global nature of the violence and the fact that all major "global" religions are somehow implicated.

3. There is a rich political and historical literature available on this topic. See Julia Mitchell Corbett's book *Religion in America* (Upper Saddle River, NJ: Prentice Hall, 1990), which provides a nice overview. See also Franklin Gamwell, *The Meaning of Religious Freedom* (Albany, NY: State University Press of New York, 1995), which gives a more theoretical perspective.

4. The United States became a country subsequent to the viscous religious-political European wars of the seventeenth century. As a result, the framers of the U.S. Constitution, historically aware and uncommonly prescient, set out new guidelines for the relationship between church and state—the Establishment Clause and Free Exercise Clause in the First Amendment. The country continues to struggle with the various ramifications of this arrangement and continues to use the courts as a virtual battleground.

5. An illustration of this concerns the rules that apply to military chaplains. Chaplains are in the uniform of their country and therefore political "targets," but because they also wear a religious insignia in relationship to a religious institution, they are specifically precluded from participating in combat. Chaplains, by law, have two conflicting identities and roles.

6. See Barry Buzan, Ole Waever, and Jaap de Wilde's sophisticated treatment of this subject in *Security: A New Framework for Analysis* (Boulder, CO: Lynne Rienner Publishers, 1998).

7. This does not imply that individuals "give up" their own deeply held religious convictions to be of value to U.S. security. It does mean that balance, integrity, and objectivity are guiding principles.

8. For example, violence is often assumed to be intrinsic to the theology, practice, and even co-optation of Islam. This assumption ignores the fact that over one billion people are at least nominally Islamic and only a few are also terrorists. It also is

in denial of the fact that the major religious wars of history have occurred in the Christian countries of Western Europe.

9. Regional experts that focus on religious violence in their area are good sources for specific information. See, for example, Abdullahi Ahmed An-Na'im, ed., *Proselytization and Communal Self-Determination in Africa* (Maryknoll, NY: Orbis, 1999); Christophe Jaffrelot, *The Hindu Nationalist Movement in India* (New York: Columbia University Press, 1998); Krishna Kumar, "Religious Fundamentalism in India and Beyond," *Parameters* (Autumn 2002): 17–33; and Manabu Watanabe, "Religion and Violence in Japan Today: A Chronological and Doctrinal Analysis of Aum Shinrikyo," *Terrorism and Political Violence* 10, no. 4 (Winter 1998): 80–100.

10. These statements represent the author's conclusions and are drawn from a number of different research agendas that include religious, military, historical, and political sources.

11. There is a paucity of good research data and analysis, possibly because scholars tend not to agree on how to define and tabulate statistics on (a) when religion is the primary factor, and/or (b) when religion plays a role in the escalation and maintenance of conflict. Current research tends to be politically or religiously motivated, thus inherently biased.

12. See Jonathan Fox, *Ethnoreligious Conflict in the Late Twentieth Century* (Lanham, MD: Lexington Books, 2002) or his very fine article, "Do Religious Institutions Support Violence or the Status Quo?" *Studies in Conflict and Terrorism* 22, no. 2 (1999): 119–39.

13. In *Ambivalence of the Sacred: Religion, Violence, and Reconciliation* (Lanham, MD: Rowman & Littlefield, 2000), R. Scott Appleby coherently and cogently describes religious "power" to be simultaneously relevant to violence and peacemaking.

14. See John D. Carlson and Erik C. Owens, eds., *The Sacred and the Sovereign* (Washington, DC: Georgetown University Press, 2003).

15. See, for example, Samuel Huntington, *The Clash of Civilizations and the Remaking of World Order* (New York: Simon and Schuster, 1996); Robert Kaplan, *The Coming Anarchy* (New York: Random House, 2000).

16. In 2003 the UN Commission on Human Security published an important global overview, at www.humansecurity-chs.org/finalreport/index.html (accessed 15 April, 2004). The authors define security in terms of people, rather than states. The assumption is that human beings are the essential element of any real definition of security.

17. S. N. Eisenstadt provides an insightful perspective on this topic in his volume, *Fundamentalism, Sectarianism, and Revolution: The Jacobin Dimension of Modernity* (Cambridge: Cambridge University Press, 1999).

18. See Kwame Bediako, "Africa and Christianity on the Threshold of the Third Millennium: the Religious Dimension," *African Affairs* (2002): 303–23.

19. See Juergensmeyer, *Terror in the Mind of God*.

20. Assassination of religious leaders seen as "not quite religious enough" seems to be a recurring pattern in international affairs. Note the deaths of Anwar Sadat, Mohandas Gandhi, and Rajiv Gandhi at the hands of fanatics.

21. See Marc Gopin, *Between Eden and Armageddon: The Future of World Religions, Violence, and Peacemaking* (New York: Oxford University Press, 2002).

2

The Politics of
Persecuted Religious Minorities

Philip Jenkins

History teaches us that men and nations only behave wisely once they've exhausted all other alternatives.

—Abba Eban

D EBATES ABOUT THE FREE EXPRESSION and practice of religion are usually framed in philosophical terms. Virtually no one questions that this freedom is, in principle, a desirable end, though controversy might arise over the precise limitations necessary for public order. Even those least sympathetic in practice to religious freedom tend to praise it in theory. The debate, then, revolves around the best means of securing the maximum degree of religious freedom possible in the circumstances of a given society.[1]

But let us ask a question rarely heard, namely, if a society fails to respect religion, what are the real-world sociopolitical consequences for that society? We may of course stipulate that the "letter of the law"—human rights covenants and international treaties—will of course be offended. But what practical harm might follow? Based on a historical and comparative perspective, I want

Philip Jenkins is Distinguished Professor of History and Religious Studies at Pennsylvania State University. He is the winner of the Theologos award of the Association of Theological Booksellers for the year's Best Academic Book and Penn State's Alumni Teaching Fellow Award. He is the author of many widely cited articles and books, including *Images of Terror: What We Can and Can't Know about Terrorism* (Aldine de Gruyter, 2003) and *The Next Christendom: The Coming of Global Christianity* (Oxford, 2002).

to suggest that a society that limits the religious rights of its subjects might suffer grave and extremely damaging consequences, injuries that may go far beyond those to international prestige or diplomatic favor. Indeed, the experience of religious minorities under persecution constitutes a major, if underexplored, element of the explanation of why some processes of nation-building fail. The politics of persecuted minorities is a topic with far-reaching consequences for national and international security.[2]

We must begin by defining the concept of persecution in the most direct and physical sense, namely an effort by government to repress major activities by a given religious group, commonly with the goal of eliminating that group in the long or short term, or at least reducing its significance to nothing. Naturally, it is often difficult to separate religious persecution from other forms of repression based for instance on ethnicity, race, or political factors. Can one properly describe the Nazi attack on the European Jews as religious in nature? Presumably not, since Jews could not save themselves by converting to another religion, even the religion of the majority of Germans. In that case, we should properly speak of racial rather than religious conflict.

In other conflicts, religious motives might not be wholly explicit, though most observers would agree that they predominated. In early modern England, the persecution of Roman Catholics that prevailed with varying degrees of severity from 1558 to the end of the seventeenth century was never explicitly religious. Rather, Catholics and especially clergy were tortured and executed for their denial of the legitimacy of the state, namely for treason or sedition. The consequence of this policy was, however, explicitly religious, so that whoever said Mass was guilty of treason. By the same standard, we might say that the repression of Shi'ite Islam in a modern nation like the Ba'athist Iraq reflected no religious prejudice, but rather a hostility to the rival political claims of the Shi'ite clergy.[3] As in early modern England, the consequence was still a massive religious and anticlerical persecution. Though a certain leeway must be granted in terms of definition, we will not generally encounter too many difficulties arriving at a reasonable consensus definition.

It should be said at the outset that religious persecution can succeed. If anyone believes that "you can't kill an idea," I would ask that optimistic person to produce a living representative of traditions like the medieval French Cathars or Albigensians, annihilated in wars and successive persecutions during the thirteenth and fourteenth centuries. Or equally, what was the story of Judaism in England during the 360 years following the total expulsion commanded by King Edward I in 1290? There might be isolated instances of crypto-Jews in England, but essentially, a long and significant communal history was snuffed out almost overnight.

But assume that persecution is not so totally successful, that it continues for decades or centuries. Based on numerous examples past and present, a number of themes can be identified that link religious persecution closely to political unrest and instability.

Going Underground

First, and perhaps most significant, persecuted communities are forced to operate clandestinely, where they learn traditions of conspiracy and secret organization. These traditions may not be overtly radical or insurrectionary, but they can create a substantial and potentially dangerous framework that can be exploited by enemies of a state in the long term. Think for instance of some of the underground networks that survived the most devastating persecutions in early modern Europe, groups like the Family of Love and the Anabaptists, and the elaborate informal networks they developed.[4] Neither provided the core of any kind of armed resistance. On the other hand, we think of the modern story of religion under Soviet rule, which especially in the Stalinist era inflicted the most savage persecution upon believers of all kinds. In the Soviet puppet state of Mongolia, for instance, the Buddhist clergy was all but annihilated.

The Muslims proved a much tougher target. While clergy could be killed or compromised, the Soviets found their deadliest enemies in the great Sufi brotherhoods that had done so much to spread Islam across Central Asia. The Soviets condemned the Sufis as the *zikristi*, those who said the *dhikr*, the sacred chant of the name of God that Sufis employ to induce a mystic state. Zikrists were savagely persecuted, but never uprooted, because of their powerful underground networks. These alone proved able to survive Soviet totalitarianism, and the Sufi orders were able to reemerge with amazing success in the post-Soviet era.[5] Their underground survival must recall that of other suppressed religious networks, like those of early modern Europe: we may think of the Catholic clergy in Protestant-dominated England or Ireland, or the Protestants in seventeenth-century France.

Orders like the Naqshbandi are critical to understanding the modern politics of Central Asia. The Sufi orders were and also are the core of the Chechen resistance in the Caucasus region, naturally enough since like many Muslims through Central and Western Asia, the Chechens were converted to Islam by the Sufi orders. It is astounding how many accounts of the Chechen/Russian conflicts fail to pay due attention to this Sufi context, and equally, how the United States has failed to exploit the massive ideological divisions that separate Sufi Islam from the intolerant puritanical traditions of the Wahhabists. Traditions like the Naqshbandi Order have proved so resilient, so skilled at clandestine survival, that we must doubt any claims by repressive Islamic states like Saudi Arabia that they have suppressed or eliminated Sufi practices. Driven them underground, perhaps, but eliminated, probably not. As in the former Soviet Union, they are rather lying dormant, ready to reemerge. Persecution may actually strengthen clandestine networks, not to mention the loyalty of ordinary believers. Sociologists of religion are very familiar with the idea that people value most that for which they suffer most.[6]

Holy Warriors

Second, if persecuted religious groups do survive, they often do so by developing quite active and effective military traditions. A simple Darwinian principle may be at work here. Groups that do not so adapt are largely doomed, unless the persecution ends spontaneously, or they find some favorable refuge: I think of the Amish and the Mennonites on American soil. But if such refuges are not available, persecuted groups often become highly effective warriors, and some of the world's toughest fighters owe their origins to the need to defend religious dissidence. Examples are quite numerous. We may think of the Sikhs, originally founded in sixteenth-century India as a tolerant and peaceful order pledged to achieve reconciliation between Islam and Hinduism. Over time they were persecuted more and more savagely by India's Mughal rulers, until by the eighteenth century, extinction seemed imminent. The solution was found in transformation into a military brotherhood, the *khalsa*, in which every man was a lion, a *singh*. The Sikhs survived and flourished in independence, and their fighting qualities deeply impressed the British Raj. Wise governments of India have respected the Sikhs' right to be left alone, a principle violated in the 1980s by Prime Minister Indira Gandhi, who attacked their Golden Temple. She of course perished soon afterwards at the hands of her Sikh bodyguards.[7]

Such stories of dissident warriors are by no means rare. In late medieval Europe, the persecuted Hussites of Bohemia formed the most formidable fighting machine of their day, and used pioneering mobile armor formations, early "tanks." Britain's religious wars of the seventeenth century produced several separate groupings subjected to appalling persecution, who responded by forming Sikh-like traditions and structures. In Scotland, the Covenanters were radical Calvinists who rejected the existing church and state as illegitimate and diabolical, and suffered terribly for it. When their allies came to power in 1689, they joined the military establishment as the Cameronian Regiment, a legendary force within the British army, and one that long retained its religious character: "It was essentially an armed congregation, and was the only unit in the British Army to carry their weapons into church. Each company elected an elder, each man carried a bible, and no church services were held without armed pickets being posted to defend it."[8]

No sophisticated theory is needed to understand the religious or political dynamic here. In a threatening environment, enemies of the state must often develop a strong military tradition if they are to survive. This is the story of the Sikhs, the Cameronians, and also of Middle Eastern groupings like the Druzes and the Maronite Christians of Lebanon and Syria. The Druze people are a classic example both of militarization and of the emphasis on the clandestine that we noted earlier. The fact that they hold views that are absolute anathema to orthodox Islam meant that they were forced to become very tough warriors, as the U.S. Marines found in their encounter with Lebanon in 1983. The Druze also practice a principle of secrecy. Followers of the Druze religion are allowed, and even encouraged, to deny their religion and to pretend that they are members of whatever the official religion may be at a particular time and place. Great value is placed on silence, secrecy, occultation—the essential tools of survival in a very dangerous environment.[9] Clearly, as Indira Gandhi was forced to realize in her country, the existence of such independent and well-armed minorities can pose real problems for state formation and the assertion of national unity.

People of Blood

Third, groups that resist and survive persecution often develop or cultivate ideologies that make sense of their suffering, and that promise rewards for themselves, and punishment for persecutors. These ideologies can in turn provide justification for resistance, and in some cases, for warfare. In practical terms, this means that persecuted groups are prone to apocalyptic ideas and to martyrdom. In approaching this, we face something of a chicken-and-egg situation. Do persecuted movements develop such ideologies as a consequence of their sufferings, or is it that groups that already possess these ideas are more likely to survive under repression, and to leave us a record of their ideas? Perhaps both processes are at work.

The popularity of Christian apocalyptic is not difficult to understand, since the most famous book that bears that name, the Revelation of Saint John, was almost certainly composed as a direct response to Roman persecution, so its mindset appeals immediately to modern counterparts in that situation. The book offers an analysis of the secular world as under the power of demonic forces, which find their seat above all in cities, and which are pledged to destroy the tiny righteous remnant of God's chosen. Persecution and martyrdom are inevitable consequences of faithfulness to God, while deceit and treachery threaten to entrap the saints at every stage. Suffering and bloodshed are not just meaningful, but perhaps essential to salvation. The only solution is a rigid rejection of the world and its evil ways, and faith in God who will shortly intervene to annihilate evil and proclaim justice. It is scarcely surprising that such ideas appealed so mightily to Christians under persecution through history. We think for instance of the Huguenots of France in the late seventeenth century. As they were persecuted and expelled, their extremists developed ever more apocalyptic and fanatical ideas, through revolutionary sects like the Camisards. Associates of the movement developed ideas of prophetic inspiration, like the notorious French Prophets whose outbursts did so much to discredit religious extremism in early-eighteenth-century England.[10]

Ideas of martyrdom need not be rooted in apocalyptic or explicit scriptural warrant. We find another classic example of a cult of martyrdom among the persecuted English Catholics of the early modern period, for whom official repression was such a standard expectation. In turn, ideas of sacrifice, martyrdom, and sacrificial bloodshed became integrated into the religious schema, and left a long historical inheritance. One of the most popular nineteenth-century Catholic hymns commemorated the "Faith of our fathers living still in spite of dungeon, fire and sword." As one of the supreme historical ironies, this hymn has now become popular among Protestants, the descendants of those who once commanded the fire and sword.[11]

In more contemporary terms, we think of the Shi'a tradition in Islam, a group that for a millennium has often known persecution and exclusion, and that has developed its ideas of sacrificial bloodshed and innocent suffering, focused on the martyr Imam Hussain and his death at Karbala. These acts are in turn commemorated by rituals that are fundamental to the lived experience of the faith, namely the Ashura festivities that provide such a close Muslim counterpart to the Christian Easter. Shi'ism is also messianic in its expectation of the return of the twelfth imam, and apocalyptic in looking to the end times.[12] None of these ideas necessarily leads to violent or subversive behavior: even if they deploy the most hair-raising rhetoric, apocalyptic groups through history commonly tend to be quietist, accepting their own bloodshed in the cause of religion, dying rather than killing. But the existence of these religious strands can potentially serve as the foundation for activities that disrupt or even destroy a state.

In practical terms, a group whose religion revolves around relics, blood, and a cult of death is commonly difficult to overawe and difficult to incorporate into a state: ask the Irish, or rather, ask the British who tried to oppress them. Often too, recalcitrance in one area, political resistance, spills over into other social areas, so that Catholic Ireland became progressively more ungovernable during the nineteenth century, as the common people rejected the legitimacy not just of the official church but of the state, its laws, and its economic order. A persecuted people is hard to govern—an obvious point, but one that is often neglected. It is easy for activists to manipulate that kind of sentiment, to manipulate the idea of the blood of the martyrs, in order to generate opposition to the state. In one of the most famous speeches in modern Irish history, Padhraig Pearse proclaimed that:

> Our foes are strong and wise and wary; but, strong and wise and wary as they are, they cannot undo the miracles of God who ripens in the hearts of young men the seeds sown by the young men of a former generation. . . . Rulers and Defenders of Realms had need to be wary if they would guard against such processes. Life springs from death; and from the graves of patriot men and women spring living nations. The Defenders of this Realm have worked well in secret and in the open. They think that they have pacified Ireland. They think that they have purchased half of us and intimidated the other half. They think that they have foreseen everything, think that they have provided against everything; but the fools, the fools, the fools!—they have left us our Fenian dead, and while Ireland holds these graves, Ireland unfree shall never be at peace.[13]

Besides the Irish, we might also think of the ordinary people of Iran, Iraq, or Lebanon, extremely long-suffering, until their patience is finally exhausted. And though the Shi'ites did not invent suicide bombings, they have since the 1980s popularized the notion of "martyrdom operations," the devastating attack by a *shahid* martyr, an idea that fits so well into their traditions of virtuous sacrifice. These ideas have of course subsequently been assimilated into Sunni Islam.[14]

Men of God

Persecution often tends to change the internal dynamic of a movement, to concentrate power and prestige in the hands of a clerical elite. The most important example of this may be the early Christian movement itself, which developed such a powerful focus on martyrdom and sacrificial bloodshed, and which came to be personified in the figure of the bishops, who were so often the successors and heirs of martyrs. They were in a sense descended from a primal act of blood offering. Elaine Pagels has argued that it was precisely the orthodox focus on martyrdom and episcopacy that gave the Orthodox/Catholic Church its edge over rival and competing sects like the Gnostics, which were ultimately stigmatized as heretics, and eventually vanished.[15] The early Church father Tertullian declared, famously, that the blood of martyrs is the seed of the church.

Similar processes can be discerned in more recent historical eras, especially in the Catholic Church of early modern and modern times. In Great Britain and Ireland, the association with martyrdom and persecution gave an enormous cachet to the Catholic priesthood, which lasted long after the actual age of rack and rope had faded into historical memory.[16] This element did much to create the powerful clericalism of Irish Catholicism in the United States, which largely survived into our own day.

These ideas of mysticism and martyrdom were much in evidence once more during the 1950s, when the persecution of the Catholic Church under Communist regimes struck such a chord among American believers, who were such enthusiastic advocates of confrontation with the Soviet Union. Catholic anti-Communism was also closely linked to ideas of apocalypse, to the Antichrist (who was commonly identified with Stalin), and to mystical revelation, through the figure of the Virgin Mary. These ideas have been powerful in our own time through the global influence of Pope John Paul II, another scion of a persecuted church, namely in Poland. Such ideas can be reinterpreted in secular terms, so that both Ireland and Poland have been presented as "martyr nations," and their heroes viewed as martyrs. It is impossible to understand the great heroes of secular Irish nationalism like Padhraig Pearse except in this sub-Catholic context of this mystical theme of secular martyrdom: the great event of the Irish nationalist calendar is of course Easter, and its symbol the Easter lily of Resurrection. Those ideas then permeate ostensibly secular nationalist guerrilla movements like the Irish Republican Army.[17]

Of course, these ideas are not confined to Christianity, since they find such powerful parallels especially in Shi'ite Islam. Shi'ism—that apocalyptic creed—is also the section of Islam most dominated by clergy, and most prone to attribute messianic hopes to specific living clergy, imams and ayatollahs. The story of modern politics in Iran, Iraq, and Lebanon can be told through the collective biographies of leading clerics and ayatollahs, whose charisma is often linked to specific families and bloodlines. As in the Catholic instance, the more a state seeks to curb these traditions through violence, the more the official violence and repression is interpreted through the language of martyrdom, and the more awe and loyalty is attached to the martyr and his heirs and spiritual successors. We think of the experience of the Shi'ite clergy in Iran, or the massive disaffection of the Shi'ites in Ba'athist Iraq.

As in the Catholic context, the view of a hostile outside world tends to support ideas of separation and withdrawal, and the creation of a whole alternative subculture of clerically dominated institutions. This process is especially evident in education. In turn, the existence of alternative schools and colleges can further generate conflicts with the established order, since they directly challenge theories of national unity and homogenization.

Brothers Across the Seas

Assume that a state has repressed, but failed to destroy, a religious minority, that has developed some or all of the characteristics that have been outlined above. The minority largely rejects the legitimacy of the state, which it views in terms of evil or demonic forces; it sees its own sufferings as part of a divine plan; it might explore ideas of apocalyptic, messianic, and redemptive violence; its cohesion and discipline are constantly reinforced by reference to the pressing dangers from the threatening outside world. Such a community is obviously deeply dangerous to the internal stability of a nation. A self-reinforcing process might also be at work. The more a community declares its opposition to the established order, the less likely it is that members of that community will be absorbed into the establishment. The more they are excluded, the more they will devote their loyalties and efforts to the religious subculture, and the more they will be seen as clannish, separatist, or subversive.

But these internal conflicts are not necessarily the worst danger faced by a persecuting state. Very few religions exist entirely within the defined boundaries of one state or nation. Some may spread over a subcontinent, or might indeed be global. A religious tradition persecuted in one nation might represent the dominant order in another, or at least might command more power and respect. People who are persecuted in one jurisdiction therefore have natural friends and allies and sympathizers in other regions. The political and diplomatic consequences are obvious. The persecuted Catholics of Tudor and Stuart England naturally found common cause with the powerful Catholic regimes of European states, especially imperial Spain. Though most ordinary English Catholics rejected treason and conspiracy, enough activists were prepared to share these schemes to create a permanent danger of subversion. And even those who rejected overt treason were sufficiently influenced by the ideologies of clericalism and martyrdom that they would be loath to betray a priest on the run. The Catholic subculture became, in effect, a ready-made nationwide resistance network, complete with safe houses.[18] A large part of the history of the Middle East in early modern times consists of the struggle between Shi'ite Iran and the Sunni Ottoman Empire, and the Shi'ites and minorities often served as an unstable factor in this relationship.

A persecuted minority can thus become an ideal fifth column, which in the correct circumstances might support an invasion or an armed incursion. It is impossible to understand the extraordinary repressive apparatus of Ba'athist Iraq except in terms of the pervasive danger posed by its domestic fifth column, the 60 percent of Iraqis who espoused Shi'ism, and who looked for support and sympathy to the neighboring Shi'ite state of Iran. Such fears naturally reached new heights during the open war between the two nations between 1980 and

1988. Apart from its potential as a fifth column, a persecuted minority can provide an intelligence service, and even a casus belli: "We" will not stand idly by and tolerate "your" persecution of our brothers and sisters.

In another area too, that of exile, the politics of persecution endanger security. Whether we are dealing with Catholics or Protestants in the early modern era, or radical Muslims today, official repression commonly drives activists and dissidents to seek exile beyond the reach of the state apparatus. Commonly, those driven from their homelands are religious leaders and exiles. Exile communities can serve many functions. They are notoriously vulnerable to the machinations of rival governments and intelligence services, who might even find in them the nucleus of an alternative government for the persecuting nation. An exile center—be it a cleric's retreat, a court, or a college—can also become a center for conspiracy and intelligence in its own right. We think of the Jesuit colleges in early modern Europe, or the household of the Ayatollah Khomeini in the 1970s, prior to the Iranian revolution. Also, exiles are free of the need to compromise with the practical realities of their homelands, and commonly drift to the most radical and extreme positions, violently opposed to the nations that drive them away. When the Spanish expelled their Jewish communities in the fifteenth and sixteenth centuries, those Jews did not simply fade into obscurity, but often found homes in Protestant nations like the Netherlands, where they served as powerful activists for radically anti-Spanish policies. The Irish Catholics forced into exile by the British state became the "Wild Geese," whose flight took them into the military service of many European Catholic states. In the wars of the eighteenth century, the Wild Geese were commonly the deadliest military enemies of the emerging British Empire.

Conclusion

Religious persecution can thus provide massive obstacles to nation-building, and to creating a stable, just, and secure international order. It also produces a vicious cycle, in which violence itself breeds theories and structures conducive to violence. And yet we know that the pattern can ultimately be ended. Apart from Northern Ireland, it has been a great many years since Protestants and Catholics have killed each other in Europe. Can anything be learned from this experience that might be applied to the contemporary world?

Ultimately, a kind of exhaustion set in. During the late seventeenth century, after decades of warfare and persecution, rival factions wearied of the cycle in which one faction would strike at another, only to be persecuted by it in turn. Gradually, people came to realize that it was in their own interests to limit the power of the state to penalize any religious interest whatever. If Baptists could force Catholics to take an unpopular oath of loyalty, then Catholics could impose their ideas when they were in the ascendant. Far better, then, to eliminate religious tests as far as possible—though the process was not complete until Victorian times. The history of civil and political rights in England and America is the story of how all factions came to this common realization.

I also think of the seventeenth-century founder of international law, the great Dutch scholar Hugo Grotius. He made one of the most important intellectual leaps in human history. He wanted to write a book on international law, but not in terms of revelation, of what God said, what the Bible said. Yet he wanted to avoid charges of religious unorthodoxy. So, he used an argument rather like this—I paraphrase shamelessly—"Now, of course, God exists. Everyone knows this. But just suppose for the sake of argument, as in a mathematical proof, just suppose God was not a given—*etsi Deus non daretur.* Just suppose that. Now, what are the intellectual consequences?" The Enlightenment can be described as the extrapolation of that principle.

That enormous principle might yet be liberating in an Islamic context. If a society could be persuaded to believe, not that God is not there, not that God does not act, but that we should look at politics and culture *etsi Deus non daretur.* Just suppose God is not a given. What follows? In the context of Europe, that proviso was a major source of the Enlightenment. Might it yet ignite future Enlightenments? And might it yet help end modern cycles of religious intolerance and violence?

Notes

1. Neera Chandhoke, *Beyond Secularism: The Rights of Religious Minorities* (New Delhi: Oxford University Press, 1999).

2. Mario Apostolov, *Religious Minorities, Nation States, and Security: Five Cases from the Balkans and the Eastern Mediterranean* (Burlington, VT: Ashgate, 2001).

3. Yitzhak Nakash, *The Shi'is of Iraq* (Princeton, NJ: Princeton University Press, 1994).

4. Christopher W. Marsh, *The Family of Love in English Society, 1550–1630* (Cambridge: Cambridge University Press, 1994).

5. See Paul B. Henze, *Islam in the Caucasus: The Example of Chechnya* (Santa Monica, CA: RAND, 1995); Anssi Kullberg, "The Sufi Resistance," *The Eurasian Politician,* October 2003, www.cc.jyu.fi/~aphamala/pe/2003/tsets-2.htm (accessed 10 January 2004).

6. See Ofra Bengio and Gabriel Ben-Dor, eds., *Minorities and the State in the Arab World* (Boulder, CO: Lynne Rienner Publishers, 1999); Malise Ruthven, *Islam in the World,* 2nd ed. (New York: Oxford University Press, 2000).

7. See Amandeep Singh Madra and Parmjit Singh, *Warrior Saints: Three Centuries of the Sikh Military Tradition* (London: I. B. Tauris in association with The Sikh Foundation,

1999); Mark Juergensmeyer, *Terror in the Mind of God: The Global Rise of Religious Violence*, 3rd ed. (Berkeley, CA: University of California Press, 2003).

8. See Stuart Hall, "Tam Recalls His Proud Days with the Real Tartan Army," *icLanarkshire*, iclanarkshire.icnetwork.co.uk/news/localnews/rutherglen/content_objectid= 12660341_method=full_siteid=50144_headline=-Tam-recalls-his-proud-days-with-the-Real-Tartan-Army-name_page.html (accessed 10 January 2004).

9. See Matti Moosa, *The Maronites in History* (Syracuse, NY: Syracuse University Press, 1986); Mordechai Nisan, *Minorities in the Middle East*, 2nd ed. (Jefferson, NC: Mcfarland & Co., 2002).

10. See Hillel Schwartz, *The French Prophets: The History of a Millenarian Group in Eighteenth-Century England* (Berkeley, CA: University of California Press, 1979); Clarke Garrett, *Spirit Possession and Popular Religion: From the Camisards to the Shakers* (Baltimore, MD: Johns Hopkins University Press, 1987). A classic analysis is found in Norman Cohn, *The Pursuit of the Millennium: Revolutionary Millenarians and Mystical Anarchists of the Middle Ages*, rev. and expanded ed. (New York: Oxford University Press, 1970).

11. John Bossy, *The English Catholic Community, 1570–1850* (New York: Oxford University Press, 1976).

12. See Juan R. I. Cole and Nikki R. Keddie, eds., *Shi'ism and Social Protest* (New Haven, CT: Yale University Press, 1986); Juan Cole, *Sacred Space and Holy War: The Politics, Culture and History of Shi'ite Islam* (London: I. B. Tauris, 2002).

13. The speech is very widely available: see for instance www.irelandsown.net/ppearse2.html.

14. See Joyce Pettigrew, ed., *Martyrdom and National Resistance Movements: Essays on Asia and Europe* (Amsterdam: VU University Press for Centre for Asian Studies, 1997); Juergensmeyer, *Terror In The Mind of God*. For a Christian variant of this tradition, see Anna L. Peterson, *Martyrdom and the Politics of Religion: Progressive Catholicism in El Salvador's Civil War* (Albany, NY: State University of New York Press, 1997).

15. Elaine Pagels, *The Gnostic Gospels* (New York: Vintage Books, 1989).

16. Robert Hugh Benson, *Come Rack! Come Rope!* (London: Hutchinson, 1912).

17. Seán Farrell Moran, *Patrick Pearse and the Politics of Redemption: The Mind of the Easter Rising, 1916* (Washington, DC: Catholic University of America Press, 1994). Compare Norman Davies, *Heart of Europe: The Past in Poland's Present* (New York: Oxford University Press, 2001).

18. See Bossy, *The English Catholic Community*.

3

Uzbekistan and the Central Asian Crucible of Religion and Security

Chris Seiple and Joshua White

The sweet dream of American political thought—reborn in each generation, it seems—is that cultural factors like religion will shrink into insignificance as blessed pragmatism finally comes into its own.

—Jack Miles[1]

IN THE PROSPEROUS DECADE before September 11, 2001, most Americans gave
only passing thought to national security, and even less to the ways in which
religion posed a risk to their way of life. Religious violence was a familiar enough
category, but far off. If asked to identify the area of the world in which religion
presented the greatest threat to their security, most Americans undoubtedly

Chris Seiple is president of the Institute for Global Engagement. Before coming to the
Institute, he was an Earhart Fellow at the Fletcher School of Law and Diplomacy at
Tufts University, where he is completing his dissertation, "U.S.-Uzbekistan Relations:
1991–2003." He was an infantry officer in the Marine Corps from 1990 to 1999 and
served in the Strategic Initiatives Group at the Pentagon. A member of the Council on
Foreign Relations and the International Institute for Strategic Studies, his publications
include *The U.S. Military/NGO Relationship in Humanitarian Interventions* (U.S.
Army War College, 1996).

Joshua White is vice president for policy at the Institute for Global Engagement and
is associate editor of *The Brandywine Review of Faith & International Affairs*. He
graduated magna cum laude, Phi Beta Kappa, from Williams College with a double
major in history and mathematics. Before coming to the Institute, he spent a summer at the U.S. State Department, where he helped to compile the annual religious
freedom report.

would have cited the Middle East generally, or perhaps a specific country like Iran or Syria. All that changed quickly after the attacks on U.S. soil, and today Afghanistan and al Qaeda are a permanent part of the American lexicon.

September 11, plainly, was an introduction not only to the immediacy of religion-inspired violence, but also to the changing geography of national threats. Americans were forced to rediscover geography as they were introduced to Central Asia—a place they had not known before, except as Afghanistan.[2] Suddenly, America had to come up to speed with the complex patchwork of national and ethnic interests (Uzbeks in Afghanistan? Russians in Tajikistan? Tajiks in Uzbekistan?) and develop a sophisticated security strategy in the region to mitigate existing and future threats, especially the religion-based terrorism of such nonstate actors as al Qaeda and the Islamic Movement of Uzbekistan. Uzbekistan—the literal center of the region, contiguous to the other five nations and home to an air base key to the pacification of Afghanistan—became a focal point of U.S. strategy. As such, Central Asia, and Uzbekistan in particular, provide both a timely and a salient case study of the nexus between religion and security concerns. There is perhaps no other part of the world where these issues are as clearly revealed and relevant to U.S. national interests.

Religion and security in Central Asia, and America's interaction with it, turn chiefly on a contextual understanding of the following: (1) Islam and stability in Central Asia; (2) present-day geopolitics; (3) American perceptions of the region; and (4) radical Islam's primary proponents in Central Asia, the Islamic Movement of Uzbekistan and the Hizb ut-Tahrir. Without such an approach—that is, without an understanding of different perspectives, ours and theirs, macro and micro—we will see only what we want to see, and will overlook the vital spiritual and geopolitical reality of religion in Central Asia.[3]

Central Asia: Islam & Stability

Central Asia was practically forgotten by the West in the twentieth century (with the exception of Afghanistan, which was viewed as globally strategic in the fight against communism). Known as Turkestan in the nineteenth century, it was conquered by Tsarist Russia and ruled from Tashkent following Russian occupation of the city in 1865. With the consolidation of Soviet power in the 1920s, the region became a part of the Soviet Union. Following the collapse of the USSR in 1991, Kazakhstan, Kyrgyzstan, Tajikistan, Turkmenistan, and Uzbekistan declared independence. In the tumultuous wake of the Soviet Union's 1989 withdrawal, Afghanistan soon succumbed to anarchy until the Taliban conquered most of it in 1996, offering stability in exchange for the harsh rule of shari'ah law.[4] The story of the region, however, is much more complex than its recent history as a Russian satellite would suggest.

Up until the twentieth century, Central Asia was anything but forgotten. It was a region hotly contested by great powers—Alexander, the Chinese, the Persians, the Mongols, and more recently, Britain and tsarist Russia in the nineteenth century, who saw Central Asia as the prize of their "Great Game" for Asian dominance. Landlocked, Central Asia became the meeting place of empires. Each successive regional power left a cultural and religious deposit of ideas and norms; perhaps the most important of these, laid down in the Arab invasion of the seventh century and developed over successive generations, was Islam.[5]

The Islamic Experience

Central Asia is predominantly Sunni Muslim, and most adherents belong to the Hanafi *madraseh*, the most tolerant and theologically flexible of Sunni Islam's four schools.[6] Shia Islam, which broke with Sunni Islam in 680 with the assassination of Mohammed's grandson in Karbala, Iraq, was less successful in gaining a foothold in the region (in part, some speculate, because it was unable to accommodate pre-Islamic traditions such as the region's long association with Zoroastrianism).[7] Shia influence, though, remains to the present day in pockets of Uzbekistan and the mountains of Tajikistan.[8] Sufism, a third and sometimes parallel perspective of Islamic thought that grew out of the Arab invasion of Persia and Central Asia, accommodated pre-existing spiritual traditions and remains deeply influential in the region and around the world. Sufism is a form of Islamic mysticism that adopts an antinomian approach to religious practice and rejects the traditional role of the mullahs in favor of a more direct, unmediated experience with God. Various Sufi orders, or brotherhoods, have been active in Central Asia; as discussed below, the most influential of these have figured prominently in the continuation of Islamic practice in the region during times of anti-Islamic repression.

Another important Islamic movement emerged in Central Asia in the late nineteenth century, in the decades before the Bolshevik revolution of 1917: Jadidism. The Jadids were intellectual Sunni reformers who sought to reconcile Islam with modernity.[9] They had, like other Islamic reformers of their day, "faith in the ability of the human intellect to solve the problems of the world," and saw "no contradiction between the notion of progress and their faith in Islam."[10] Highly literate, the Jadids published books and newspapers that were instrumental in the development of the modern Turkic culture.[11] Jadidism never materialized into a mass movement, though its influence in Central Asia, particularly as a social-political force in the context of Russian imperial rule, was widespread. Its success (however short-lived) broadly illustrates the historically tolerant nature of indigenous Central Asian Islam.[12]

The Jadids and other practicing Muslims were generally tolerated in the early days of Russian rule. But under the Soviet regime, beginning in the 1920s, Islam was harshly repressed and forced underground; some movements, like the Jadids, were eliminated entirely during Stalin's purges. It was not until the 1960s that the Soviets, seeking to gain support among Muslim states for the worldwide expansion of communism, developed a state-sponsored Islam—complete with mosques and madrassas—to showcase to the world.[13] The state's control of Islam continued, more or less, through the fall of the Soviet Union and into the new era of the independent republics, which began in 1991. (In Uzbekistan, for example, there is a national *muftiate*, and the state approves the message given by all mullahs throughout the country for Friday prayers.)

The reemergence of Islam in Central Asia in the 1990s as a religious practice, an identity, and a political force should not have come as a surprise. Islam was never completely suppressed under Soviet rule, and indeed it persisted quite successfully. Part of this persistence must be credited to the success of the Sufis. The Naqshbandi order, founded in the fourteenth century by Muhammad ibn Baha ad-Din Naqshband in Bukhara, is perhaps the most influential Sufi order in Central Asia. Its ability to continue in secret during periods of repression was central to the reemergence of Islamic practice in the last decade.

In congruity with Central Asia's predominantly Turkic culture of hospitality and respect, and its diverse religious traditions, Naqshbandi Sufism tends toward tolerance in matters religious. This does not mean that, politically speaking, the Naqshbandi have been passive or uninvolved. Quite the contrary. The leader of an 1898 revolt in Andijan (in the Fergana valley) was Naqshbandi, and Sufi leaders led later revolts against tsarist and communist domination into the early twentieth century.[14] More recently, Sufi leaders in the Fergana valley have been known to exercise political influence.

Naqshbandi Sufism's historical connection to nationalistic movements is a key to understanding the political-religious dynamics in modern-day Central Asia. Indeed, it is important to note that the Chechen nationalist movement has wielded Naqshbandi Sufism as a legitimating force for nearly two centuries. Although the Islamic theological underpinnings of Sufi thought have decidedly not been the driver of that conflict, the Chechens do however trace their resistance to an early-nineteenth-century Naqshbandi sheik. As a result, the Sufi identity has been used quite effectively "to create solidarity and [help] solicit the direct support of the Muslim world."[15] Jadidism, similarly, had a striking protonationalist impulse (which accounts at least in part for its harsh treatment under the Soviet rule). Adeeb Khalid, a leading scholar of the movement, notes that the Jadidists were influential in promoting the importance of a national identity in a region historically centered around dynasties and tribes.[16]

Central Asians tend to be religiously tolerant, in part because 90 percent of them are Muslims of the liberal Hanafi school or of various Sufi orders that are generally accommodating of diverse religious practice. Yet it is precisely because of this overwhelming religious belief that Sufi and Jadidist communities, with the right leader, have had so much political influence as underground or national resistance movements.

Given today's precarious geopolitical context, the potential for Islam to be the deciding factor in stability for the region's future is great. Unfortunately, according to the near-term priorities of geopolitical power, Islam has been used by radical groups to teach violence (the Islamic Movement of Uzbekistan) or hate (the Hizb ut-Tahrir) while governments in the region, especially Uzbekistan, have sought to repress and control Islam. If Islam is not embraced according to the best of its spiritual and intellectual traditions then there is little long-term hope for stability in this part of the world.

The Geopolitical Lens

Stalin redrew the map of Central Asia in the 1920s, dividing Turkestan into five republics that cut across ethnic divides and historic allegiances. The result facilitated Soviet control of these former Russian provinces by preventing consolidated opposition of any kind. To this day, however, the region is characterized by a patchwork of ethnic identities that do not cleanly align with political boundaries. Over a million ethnic Tajiks, for example, live in Uzbekistan, and a quarter of Tajikistan's nearly seven million people are ethnically Uzbek. Kyrgyzstan is only about half ethnic Kyrgyz, and has sizable Russian and Uzbek minorities.[17] The Fergana valley, where Uzbekistan, Kyrgyzstan, and Tajikistan meet, includes four Uzbek enclaves surrounded by Kyrgyz territory, a Kyrgyz enclave inside of Uzbekistan, and three Tajik enclaves surrounded by Uzbek and Kyrgyz territory.

Geography is another challenge. The region is landlocked, and Uzbekistan—which sits at the center, bordering the other four Soviet Central Asian republics plus Afghanistan—is, in fact, one of only two doubly landlocked countries in the world. Trade, especially exports of key natural resources, must therefore pass overland. Water rights are likewise contentious. Uzbekistan, for example, is still overdependent on its top export, cotton, which requires twice the annual amount of rainfall that the country receives. Poor irrigation methodologies and catastrophic environmental policies continued from the

Soviet era have left the region with an impending water crisis as people begin to leave the areas where water is unavailable (e.g., around the Aral Sea, which will likely disappear sometime in the next decade). For a country like Uzbekistan in which over 60 percent of the population derives its living from agriculture, this has enormous economic import.[18]

The combination of these demographic and geographic realities should, if economic and political stability is to result, provide a sort of forcing function for Central Asia in the direction of regional cooperation. Unfortunately, the first ten years of the newly independent republics were hardly characterized by stability. With the collapse of the Soviet Union came, in short order, the pullout of Russian expertise, troops (except in Tajikistan), subsidies, and, to a certain degree, markets. Ahmed Rashid notes that "every international telephone line to Central Asia went through Moscow," a problem indicative of Central Asia's complicated interconnection to the Soviet system.[19] To add injury to insult, these countries competed against each other, often turning off, or not paying for, each other's gas, electric, or water supplies.[20]

These republics, by virtue of their location in the "heartland" of Asia (to use Sir Halford Mackinder's memorable phrase)[21] found themselves in the figurative backyard that everyone shares. Surrounded by four regional powers equipped with nuclear weapons (Russia, China, India, and Pakistan) and one that seeks them (Iran), Central Asian leaders did what Central Asian leaders have always done: they instinctively turned to balance-of-power, realpolitik decision making.

Consider the perspective of Uzbekistan. Looking north, Kazakhstan possesses tremendous oil reserves and a relatively strong economy that grew by 10 percent last year. Uzbeks do not like to be second to anyone (not least the Kazakhs), something brought into painful relief in 2004 as more and more Uzbeks migrated to Kazakhstan to find work. Farther north, the Uzbeks still harbor fears about Russia's undue influence in the region, exercised through economic clout, especially regional control of oil and gas exports through preexisting Soviet pipelines. Continuing clockwise to the east is Tajikistan, a failed state still recovering from a five-year civil war (1992–1997) between pro-Islamic groups and the government that claimed 50,000 lives. The fact that 15,000 Russian troops are stationed there to this day is both a comfort and a concern to Uzbek strategists. Farther east is China's Xinjiang province, a Turkic Uighur semiautonomous region that has closer cultural ties to Central Asia than to China proper. The Chinese are concerned about the region's Islamic terrorists, especially the Eastern Turkestan Islamic Movement, which was declared a terrorist group by the State Department in 2002. The Uzbeks are traditionally wary of Chinese influence; a regional proverb cautions, "When the Chinese are in Central Asia, catastrophe follows."

Looking south is Afghanistan. The Uzbeks were understandably threatened by the neighboring Taliban, who, until the U.S.-led invasion in late 2001, controlled over 90 percent of Afghanistan's territory, provided safe harbor to the Islamic Movement of Uzbekistan, and produced a vast majority of the world's supply of heroin. To the west is Turkmenistan, a closed, repressive society sitting on tremendous gas reserves; a seventeenth-century khanate in no rush to participate in the twenty-first century, Turkmenistan's president Saparmurad Niyazov has established a personality cult and shunned foreign alliances. Farther south is Iran, a major exporter of Shi'ite radicalism (despite the democratic tendencies of its youthful majority).

It is in this geopolitical context that Uzbekistan and its neighboring states operate. The post–September 11 U.S.-Uzbek strategic partnership that allowed for a U.S. military base in Karshi-Khanabad was a clear attempt on the part of the Uzbek government to use its U.S. alliance to balance out the influence of its neighbors, especially Afghanistan, and regional powers while providing legitimacy to its repression of Islamic radical groups at home.

There is a threefold irony in America's discovery of Central Asia in the last several years. As a great power, it has discovered a region of the world that has long been recognized by past great powers as an important geopolitical fulcrum of Asia. Second, the Central Asia that America is discovering is a frighteningly less tolerant place than it once was, as the specter of radical Islam increasingly shadows the region, inviting greater repression. This repression, in turn, makes radical Islam more legitimate in the absence of economic and political reform. Third, the reasons that prevented America's discovery and understanding of Central Asia prior to September 11 still persist. Unless we come to grips with these faulty assumptions, they almost guarantee that U.S. policy in the region will not only fail to succeed, but will make matters worse.

Misguided Preconceptions

The fall of the Soviet Union created both a strategic vacuum in Central Asia and a profound spiritual-psychological dislocation (reinforced by the accelerating pace of globalization). As people looked for meaning amid instability, religious, ethnic, national, and clan identities took on new power, despite the rosy forecasts of Western thinkers and policymakers that this was not a new era but the very end of history. The dream that progress, cooperation, and benign globalization would rule a common understanding of the world, irrespective of geography or culture, is being replaced by the realization that there is now an unprecedented global competition for "hearts and minds." The question of who steps into this spiritual-strategic vacuum is one that is at the

center of the discussion of religion and security. For whoever steps in to provide spiritual meaning in a given region or context will also invariably shape
the strategic direction of that context.

In Central Asia this has taken several forms. Islamic radicalism grew quickly
after the collapse of the Soviet Union as fundamentalist Muslim missionaries
began educating Central Asians about the need for an Islamic state. In Uzbekistan, for example, President Karimov's response to this has been to invest heavily in education, a project that includes the establishment of a national myth
around Timur the Lame. This fourteenth-century ruler and descendant
of Ghengis Khan ruled the Middle East from the present-day Uzbek city of
Samarkand; today (in a feat of historical imagination) he is hailed as the original
hero of the Uzbek people and the George Washington of the Uzbek state.[22]
Alongside these responses, still others—from the growth of evangelical Protes-
tantism to the renewed interest in traditional Muslim practice—demonstrate the
range of offerings that have been proffered to fill the post-Soviet "identity gap."

The West, and the United States in particular, has been slow to understand, let
alone address, this strategic and spiritual vacuum due to three disabling preconceptions.

Cartographic Camouflage

Following the Cold War, the United States by and large did not pursue a
comprehensive, regional strategic approach to Central Asia. Within the State
Department bureaucracy, Central Asia was first grouped under the imagina-
tive rubric of the "Former Soviet Union" before migrating to the more progressive "Newly Independent States." Naturally, the region took a second seat
to U.S.-Russian bilateral relations under Deputy Secretary of State Strobe Tal-
bott's de facto "Russia first" policy. Today, Central Asia falls under the State
Department's Bureau of European and Eurasian Affairs, placing it, in diplomatic shorthand, in the European and Russian sphere of influence. This geographic grouping, which is still the former Soviet Union, implicitly suggests
that Central Asia should be oriented north and west. This may be a sensible
assumption for the South Caucasus—the western Caspian region that includes Armenia, Georgia, and Azerbaijan—as these countries have greater cultural affinity with Europe. But aligning Central Asia under the same bureau
has, especially since September 11, proved to be a questionable arrangement.

Tellingly, the Defense Department's regional divisions did not align with
those of the State Department. This is indicative of the disjuncture between
the diplomatic and military components of U.S. strategy, but also of the Defense Department's accidental foresight in drawing its map to better reflect
emerging geopolitical realities. Under the Pentagon's organization, U.S. Cen-

tral Command (CENTCOM), activated in 1983 as a permanent successor to President Carter's Rapid Deployment Joint Task Force (itself a reaction to the U.S. inability to operate militarily during the Iran Hostage Crisis), has an Area of Responsibility that stretches from the Horn of Africa to Central Asia.[23]

This alignment better reflects what has become known as the arc of instability, or the crescent of crisis. This arc begins in the Horn of Africa, extends northeast through Palestine, Iraq, and Iran up to Central Asia before curving southwest down through Pakistan, India, and into Southeast Asia. Many factors contribute to the instability of this arc, but the one common factor to all is the role of radical Islam. Islamic radicalism in Central Asia has, sadly, validated those like Anthony Zinni who saw important strategic reasons for grouping the region with the Middle East and South Asia. History demonstrates that all maps are in part political propaganda, demarcating—often unconsciously—the expectations, dreams, and fears of those who craft them. That the diplomats of the post–Cold War West would envision the entire Caspian region as the "Former Soviet Union" was bureaucratically natural but mentally lazy. It was a linear extrapolation of a long-standing preconception from the past, but it missed the religious radicalism and instability of the present.

The "Sweet Dream"

Since the Enlightenment, the West has divided state from religion in the name of good governance. The result has been admirable, but too often the casualty has been holistic analysis. For a host of reasons—some of which are outlined in this volume by Pauletta Otis—the United States has traditionally neglected religion and other cultural factors in its security analysis. Though one would expect that, following September 11, there would have been a resurgence of interest in religion's role in security considerations, the interest by the U.S. government in these issues has in fact been uneven. To the extent that religion is included as a factor of analysis, it is often framed as a simplistic ideology ("those who hate freedom," etc.) and catalyst to conflict, rather than a complex worldview that forms and informs culture and action, and therefore deserves more subtle discussion.

As a motivating force, there is of course an ideological element to radical Islam. But a singular focus on Islam-as-ideology obscures the other elements—some theological, some deeply pragmatic—of the movement. (And we should point out that, placed in the perspective of the worldwide Muslim *umma*, or global community of believers, radical Islam is a decidedly minority movement.) As Graham Fuller has noted, "Islamism is . . . not an ideology but a religious-cultural-political framework for engagement on issues that most concern politically engaged Muslims."[24] Sound analysis needs to account for the fact that political actions are sometimes genuinely birthed out of actual religious conviction, and that belief systems are cultural-political drivers of conflict that have real security implications. Such analysis must properly name the religious dynamics at play and also seek to provide a place for religion in any comprehensive solution.

The U.S. government, for example, was wise in the wake of September 11 not to associate its response in Afghanistan and beyond with a "War on Islam." There was a clear understanding that the conflict could not—and must not—be understood in predominantly religious terms. This insistence, helpful as it was, unfortunately precluded much discussion within the U.S. bureaucracy of the cultural-religious motivations of its enemy. This is beginning to change, as policymakers come to realize that the rational-actor model is not sufficient to address the complexity of factions and motivations within the radical Islamic movement.

As the epigraph to this chapter reminds us, it is, regretfully, the "sweet dream of American political thought . . . that cultural factors like religion will shrink into insignificance as blessed pragmatism finally comes into its own." This is the dream that accompanied idealism about "the end of history," and while enthusiasm for the latter has faded, the same cannot be said of the former. Consideration of religion is still commonly sidelined in policy discussions and counterterrorism strategies (witness Iraq). Central Asia, however—with its multiplicity of religious influences—is a place where analysis that neglects the subtleties of religion and presupposes only pragmatism is bound to come up short.

State or Society?

A third preconception applicable to U.S. engagement in Central Asia is one that has very deep roots, and is not isolated to this region of the world. It is the assumption, dating from the 1648 Peace of Westphalia, that the state is the primary unit of analysis in global affairs. The Westphalian assumption is slowly beginning to lose its hold on Western patterns of analysis, due in no small part to the events of September 11. The paramount role of "nonstate actors" is now widely acknowledged. When state actors engage non-state actors there is necessarily a certain degree of asymmetry involved: terrorism, for example, is a threat best countered by good intelligence and special operations forces, not a conventional military force. A state's military will necessarily have a hard time, literally and figuratively, matching its strengths (e.g., tanks) against the strengths and weaknesses of nonstate actors who can employ guerrilla tactics or hide for long periods of time in the "open space" of free societies. As has often been said, nonstate actors have no home address.

One nonmilitary form of asymmetric engagement that is beginning to emerge as a key piece of U.S. strategy involves state-to-society relationships. There has been much talk the last three years about reinvigorating U.S. public diplomacy, though the results thus far have been mixed. Inevitably, if this project is to be successful in the context of the "war on terror," it will have to deal head-on with issues of religion.[25]

Religion clearly has an important place in the evaluation of symmetric threats; states have religious histories, laws, and characters that can be taken into account. In the evaluation of asymmetric threats, however, the role of religion is often even more important. In a region like Central Asia, where the primary nonstate actors have ties (some tenuous, some very deep) to religious traditions, and are consciously acting in accordance with publicly declared moral norms, it would be foolish to take religion off the table as part of an overall, state-to-society engagement. Discussion of religious freedom is a necessary part of any such engagement strategy and is particularly important in those parts of the world that have a history—but no current political implementation—of religious tolerance. To quote Jack Miles again:

> It is an oft-repeated truism that democratic capitalist states do not make war on other democratic capitalist states in the pursuit of political or economic power. This can be expanded to include religion: societies in which there is freedom of religion do not make religious war on other religiously free societies. It must be stressed, though, that the unit of comparison here is not the state but the society. But how does a state engage a society about the society's religion? State-to-state diplomacy, even as it touches upon religion, is well enough understood. Informal society-to-society diplomacy or "public diplomacy" is equally well understood; religious delegations undertaking people-to-people missions are increasingly familiar. But asymmetrical, state-to-society diplomacy with religious reform as its target is virtually without precedent in the modern West.[26]

The impulse to engage in this sort of diplomacy on issues of religion need not stem simply from progressive liberal values, and ought not stem from any sectarian impulse to proselytize on behalf of the "national faith." It is, rather, a necessity of strategy.

Strategy is the ultimate dialectic. In any conflict, the enemy gets a vote. In any plan of our devising, "the other" has a say by way of his or her response. The imperative, therefore—and the purpose for this discussion of U.S. preconceptions—is to address not only how "we" think, but how "they" think. This means, among other things, redrawing our maps, geographic and psychological, to better describe how they see the world; taking seriously, when appropriate for the purposes of analysis, their genuine religious motivations; and viewing regional issues through the eyes of those who do not consider strategy through the lens of the state. These are changes to which we in the West are not inclined; but the security issues they highlight are ones to which we are not immune. For its part, the United States has little choice but to deal with this global reality in accordance with its regional contexts. If it cannot, its interests and values will suffer.

Uzbekistan: Islam and Political Grievance

Uzbekistan is the key to Central Asian stability. It has the region's largest population and strongest military, and it is contiguous with the other four former Soviet republics, plus Afghanistan. With a population that is nearly 90 percent Muslim (with the balance mostly Russian Orthodox), it is also fairly representative of the region's religious demographics.[27] Economically, the country has little to show for over a decade of independence: foreign direct investment is low, corruption is high, the currency has only recently been convertible, and real wages are by most accounts stagnant.[28] There are still other reasons to be concerned: With nearly one-third of its population unemployed, Uzbekistan has seen a rise in illicit drug use, HIV infection rates, and suicides. Combine this with a population in which 60 percent is under the age of twenty-five; something has to give.[29]

The government, led by former Communist Party boss and now President Islam Karimov, has not lived up to its promises of reform. Press freedom is almost nonexistent. Torture is widespread. Freedom of religion is severely circumscribed. In spite of Uzbekistan being a nation of great promise and resources, the government has taken only a few small steps forward toward respect for human rights and a functioning market economy. This harsh political environment does not, however, exist in a vacuum. The government has been challenged by radical Islamic groups, and the state's political repression must be seen as both a consequence and a cause of this confrontation. Two Islamic groups feature prominently: the Islamic Movement of Uzbekistan and the Hizb ut-Tahrir.

The Islamic Movement of Uzbekistan: Ulterior Ends

On February 16, 1999, Tashkent was rocked by several bomb blasts. In what was an apparent assassination attempt on Islam Karimov, five coordinated blasts occurred simultaneously around the capital. Karimov narrowly avoided the blast meant for him at the Cabinet of Ministers' Building. Never late, he had been delayed momentarily at his previous location by a minute or so. The government attributed the blasts to the Islamic Movement of Uzbekistan

(IMU)—a shadowy, radical Islamic group whose leaders, Juma Namangani and Takhir Yuldashev, had connections to al Qaeda's Osama bin Laden, the Taliban in Afghanistan, Chechen separatists, and the Tajik opposition from that country's civil war in the mid-1990s.[30] Following the blasts, Namangani and Yuldashev were sentenced in absentia, and fell back to Tajikistan and Afghanistan. From these locations they launched limited guerrilla infiltrations into Uzbekistan in 2000 and 2001. Namangani was killed in Afghanistan in late 2001 (where the IMU was fighting alongside al Qaeda and the Taliban), and the current status of the movement remains uncertain.

The IMU effectively dates back to 1991, when Yuldashev and Namangani—both in their twenties and influenced by fundamentalist missionaries—formed an Islamic "neighborhood crime watch" in Namangan (they called it "Adolat," which means "justice"). In a face-to-face confrontation with President Karimov in Namangan in December of 1991, they called for the establishment of an Islamic Uzbek state, which President Karimov rejected.[31] (It was this confrontation that led to Karimov's first crackdown on radical Islam in March of 1992.) The goal of the IMU from that date onward was framed in religious terms, superficially rooted in a simplistic understanding of Islam. In contrast to other Islamic revivalist groups, the IMU "had no respect for official Islam, no patience with tradition, and no fear of the political regime, which they overoptimistically considered to be on the verge of disintegration and collapse."[32] Namangani, who served as the almost mythical rebel leader of the IMU, was a skilled warrior and organizer whose religious message functioned as a means to his more pragmatic ends: destabilizing the Uzbek regime. Congruent with this approach was the IMU's heavy involvement in narcotics trafficking between Afghanistan and Russia, which also created political instability in Uzbekistan. It is likely that the political and financial goals of the IMU were symbiotic, and that the organization's Islamic identity was used to provide rationale, networks, and funding.[33]

As a result of the poor economic situation in Uzbekistan, the IMU was able to garner some support among the common people, particularly in the Fergana valley. On the whole, though, its approach was nonideological and insufficiently managed to channel local discontent in such a way as to make the IMU a legitimate broad-based political alternative to the Karimov regime.[34]

The Hizb ut-Tahrir: Undefined Means

If the IMU can be described as tactically inadequate, strategically bereft, and ideologically shallow, the Hizb ut-Tahrir (HT), or Party of Liberation, is at least in some respects the opposite. It is heavy on ideology and strong on tactics and organization; and, as of yet, it is uncommitted to the use of violence to achieve its ends. But while the HT has developed an advanced organization based around superior recruiting and secretive cells of five to seven people, the organization apparently lacks a pronounced strategy.[35] (Whether this is intentional or not, remains to be seen.) The HT was founded in 1953 in Saudi Arabia and Jordan by a Palestinian sheik.[36] It once had close ties to the Muslim Brotherhood in Egypt, the ideological forebear of many of the modern-day radical Islamic groups. The HT's goal, which envisions the establishment of a Central Asian caliphate, is pursued through an intentional three-stage strategy modeled on the life of the prophet Muhammad. The first stage is quiet recruitment and outreach; the second stage involves persuading the worldwide Muslim community of the rightness of the group's Islamic practice; and the third stage is the establishment of an Islamic government in accordance with shari'ah law.[37] Two things are striking about this agenda. The first is its ideological incompatibility with traditional Central Asian Muslim values. The second is the HT's seemingly ill-defined plan to move from the first stage to the agenda's ultimate ends.[38]

The HT's ideology is, on multiple counts, alien to Central Asian values and to the region's experience of Islam. Although the HT has split from the Saudi Arabian Wahhabi movement that helped to inspire it, the two groups share very similar beliefs, and maintain connections, though perhaps primarily at lower levels.[39] (We should note, though, that the government of Uzbekistan still conveniently attaches the pejorative Wahhabi label to the HT.) Ideologically speaking, the HT is basically Middle Eastern in origin, and thus culturally dissimilar from traditional Central Asian Islam. Whereas Islam in Central Asia has generally been flexible in applying religious law to public matters, the HT advocates the establishment of a much more rigorous, exclusive, political expression of the faith. And whereas Central Asia has a history of religious tolerance among the various Muslim sects, the HT is both virulently anti-Sufi and anti-Shi'ite. Add to this the HT anti-Semitic rhetoric that simply does not square with the long-standing, peaceful history of Jews in Central Asia (who were once a sizeable minority based in Bukhara), and the HT agenda is clearly at odds with Central Asian values.

Not only is the HT ideology foreign to Central Asia, but its plan for bringing about a caliphate is extraordinarily ill-defined. Claiming to eschew violence, the HT has never explained how its dream would ever materialize. One is left to conclude that either the HT plan is naïvely idealistic about the possibility of peaceful reform, or that the HT's network could one day be mobilized in support of a violent rebellion. Whichever it may be, though, one thing is certain: the movement is growing quickly. Introduced in Uzbekistan in 1995, the group already has a support base of at least 15,000 members.[40] How to explain such rapid growth?

There are a couple of important underlying reasons for the HT's success, reasons that again place Uzbekistan at the forefront of discussions of religion and security. The first reason is that for all of the distance between the HT ideology and traditional Central Asian Islam, there are still points of congruity between HT tactics and Uzbek culture. The fact that the HT is nonviolent appeals to the Uzbek sensibility (and lays the foundation for future manipulation by shrewd political entrepreneurs); Uzbeks, unlike some of their ethnic neighbors, are a largely passive people. The HT approach—organizing converts through relational networks into study cells—is bound to resonate with many Uzbeks. As Ahmed Rashid points out, some Uzbeks are also taken with the idea of a revived Ottoman Empire (though they fail to note that, unlike the HT, the Ottomans tolerated different Islamic schools of thought, and frequently non-Muslims as well).[41]

Second, the HT functions as a popular grievance mechanism for Uzbeks who are frustrated with a poor economy, official corruption, and government repression. With all opposition parties effectively banned and mass media outlets tightly controlled, Uzbeks have little opportunity to voice dissent. The hopes of the last decade have slowly dissipated, and resentment has taken their place. The police are particularly resented. Their bribe-taking and harsh closing of local bazaars have engendered quiet anger on the part of many Uzbeks. The March 2004 bombings across Uzbekistan were carried out as retaliation against these police forces and what they represent: a government that is corrupt and either unable or unwilling to provide jobs and a better economic future.[42]

Related to, and building upon, this anger is deep resentment about the government's response to the HT. As has been well documented, over 5,800 Uzbeks have been incarcerated in recent years on allegations of affiliation with the group.[43] Many innocent, pious Muslims have been caught up in this dragnet, and in the population centers nearly everyone has a friend whose father or brother has been taken away under this suspicion. The impact of this government campaign on the growth of the HT cannot be underestimated; it is, without a doubt, fueling the growth of the organization. In its attempt to rein in what it considers to be a threatening movement, the government has in fact exacerbated its own security problem. Most Uzbeks today are sympathetic to the HT because they are wrongly oppressed. The HT promise of social justice resonates loudly, especially in the cities.

Here the nexus between religion and security is particularly subtle. There is the real possibility that the HT will, in the words of a Kyrgyz journalist, "change lanes" as the Muslim Brotherhood did in Egypt, and move from peaceful advocacy to violent radicalism.[44] As Philip Jenkins observed earlier in this volume, it is not difficult to leverage clandestine networks into "a substantial and potentially dangerous framework that can be exploited by enemies of a state in the long term." Under this scenario, the HT is justly considered a threat to state interests.[45]

But the political context must be considered. The HT has been successful in recruiting because of its status—legitimized, ironically, by the government repression—as an outlet for political grievance. The organization's agenda lacks broad-based cultural and religious appeal, and, depending on the context, it remains uncertain as to whether or not it would thrive "above ground." Were it no longer to wear the badge of the "persecuted opposition," the HT would be forced to explain its agenda and its solutions more clearly. That is a losing proposition for the organization. Unfortunately, the government seems intent on writing its own losing proposition, and thus making it more likely for HT to survive above ground in a future political context where the HT is legitimately popular. By providing no outlet for political grievance, and little outlet for genuine religious devotional practice, the government is, in the name of stability, working against its own security interests. Whether such an approach will eventually pressure HT networks into open foment is still to be seen.

Calculating the Risks

To its credit, the government of Uzbekistan recognizes that, of the two radical Islamic movements that it faces, the HT poses the greater risk. The combination of potent ideology and effective organization is a hallmark of successful resistance movements. That the HT's ideology is not at home in Central Asia will be beside the point if the government crackdown continues to afford the group the privilege of being an outlet for political and economic frustration. The IMU and its successors (and there will be successors) lack the fervent faith dimension that has the potential to make the HT so dangerous.

Judged against Jenkins' rubric, there is plenty to be worried about if the government crackdown continues. Of the five themes he identifies in chapter 2 linking religious persecution to political instability (see pages 27–34), the scorecard for the HT is troubling. *Going Underground:* The HT employs a secretive cell structure in all of those countries in which it is politically threatened. *Holy Warriors:* Not yet applicable, but some HT leaders hint that they would not oppose violent action if other groups initiated it. *People of Blood:* The apocalyptic is already a part of the HT ideology, and just as the idea of martyrdom has been assimilated from Shi'ite to Sunni Islam, it could easily be brought into the HT context. Tragically, it already exists in the Uzbek context with the March 2004 terrorist acts of female suicide bombers. *Men of God:* The hierarchical structure and declared aims of the HT organization would lend themselves to the creation of a clerical elite were the movement to be brought aboveground. *Brothers Across the Seas:* The links, both historical and contemporary, between HT and other Islamic organizations are well known, and are only likely to grow with time.

In addition, there is reason to be concerned about the kind of followers the HT is recruiting: many are young, reflecting Uzbekistan's burgeoning youth population. Many are well educated and drawn from outside the rural areas. And even those who are recruited without significant education are brought into an extended process of theological and ideological training. This, as Samuel Huntington has observed, has real security implications: "The higher the level of education of the unemployed, alienated, or otherwise dissatisfied person, the more extreme the destabilizing behavior which results. Alienated university graduates prepare revolutions; alienated technical or secondary school graduates plan coups; alienated primary school leavers engage in more frequent but less significant forms of political unrest."[46] In other words, it is easy to imagine the emergence of a "Lenin" in such a context, promising "land, peace, and bread" as simple answers to complex problems, even as those answers cover the real motives behind the revolution.[47]

All of these factors combine to produce a picture of an organization that, unless properly neutralized, could—perhaps in conjunction with more pragmatic movements like the IMU, or a spontaneous local resistance movement—rise up in opposition to the current regime, thus destabilizing the entire region.

Conclusion

Even a cursory overview suggests that a comprehensive security strategy in Central Asia must take account of religious history and motivation, and that the role of religion in the social context can be a potent force for instability. A second conclusion, further examined in this volume, is that religion's role also has the potential to be positive—a force for regional security and social stability. One does not have to look too far back into the past to find a Central Asia where religious mores—say, those of the Sufi and Jadidist traditions—were conducive to security rather than destabilizing in nature.

An examination of the HT's popularity also suggests quite strongly that religious freedom has a key role to play in the establishment of secure states. Most people in Uzbekistan will tell you openly that, were a culturally congruent form of religious freedom to be endorsed in Uzbekistan that legalized the HT and its practices, the group would quickly lose its "opposition" cachet, and, failing to attract members on the basis of ideology alone, would dramatically recede as a security threat. It does not require American-style religious freedom to see this through. As many historians of religion have noted, religious freedom has to emerge from within a cultural context, and does not easily take root in a culture when imposed from the outside. Uzbekistan would be wise to cultivate a set of religious freedoms that reclaim the region and nation's tolerant Muslim identity, and still protect against groups that might do serious harm to national security or social stability.

The decision to pursue such a policy is often a difficult one, because in the short term, religious freedom—and indeed, all freedoms—can sometimes produce instability associated with change. But over the long term, as Thomas Farr has persuasively argued, religious freedom "will almost certainly be stabilizing because it channels and protects a human activity which is stabilizing and productive, not only on personal terms but in civil society terms. . . . If we shut people out of society because of their religion we risk radicalizing them."[48] This is truer today in Central Asia than perhaps any other part of the world, and it flies in the face of that region's control-oriented bureaucratic culture inherited from the Soviet system. But in the long run, as Central Asian states look to preserve public order amid growing domestic discontent and religious radicalism, they would do well to be reminded that religious freedom is undeniably central to the preservation of regional security.

Those in the U.S. policy community can facilitate this process, both formally and informally. The balancing of hard and soft power is the ongoing challenge of U.S. policy in Central Asia. The Uzbeks, for example—not without some justification—have since 1995 seen the State Department as the "bad cop" and the Pentagon as the "good cop." To be sure, there is room for both roles. But until the "hard power" Pentagon learns to advocate "soft power" issues like religious freedom in a security context, U.S. influence in Uzbekistan will necessarily be limited, as will the effectiveness of the Uzbek security policy with which the U.S. government is complicit.[49]

The case of Central Asia, and how the United States responds, will have profound implications for the projection of national power over the coming years in both the region and the world. Make no mistake, we are now creating patterns in international relations that will determine the course of the twenty-first century. If the United States cannot find a way to credibly represent its societal values—not least of which is religious freedom, dating back to Roger Williams in 1636—and place these values in the context of real regional security issues, it will not have learned the lessons of the last century.

Notes

1. Jack Miles, "Religion and American Foreign Policy," *Survival* 46, no. 1 (Spring 2004): 25.

2. We define Central Asia as the five former Soviet republics—Kazakhstan, Kyrgyzstan, Tajikistan, Turkmenistan, and Uzbekistan—plus Afghanistan.

3. The sources cited in this paper have been supplemented by the authors' interviews with U.S. and Uzbek officials in Washington, D.C., and Tashkent during the period 1999–2004. Names withheld upon request.

4. The Taliban was fueled by radical Islamic students (or "talibs") who had been trained in the Islamic seminaries (*madrassas*) of neighboring Pakistan.

5. Troy S. Thomas and Stephen D. Kiser, "Lords of the Silk Route: Violent Non-State Actors in Central Asia," Occasional Paper #43 of the U.S. Air Force Institute for National Security Studies, May 2002, 61.

6. Roald Sagdeev, "Central Asia and Islam: An Overview," in *Islam and Central Asia*, eds. Roald Sagdeev and Susan Eisenhower (Washington, DC: Center for Political and Strategic Studies, 2000), 7.

7. Zoroastrianism is an ancient religion founded by Zarathushtra (also known as Zoroaster) sometime between 1400 and 600 B.C.E. It was the state religion of various Persian empires through the seventh century C.E. The principal symbol of the Zoroastrian cult is the sacred fire, which represents the supreme deity.

8. Ahmed Rashid, *Jihad: The Rise of Militant Islam in Central Asia* (New York: Penguin Books, 2003), 26. See also Sagdeev, "Central Asia and Islam," 7.

9. Adeeb Khalid, *The Politics of Muslim Cultural Reform: Jadidism in Central Asia* (Berkeley, CA: University of California Press, 1998), 93.

10. Rashid, *Jihad*, 12.

11. Rashid, *Jihad*, 30.

12. See T. Jeremy Gunn, "Shaping an Islamic Identity: Religion, Islamism, and the State in Central Asia," *Sociology of Religion* 64, no. 3 (Fall 2003): 389–410.

13. Rashid, *Jihad*, 39.

14. Rashid, *Jihad*, 28.

15. Sagdeev, "Central Asia and Islam," 17.

16. Khalid, *The Politics of Muslim Cultural Reform*, 184.

17. CIA World Factbook 2003, www.cia.gov (accessed 15 April 2004).

18. Interview by the author (Chris Seiple) with Uzbek and USAID officials, April 2004. There are about 2.2 million farmers in Uzbekistan, working on 250,000 hectares of land along 1,000 miles of irrigation channels.

19. Rashid, *Jihad*, 47.

20. For an overview of the potential for cooperation and competition among the Central Asian states, see Martha Brill Olcott, "Central Asia: Common Legacies and Conflicts," in *Central Asian Security: The New International Context*, eds. Roy Allison and Lena Jonson (London: Royal Institute of International Affairs, 2001), 24–48.

21. Halford J. Mackinder, "The Geographical Pivot of History," *Geographical Journal* 23 (April 1904): 421–37.

22. The mythologizing of Timur the Lame as the original Uzbek hero is all the more striking when one considers that he predates the anthropological consolidation of the Uzbeks as an ethnic group. See Edward A. Allworth, *The Modern Uzbeks: From the 14th Century to the Present: A Cultural History* (Stanford, CA: Hoover Institute Press, 1990).

23. U.S. European Command (EUCOM) originally argued that Central Asia should be in its Area of Responsibility, but then–CENTCOM Commander-in-Chief Gen. Anthony Zinni carried the day. (This was in part because EUCOM was consumed by the conflict in Kosovo and did not have the political capital to wage a bureaucratic war for five more countries when it already had more than ninety, and CENTCOM, at the time, only sixteen.)

24. Graham Fuller, *The Future of Political Islam* (New York: Palgrave/Macmillan, 2003), 193.

25. For further discussion of this approach, see Chris Seiple, "The Grand Strategy: Sustainment" in *In the Shadow of War* (vol. 4 in the "Defeating Terrorism, Developing Dreams" series) (Philadelphia, PA: Chelsea House Publishers, 2004); "Religion and the New Global Counterinsurgency," in *The Iraq War* (vol. 5 in the "Defeating Terrorism, Developing Dreams" series).

26. Miles, "Religion and American Foreign Policy," 32–33.

27. "Central Asians Differ on Islam's Political Role, But Agree on a Secular State," *Opinion Analysis* (Washington, DC: Office of Research, U.S. Department of State, M-95-00, July 6, 2000).

28. See, for example, Transparency International Corruption Perceptions Index 2003 (accessed October 7, 2003), www.transparency.org. For economic data on Uzbekistan, see U.S. State Department Background Note on Uzbekistan, www.state.gov/r/pa/ei/bgn/2924.htm; www.bearingpoint.uz; and www.cer.uz.

29. Interview by the author (Chris Seiple) with an Uzbek official, April 2004.

30. The 1999 bombings were never confirmed to have been carried out by the IMU; it is possible they were planned by one of Karimov's political rivals, or, as some theories hold, by Karimov's government. See Abdumannob Polat and Nickolai Butkevich, "Unraveling the Mystery of the Tashkent Bombings: Theories and Implications," *Demokratizatsiya* 8, no. 4 (2000).

31. Various interviews by the author (Chris Seiple). See also Chris Seiple, "Questions and More Questions: The Islamic Movement of Uzbekistan, Uzbek National Security, and U.S. Policy," unpublished paper, December 11, 2000.

32. Rashid, *Jihad*, 139.

33. Selling drugs to European or "Christian" markets is often portrayed as another kind of *jihad* because the end users are "infidels."

34. In this respect, the IMU provides interesting analogues to Che Guevara's methodology of insurgency. This method, based on the unique circumstances that brought Castro's band of several hundred guerrillas to power as the Batista regime collapsed from corruption, focused on military action before political activation. Guevara felt that the peasants would rise up if they saw someone taking up their cause. He did not take into account local realities or the need for local ownership of the ideology (cf. Mao Tse-tung, who spent years on political activation before taking up arms). It is no accident that Guevara died basically alone in a foreign country that did not understand his ideology or methodology.

35. Alisher Khamidov, "Countering the Call: The U.S., Hizb-ut-Tahrir, and Religious Extremism in Central Asia," Brookings Analysis Paper no. 4, July 2003, 7.

36. Rashid, *Jihad*, 116.

37. Khamidov, "Countering the Call," 6.

38. For a thorough overview of the HT, see "Radical Islam in Central Asia: Responding to Hizb Ut-Tahrir," International Crisis Group, June 30, 2003 (ICG Asia Report no. 58).

39. While Central Asia developed the most liberal form of Sunni Muslim practice, Saudi Arabia developed Wahhabism, based on the eighteenth-century puritan teachings of Muhammad ibn Abd al-Wahhab; if oil had never been discovered in the Arabian peninsula, we would probably never have known his name. As it now stands, the Uzbek government attaches his name to any Islamic threat, real or perceived.

40. Uzbek officials report that Tashkent alone has 6,000 HT members, a conservative number, and that the group is particularly strong in all of the major cities.

41. Rashid, *Jihad*, 122.

42. For further analysis, see Chris Seiple, "Implications of Terrorism in Uzbekistan," Foreign Policy Research Institute E-Note, April 12, 2004, www.fpri.org.

43. See "Creating Enemies of the State: Religious Persecution in Uzbekistan," Human Rights Watch, March 30, 2004.

44. Khamidov, "Countering the Call," 7–8.

45. Legal in the U.K., the HT is in fact banned in Germany.

46. Samuel Huntington, *Political Order in Changing Societies* (New Haven, CT: Yale University Press, 1968), 48.

47. It would not be surprising if future historians were to find among HT literature the equivalent to Lenin's 1902 Treatise, "What is to be Done?" where he bridges the intellectual gap between agrarian Russia and Marxist labor by creating a "Vanguard of the Proletariat" that resulted in the 1917 Bolshevik revolution and seizure of power.

48. Thomas Farr, "First Freedoms," *The Brandywine Review of Faith & International Affairs* 2, no. 1 (Spring 2004): 43–48. Interview by the author (Joshua White).

49. For further policy recommendations, see Chris Seiple, "Heartland Politics and the Case of Uzbekistan," Foreign Policy Research Institute E-Note, January 25, 2004, www.fpri.org; and "Strategic Objectives: Central Asia," a presentation to the President of Uzbekistan's Institute for Strategic and Regional Studies, September 19, 2001, www.globalengagement.org/issues/2001/09/cseiple-uzbek-strategy.htm.

PERSPECTIVES ON PLURALISM:
MAKING A WORLD SAFE FOR DIVERSITY

4

Choosing Exclusion or Embrace:
An Abrahamic Theological Perspective

Manfred T. Brauch

IN THE AFTERMATH OF THE GENOCIDAL VIOLENCE in post-Communist Yugoslavia, where Croatian Catholics, Muslims, and Jews became the victims of Orthodox Serbian *cetnik*, Croatian author Miroslav Volf penned one of the most profound theological treatises of our time: *Exclusion and Embrace: A Theological Exploration of Identity, Otherness and Reconciliation.* "For months," writes Volf, these notorious Serbian fighters "had been sowing desolation in my native country, herding people into concentration camps, raping women, burning down churches and destroying cities."[1] Volf had witnessed nothing less than Europe's worst massacre since the Second World War. Ironically, Srebrenica had been declared a "safe zone" by the United Nations peacekeeping forces when it was overrun by Serbian soldiers in July 1995, who summarily executed nearly 8,000 Muslims, most of them men and boys.

In the context of this tragedy, which in various ways implicated the Abrahamic faith traditions, Volf's rich book struggles with the tension between God's embrace of humanity, on the one hand, and on the other hand the human proclivity to exclude "the other" in ways that lead to horrific violence.

Manfred T. Brauch is the James A. Maxwell Professor of Biblical Theology at Eastern Baptist Theological Seminary. Previously, he served the seminary as academic dean (1978–1986) and president (1989–1997). His articles have been published in numerous journals including *Christianity Today* and *Tyndale Theological Bulletin,* and he has contributed essays to *Dictionary of Paul and His Letters* (InterVarsity, 1993), *The Evangelical Roundtable* (Princeton, 1986), and *Paul and Palestinian Judaism* (Fortress, 1977). He is the author of *Hard Sayings of Paul* (InterVarsity, 1989) and *Set Free to Be* (Judson, 1975).

Why, despite many shared theological resources for choosing embrace, do the children of Abraham choose exclusion? It is a question that now haunts not only the Balkans but the whole post-9/11 world. Lasting peace and security in our present context of religiously motivated terrorism and "civilization conflict" will only be achieved by choosing reconciliation—a choice that is only sustainable when "embrace" is seen as theologically and spiritually legitimate to all parties.

The connection between Volf's treatise and the present-day struggle for security among the literal and spiritual descendants of Abraham, via Ishmael or Isaac, is strikingly illustrated by the book's cover photo, *Abraham's Farewell to Ishmael.*[2] This moving sculpture presents the figures of Abraham and his son Ishmael in tender embrace, while Ishmael's mother, the Egyptian Hagar, stands hidden in the shadows and Abraham's wife Sarah (who, according to the biblical Genesis narrative, demanded the expulsion of Hagar and Ishmael) stands with back turned toward Abraham and Ishmael, in a gesture of cold exclusion.

In light of this image, in this chapter we shall reflect biblically and theologically on the gap between the actual scriptural vision—in which God has a blessing for each of the major groups in the Abrahamic lineage—and the ongoing reality among the Abrahamic faith traditions, namely exclusion and insecurity. I will contend that the pluralism of the Abrahamic "family" will only offer authentic and stable security and freedom when each member of the family finds the courage to deal honestly with areas of theological common ground in scripture, thereby enabling each to choose to embrace "the other" in a way that does not sacrifice theological integrity.

After surveying the Abrahamic lineage of Judaism, Christianity, and Islam, as well as the history of conflict between these traditions, our primary example of Abrahamic common ground in scriptural terms will be the Prophet Isaiah's vision for Israel, Assyria, and Egypt. Isaiah, proclaiming his message to Judah and Jerusalem in the latter half of the eighth century B.C.E. (742–701) during a time of national crisis, articulated a bold vision: Historic enemies—Assyria, Israel and Egypt—shall be reconciled and become a blessing in the midst of the earth (Isaiah 19:23–25). The foundation for this radical vision is Isaiah's affirmation that the same God who calls Israel "my heritage" also calls Egypt "my people" and Assyria "the work of my hands." Why has this vision not been a more effective resource for peace and security? The problem is not with the prophet's original words, but with the way those words were deliberately recast (and mistranslated) in succeeding centuries by the political-religious establishment into an ethnocentric religious exclusiveness.

It is but one example of the kind of theological habit we must learn how to break. For the sake not only of "our" security, but the security of "the other," we must find a way to be true to our own traditions *and* answer the prophetic call to *embrace.*

Our Father Abraham

Three major monotheistic religious traditions—Judaism, Christianity, and Islam—locate their distant origins in the biblical figure of Abraham and his descendants. As John Esposito has aptly described it, "Jews, Christians and Muslims are . . . children of Abraham. However, they belong to different branches of the same family."[3]

For the first of these traditions, Judaism, the connection with Abraham is rooted in the patriarchal narratives of the book of Genesis, and particularly in the story of God's calling of Abraham (Genesis 12:1) and the promise that his progeny would become a great nation and a blessing to "all the families of the earth" (Genesis 12:2–3). Israel's patriarchal traditions are most likely to be dated in the middle of the second millennium B.C.E. The ancestry of Judaism in Abraham and his descendants is affirmed throughout the Torah. A frequent designation of the God of Israel in the Hebrew Bible is "the God of Abraham, the God of Isaac, and the God of Jacob" (e.g., Exodus 3:6; 4:5; I Kings 18:36; I Chronicles 29:18). Jacob's progeny, through his twelve sons and their descendants, constituted the Israelite tribes resident in the land of Egypt (Genesis 46–50), whom Moses led from Egyptian bondage through the wilderness toward the promised land of Canaan.

Throughout this period of their history, they are reminded that they are the descendants of Abraham, Isaac, and Jacob (Exodus 32:13), that Yahweh (the name of God in the Hebrew scriptures) is faithful to the covenant with them and their descendants (Leviticus 26:42) and that Yahweh's promise of land to their ancestor Abraham will be fulfilled (Deuteronomy 1:8; 30:20; 34:4). Poised for entry into the land of promise, the people of Israel are exhorted by Moses to remember that "a wandering Aramean was my father" (Deuteronomy 26:5) and to recite this fact of their collective identity, together with the history of Egyptian bondage and divine deliverance, regularly in their cultic worship.

Toward the end of his life and the conclusion of his leadership of the tribes of Israel in the conquest and settlement of much of the land of Canaan, Joshua gathers the tribes at Schechem and rehearses for them their divinely led history, beginning with "your father Abraham" (Joshua 24:1–13). Centuries later, Yahweh proclaims through his prophet: "Look to the rock from which you were hewn. . . . Look to Abraham your father and to Sarah who bore you" (Isaiah 51:1–2). On the basis of this extensive confessional history, "all the Jews trace their ancestry to Abraham as father of the Hebrew nation."[4]

Chronologically, the second Abrahamic faith tradition, whose roots are deep in the soil of Judaism, is Christianity. Its beginnings in the third decade of the first century C.E., under the impulse of the teaching and ministry of the prophetic figure Jesus of Nazareth (Matthew 21:11; Luke 7:16; Acts 2:22), is marked in the Christian scriptures (the New Testament) by numerous affirmations of both the connection between Jesus and Abraham, and the continuity between the Abrahamic covenant community (Israel) and the new covenant community constituted by Jew and Gentile.

The Gospel of Matthew begins its account of Jesus' life and ministry with these words: "An account of the genealogy of Jesus the Messiah, the son of David, the son of Abraham" (1:1), and then traces the genealogy from Abraham through forty-two generations to Jesus. Whereas the Gospel of Luke emphasizes the universal orientation of early Christianity, and therefore traces the genealogy of Jesus all the way to Adam at the head of the human race, the heritage of Jesus nonetheless passes through Abraham (Luke 3:23–38).

The grounding of the Jesus story in the story of Abraham and his descendants is focused particularly on the connection between the promise to Abraham—that through his progeny the nations would be blessed (Genesis 12:1–3)—and the life and work of Jesus. That is clear in the narratives surrounding the birth of Jesus. In the "Magnificat" of Mary, the coming of Jesus is celebrated in these words:

> [God] has helped his servant Israel,
> in remembrance of his mercy,
> according to the promise he made
>   to our ancestors,
> to Abraham and to his
>   descendants forever.

> (Luke 1:54–55)

The doxology on the lips of the priest Zechariah—in response to the birth of John and in anticipation of the deliverer whom John would announce—begins with the affirmation:

> Blessed be the God of Israel
>   for he has looked favorably on
>   his people and redeemed them.

> (Luke 1:68)

and goes on to confess that

> [God] has shown the mercy
> promised to our ancestors,
> and he has remembered his
> holy covenant,
> the oath that he swore to our
> ancestor Abraham.

(Luke 1:72–73)

These connections with the Abrahamic faith tradition of Judaism are strongly affirmed in subsequent decades when early Christian identity is being shaped as the "Israel of God" (Galatians 6:16), in which "the Gentiles have become fellow heirs" with Jews (Ephesians 3:6) and where Jew and Gentile are brought together as "members of the household of God" (Ephesians 2:19). This faith community is addressed as "a chosen race, a royal priesthood, a holy nation, God's own people" (I Peter 2:9), in language that clearly affirms continuity with the people of Israel. Followers of Jesus, both Jewish and Gentile, are said to be "Abraham's offspring, heirs according to promise" (Galatians 3:29). That reality, says Paul the Apostle, is the result of God's promise to Abraham that "All the Gentiles shall be blessed in you" (Galatians 3:8). Therefore, Jewish and Gentile believers "are blessed with Abraham who believed" (Galatians 3:9; cf. Romans 4:12).

In agreement with this Pauline understanding of early Christian identity, John's Gospel insists that those who display Abraham's faith and deeds are Abraham's offspring (John 8:31–41). The Epistle of James, addressed to "the twelve tribes in the Dispersion" (James 1:1), calls Christians to emulate Abraham's faith and its manifestation in good works and refers to Abraham as "our ancestor" (James 2:21). Since the term "Dispersion" described Jews living outside Palestine (the Diaspora), its metaphorical use to identify Jesus' followers (perhaps Jewish Christians) testifies to the earliest Christians' sense of connectedness with Israel (cf. I Peter 1:1). Finally, as Marvin Wilson has noted, "according to the book of Hebrews, Abraham's faithful obedience, from the moment God called him (Hebrews 11:8f) serves as an inspiring witness to the Church (12:1), that new people of God both rooted in Abraham and numbered among his children."[5]

The third Abrahamic faith tradition, Islam, emerged from the life and teaching of the prophet Muhammad on the Arabian peninsula in the period 610–632 C.E. What is of particular note is that Muhammad did not see himself as the founder of a new religion. John Esposito argues rightly that Muhammad was instead a religious reformer, seeking to call people "back to the one, true God and to a way of life that most of his contemporaries had forgotten or deviated from Worship of Allah was not the evolutionary emergence of monotheism from polytheism but a return to a forgotten past, to the faith of the first monotheist, Abraham."[6]

Throughout the Qur'an—the deposit of the recitations of Muhammad—
Abraham is recognized as the first true believer and the prototypical Muslim—that is, "one who submits to God."[7] In Sura 16:120–123, Muhammad is
urged by *Allah* (the Arabic word for God, like the Hebrew cognate *Elohim*) to
adopt the way of Abraham, his predecessor in the faith (cf. Sura 3:95; 2:135).
This affinity with the earlier Abrahamic faiths is expressed as follows in Sura
2.135–136:

> They say: "Become Jews or Become Christians
> and find the right way."
> Say: "No, we follow the way of Abraham
> the upright, who was not a idolater."
> Say: "We believe in God
> and what has been sent down to us,
> and what has been revealed
> to Abraham and Ishmael
> and Isaac and Jacob and their progeny,
> and that which was given to Moses and Christ,
> and to all the other prophets of the Lord.
> We make no distinction among them
> And we submit to Him.[8]

The above citation from the Qur'an reveals a unique aspect of Islamic tradition vis-à-vis both Judaism and Christianity. Namely, Ishmael appears in the
catalog of those to whom God has revealed his will. According to Genesis 16,
Ishmael was Abraham's firstborn son by his Egyptian wife Hagar. Although
excluded from the covenant God established with Isaac (Abraham's son by his
wife Sarah, Genesis 17:15–19, 21; Genesis 21:1–5), Ishmael nonetheless receives the blessing of God:

> As for Ishmael, I have heard you; I will bless him
> and make him fruitful and exceedingly numerous;
> he shall be the father of twelve princes
> and I will make him a great nation.
>
> (Genesis 17:20)

Within this patriarchal narrative we are also told that God's covenant with
Abraham (Genesis 17:9–14) is sealed in the sign of circumcision of Abraham
and Ishmael and the entire clan (Genesis 17:23–27). Thus, Ishmael is included
in the Abrahamic covenant. When Hagar and her son Ishmael are exiled from
Abraham's family (Genesis 21:8–14), the promise of God's blessing of, and
presence with, Ishmael and his descendants is reaffirmed (Genesis 21:13, 18).

Ishmael marries an Egyptian woman (Genesis 21:21) who, according to the narrative in Genesis 25:12–17, bears him twelve sons. They and his descendants settle in Havilah and Shur, in the southwest region of Arabia (Genesis 25:18).

What is noteworthy about this biblical Israelite tradition is that, while Abrahamic descent in Israel is traced via Isaac (Abraham's son by Sarah), the Islamic faith tradition claims its ancestry in Abraham via Ishmael. "The Qur'an (3:95) and Muslim tradition portray [pre-Islamist Arab monotheists, called *hanifs*] as descendants of Abraham and his son Ishmael."[9]

In keeping with this tradition, the biblical narrative is expanded in the Qur'an to include the building of a place of worship, called the *Ka'bah* (at Mecca) and its purification by Abraham and Ishmael as a place of pilgrimage, contemplation, prayer, and prostration (Sura 2.125–126). Upon the completion of this place of worship, Abraham and Ishmael offer this dedicatory prayer:

> Accept this from us, O Lord . . .
> and make us submit, O Lord, to your will
> and our progeny a people submissive to you.
> Teach us the way of worship
> and forgive us our trespasses,
> for you are compassionate and merciful.
>
> (Sura 2:127–128)

Several of Islam's central convictions are revealed in these texts: (1) that Islam is rooted in the covenant God made with Abraham via Ishmael; (2) that submission to God (Muslim = one who submits) is a central tenet of faith and practice; and (3) that God is compassionate, merciful, and forgiving. The dedicatory prayer ends with the plea that God would send to their descendants a messenger from among them who would recite (Qur'an = recitation) to them his revelation (Sura 2:129). The conclusion is inescapable, namely, that Muhammad, the messenger of God, is understood to be the divine answer to this prayer by Abraham and Ishmael. Indeed, this prayer "has the specific function of bracketing Abraham and Muhammad together."[10]

Abrahamic Pluralism, Abrahamic Common Ground

As we have seen, Jews, Christians, and Muslims are the "children of Abraham." They are also "People of the Book" (e.g., Sura 3:64, 70, 199; 4:47; 5:59, 68, 77), a frequent designation in the Qur'an for Jews, Christians, and Muslims and their sacred scriptures (Hebrew Bible, Old Testament and New Testament, and

Qur'an). They belong to the same family tree in which Abraham's faith in God and the sovereignty of God's will over all human life is extolled. They believe in the one and only God who is Creator and Lord of the world (Deuteronomy 6:4; Isaiah 45:5; 40:18–23; I Corinthians 8:4–6; Romans 1:18–25; Sura 2:255, 3:18; 57:1–6). They are the recipients of divine revelation from the one and only God, revelation intended to guide human life in the ways purposed by God.

Thus, one of Israel's psalmists confesses:

> Your word is a lamp to my feet
> and a light to my path. . . .
> Teach me your ordinances. . . .
> Hold me up, that I may be safe
> and have regard for your statutes continually.
>
> (Psalm 119:105, 108, 117)

Centuries later, the teaching of Jesus affirms his people's scripture as authoritative:

> Do not think that I have come to abolish the law
> and the prophets; I have not come to abolish, but to fulfill.
> For I tell you, until heaven and earth pass away,
> not one letter, not one stroke of a letter, will pass away
> until all is accomplished.
>
> (Matthew 5:17–18)

Likewise, the Apostle Paul writes that

> All scripture is inspired by God, and is useful for teaching,
> for reproof, for correction and for training in righteousness,
> so that everyone who belongs to God may be proficient,
> equipped for every good work.
>
> (II Timothy 3:16–17)

In continuity with these convictions, we find the following words received by Muhammad and recited in the Qur'an:

> He has verily revealed to you this Book,
> in truth and confirmation
> of the books revealed before,
> as indeed He had revealed the Torah and the Gospel
> before this as guidance for men . . .
>
> (Sura 3:3–4)

The scriptures of the children of Abraham call the faithful to walk in the ways of righteousness, justice, and peace. After a devastating critique of Israel's moral degeneration, social corruption, and empty cultic practice (Amos 2:4–5:23), the prophet Amos calls upon his people to

> Let justice roll down like
> waters
> and righteousness like an
> ever-flowing stream.
>
> (Amos 5:24)

Several decades later, the prophet Micah calls the people of Israel beyond the false security of sacrificial ritual:

> He has told you, O mortal, what
> is good.
> And what does the Lord require
> of you
> but to do justice, and to love
> kindness,
> and to walk humbly with
> your God?
>
> (Micah 6:8)

These themes are reaffirmed in the Christian scriptures of the New Testament. The announcements of Jesus' birth in the Gospel narratives are accented with the expectation that he would usher in an era of peace, justice, and righteousness (Luke 2:14). God's mercy and forgiveness would lead to holiness and righteousness (Luke 1:22–75) and "guide our feet into the way of peace" (Luke 1:79). Jesus' teaching about God's will in human life reverberates with these themes:

> Blessed are those who hunger
> and thirst for righteousness,
> for they will be filled.
> Blessed are the merciful,
> for they will receive mercy. . . .
> Blessed are the peacemakers
> for they will be called children of God.
>
> (Matthew 5:6–9)

He called his disciples to a higher standard of righteousness than even that required by the strictest sect in Judaism (Matthew 5:20). In his teaching about the realization of God's reign (the kingdom of God) in human affairs, he called for compassion and mercy (Matthew 18:23–25; Luke 10:30–37), forgiveness (Luke 6:37–38), righteousness (Matthew 6:33), humility (Mark 10:13–16; Luke 14:11), and love of neighbor (Luke 10:27–28), as well as love of the enemy (Matthew 5:43–48; Luke 6:27, 35) and concern for the poor (Luke 16:19–31; Matthew 25:31–46) and for justice (Luke 18:1–8).

This understanding about the embodiment of God's will in society is echoed in the writings of Jesus' followers. Christian responsibility for the poor is a central concern (Acts 4:34–35; I John 3:17–18; Romans 12:13, 15:25–26; James 2:1–7), as well as justice in human affairs (James 5:1–6). An excellent summary of righteous Christian behavior is found in Paul's ethical teaching:

> Bless those who persecute you;
> bless and do not curse them. . . .
> Do not repay anyone evil for evil,
> but take thought for what is noble in the sight of all.
> If possible, so far as it depends on you,
> live peaceably with all.
> Never avenge yourselves. . . .
> No, if your enemies are hungry, feed them;
> if they are thirsty, give them something to drink. . . .
> Do not be overcome by evil,
> but overcome evil with good.
>
> (Romans 12:14–21)

In the letter to the Ephesians—which many scholars consider a circular letter intended as an introduction to a collection of Paul's other letters[11]—the central purpose of God's work in Christ is said to be the shattering of the dividing wall of hostility between Jews and Gentiles, so that

> he might create in himself
> one new humanity in place of the two,
> thus making peace. . . .
>
> (Ephesians 1:14–15)

Finally, the recitations of Muhammad, gathered in the Qur'an, reaffirm these Jewish and Christian convictions about God's will for his people. Allah is the Lord of Mercy (Sura 3:8–9), the Lord of Peace (Sura 3:19), the upholder of justice (Sura 3:18), the one who forgives and extends compassion (Sura 2:128; 3:31–33).

Therefore, his human children are called upon to manifest these virtues in their dealings with one another. Muslims are exhorted to be "custodians of justice" and not to "swerve from justice" (Sura 4:135). The injunction, "verily, God loves those who are just" (Sura 49:9) is concretized in these admonitions:[12]

> Handle the property of orphans with all integrity,
> until he comes of age, seeking only its improvement.
> Keep your bond, for you are accountable.
>
> (Sura 7:34–35)

> Woe to those who act fraudulently,
> Who exact their full measure when in receipt from others,
> yet give short measure
> when they reckon out for others.
>
> (Sura 83:1–6)

Deeds of kindness and generosity toward the poor and needy are lauded (Sura 30:38–39; 2:261–274). Those who ask what they should give in charity are answered:

> Tell them: the utmost you can spare.
>
> (Sura 2:219)

> What you can spare of your wealth
> as should benefit the parents, the relatives,
> the orphans, the needy, the wayfarers;
> for God is not unaware of the good deeds that you do.
>
> (Sura 2:215)

The yearning for harmony and peace among peoples finds voice in this affirmation:

> Humanity! Truly We have created you
> male and female,
> and made you to be nations and tribes
> in order that you might know each other.
>
> (Sura 49:13)

In his analysis of Islamic teaching, Esposito contends that it is "egalitarian; it transcends regional, family, tribal, and ethnic boundaries. It does not recognize social class or caste differences."[13]

A Story of Conflict

None of this is to suggest, of course, that there are no irreconcilable theological differences among the Abrahamic faith traditions. Still, the question remains: why hasn't the social context of robust Abrahamic differences more often been one of peaceful coexistence, dialogue, and persuasion? One would expect that the common ground briefly sketched above would have provided the basis for respectful, mutually affirming, and peaceful relationships. But, as John Kaltner notes, "The sad fact is that for a long time [they] have rarely been on speaking terms and, when they have communicated, they have usually not had nice things to say to each other."[14] Indeed, they have been engaged in bitter conflict for centuries.

This historical acrimony, which continues to be a contemporary reality here at the beginning of the third millennium C.E., has its roots in the age-old disparity between vision and reality within and between these faith traditions. Internally, the result has been fragmentation, schism, rejection, persecution, and violence. Externally, the relations between Judaism, Christianity, and Islam have been marked by ethnocentric exclusivity, religious bigotry, hostility, and often hatred, persecution, violence, and even attempted genocide. Given the nature of today's complex international security challenges, it is the conflicted and hostile relationships between the Abrahamic traditions that most urgently need to be confronted—and, it is hoped, transformed.

Consider the history of Israel's "holy war" tradition, focused on the subjugation and destruction of other cultures and faith traditions and the conquests of their lands.[15] This is amply documented in its sacred texts, particularly in the books of Joshua and Judges. These deal with the settlement of the tribes of Israel in Canaan during the last century of the second millennium B.C.E. Israel's monarchy period, from c. 1000–600 B.C.E., continued to be characterized by significant conflict with neighboring ethnic and religious groups, including such events as the massacre of the priests of Baal under the order of the prophet Elijah (1 Kings 18), and the slaughter of the worshippers of Baal under King Jehu (2 Kings 10).

Four centuries later, during the Hasmonean dynasty (c.140–60 B.C.E.) that followed the Maccabean revolt and the expulsion of the Syrian oppressors (168–163 B.C.E.), the Jewish state developed "territorial ambitions and conquered Moab, Samaria, and Edom, on whom the Jews forcibly imposed their religion."[16]

For its part, the Christian faith's legacy is also scarred by numerous forms of exclusion and conflict. Birthed as a Jewish sectarian movement in the context of Palestinian Judaism, Christianity was known as "the sect of the Nazarenes" (Acts 24:5). However, the claim that Jesus was the Messiah, challenges to the authority of temple and Mosaic religion (Acts 3–7), and the increasingly prominent presence of Gentiles in the early Christian communities gradually led to the separation of church and synagogue over a period of approximately 100 years. This process toward separation was marked by persecution (Acts 8:1–3), executions (Acts 7), violent opposition (Acts 17:1–10; 21:27–36) and exclusions of the *notzrim* (the Nazarenes, i.e., Christians) from the synagogue.[17]

Partly in response to these external pressures, by the middle of the second century C.E., the Christian movement began to define itself as apart from Judaism and in opposition to it. As Marvin Wilson states, "From the biblical period to the present day, one would be hard pressed to find a single century in which the Church has not in some significant way contributed to the anguish of the Jewish people."[18]

And then there is Islam. Notwithstanding the common ground in Abraham, the historic tensions and conflicts between Islam, on the one hand, and Judaism and Christianity, on the other hand, have their origin in the earliest teaching of Muhammad, "who believed that both the Jewish and the Christian communities had distorted God's original revelation to Moses and later to Jesus."[19] This belief is attested repeatedly in the Qur'an:

> O People of the Book,
> why do you mix the false with the true,
> and hide the truth knowingly?

> (Sura 3:71)

While Jesus is seen as a servant of God, in line with the earlier prophets (Sura 5:46–47), the claims of Christians regarding his divine sonship and the Trinitarian understanding of God are rejected:

> They are surely infidels who say:
> "God is the Christ, son of Mary."
> But the Christ had only said:
> "O children of Israel, worship God
> who is my Lord and your Lord."

> (Sura 5:27)

> The Messiah who is Jesus, son of Mary
> was only an apostle of God . . .
> So believe in God and his apostles,
> And do not call him "Trinity."

> (Sura 4:171)

These theological convictions, coupled with the resistance of Jewish tribes and Christian Arabs in Medina to both political and religious cooperation with the Muslims, became the seedbed for centuries of hostility and often violence. It is a history that includes such events as the expulsion of all Jews from Medina by Muhammad (624 C.E.) and all Christians and Jews from Arabia under Caliph Umar bin al-Khattab (634 C.E.); the promulgation of discriminatory laws against Jews and Christians by Caliph Matawakkil (850 C.E.); persecution of Christians in Egypt under Caliph al-Hakim (1000–1021 C.E.); the destruction of synagogues in Morocco during the Berber dynasty (1147–1269 C.E.) and the persecution of Jews who were forced to choose between conversion to Islam and death.[20]

This history is also marked, at the same time, by humanitarian impulses in the Qur'an and its affirmation of the righteous among Jews and Christians:

> Certainly among the People of the Book
> are some who believe in God . . .
> and they bow in humility before God.
>
> (Sura 3:199)

Consequently, the "Covenant of Umar" (638 C.E.) granted to Christians and Jews freedom of worship and protection of their lives and property—in return for submission to Islamic social and political order. But it was a peace that would eventually give way to war. "[C]enturies of relative peaceful co-existence that followed Umar I's treaty . . . was shattered by holy wars."[21]

Negative views of Christianity among Muslims, right down to the present day, are in large part a legacy of the Crusades, which sought to wrest control of the Middle East from the Muslims. In 1099 C.E., the Crusaders invaded Jerusalem and slaughtered the Muslim and Jewish populations, including women and children.[22] In 1187 C.E. Saladin recaptured Jerusalem, exercising compassion toward noncombatants and extraordinary tolerance for the maintenance of Christian holy sites. To be sure, in certain regions, such as in Egypt and Syria during the Sultanate of Babir Momduke (1250–1382 C.E.), Jews and Christians suffered periodic persecution; some were forced to convert to Islam and churches and synagogues were destroyed. In 1855 C.E. the status of *dhimmis* (religious minorities protected by Islamic rule) was abolished in Egypt, and subsequently in other Muslim countries.[23] Still, on the whole, the Ottoman Empire (1281–1918 C.E.), which had extended the reach of Islam into the Balkans, treated the "People of the Book" living within its borders magnanimously.[24]

The rise and onslaught of Western (Christian) colonialism in the eighteenth to early twentieth centuries upon the world of Islam (accompanied often by aggressive Christian missionary activity); the collapse of the Ottoman Empire at the end of the Second World War; the occupation of the Muslim world's heartland by governments of Christian nations; the establishment of the state of Israel in 1948 and its expansion into Muslim territory as the result of subsequent wars; and the resurgence of Islam in the latter half of the twentieth century—all these conspired to produce what is now arguably one of the most intense periods in the long, sad history of Abrahamic insecurity.

Exclusion or Embrace?

I contended earlier in this essay that these conflictual relationships have their deepest roots in the disparity between *vision* and *reality* within our three faith traditions—their loftiest ideals, commitments, and values have again and again stepped into the background and have capitulated to baser instincts. It is, of course, an enormously complex and shifting array of historical and geopolitical factors that has led to the failure of the Abrahamic tradition to handle its plurality in a way that preserves security. But I want to suggest that one important, though often overlooked, factor explaining this failure is not so much structural as theological. That is, there is often a deliberate, willed choice by religious and theological leaders to ignore, underutilize, or even distort beyond recognition those theological resources that lend spiritual dignity to "the other." Those who take their faith seriously rightly take their scripture seriously, but too often leaders have allowed scriptural messages of "embrace" to be overtaken by messages of "exclusion."

By way of illustration, consider the prophetic word of Isaiah proclaimed to Judah and Jerusalem during the waning years of the eighth century B.C.E. It was a time of political crisis in which the very survival of the kingdom of Judah was at stake, threatened by the Assyrian empire to the northeast and by Egypt to the southeast.[25] Some scholars assign Isaiah's visions in 19:16–25 to a later editor and a time around 300 B.C.E., when Israel was caught up in the conflict between the Seleucids (Syria) and the Ptolemies (Egypt).[26] Others assign the passage to the early second century B.C.E. when Israel was dominated by the Seleucids.[27] But whether an earlier or later date is accepted, the prophetic vision remains the same and it is nothing short of revolutionary.

After an oracle against Egypt, in which the images from the Exodus event of about 600 years earlier are evoked, the prophet Isaiah astounds and shocks his hearers with an oracle in which God promises to send to Egypt a savior to heal them (19:22). Egypt, we are told, will give allegiance to Yahweh (19:18). An altar to Yahweh will be erected in the center of the land of Egypt as a sign and witness to Yahweh's presence there (19:19). And Yahweh will make himself known to the Egyptians, and the Egyptians will know Yahweh and worship him (19:21).

Then follows a passage in which the prophet Isaiah speaks an astounding word from Yahweh, which was deeply troubling to, and in tension with, a more pervasive particularism and exclusivism in Jewish thought. The text reads:

> On that day there will be a highway from Egypt to Assyria,
> and the Assyrian will come into Egypt,
> and the Egyptian into Assyria,
> and the Egyptians will worship with the Assyrians.
>
> On that day, Israel will be the third with Egypt and Assyria,
> a blessing in the midst of the earth
> whom the Lord of hosts has blessed, saying:
> "Blessed be Egypt my people, and Assyria the work of my hands,
> and Israel my heritage."
>
> (Isaiah 19:23–25)

In this startling vision we see Israel's nemesis—Assyria in the north—and its former oppressor and continuing threat—Egypt in the south—united with Israel by a highway that runs from the one to the other through Judah (v. 23a); by their common worship of Yahweh, the Lord of hosts (v. 23b); by their common calling to be a blessing to the nations (v. 24); and by their common identity as the people of God: *Blessed be Egypt my people, and Assyria the work of my hands, and Israel my heritage* (v. 25).

As Walter Brueggemann has argued, the prophetic oracle suggests that social, economic, and military harmony—via a highway uniting old enemies—"has as a defining component common worship of the true God."[28] The movement from terror (19:16) to reconciliation, harmony, and peace (19:23) climaxes in a vision where a region in the middle of the known world—saturated with war, blood, hostility, and intrigue, even until now—becomes "a blessing in the midst of the earth" (19:24).

However, such a blessed community of nations is only possible when exclusive claims are surrendered to God's inclusive embrace. Thus, in the remarkable closing words of Isaiah's vision (19:25), terms that were previously restricted and solely designations of Israel by Yahweh are now applied to both Egypt and Assyria.[29] Egypt is called "my people" (a designation for Israel in, for example, Isaiah 10:24; 43:6; Hosea 1:10; 2:23; Jeremiah 11:4). Assyria is given the honor of being named "the work of my hands" (a special designation of Israel in, for example, Isaiah 60:21; 64:8; Psalm 119:73; 138:8). Brueggemann gets at the heart of Isaiah's vision:

Israel's long-standing enemies are now renamed and re-defined according to pet names now to be used for Assyria and Egypt as well as Israel. . . . By this astonishing renaming, the enemies are renamed as fellow members of the covenant and are invited to accept new identity in the world. But we also notice that to make this possible, Israel must relinquish its exclusive claims and its unrivaled relation to Yahweh and be willing to share the privileges of such identity.[30]

We have come full circle. The promise to Abraham (Genesis 12:1–3) that through his progeny all the world would be blessed—a promise in which the three Abrahamic faith traditions are rooted—attains its fullest expression and hope in Isaiah's vision. But, not surprisingly, the idea that God is not even the enemy of God's own enemies was extremely difficult to grasp and accept. The possibility that God is in the business of creating a new community of belonging out of former enemies could not be seriously entertained. And so, in the age-old contest between exclusion and embrace, God's inclusive embrace lost out to the ideology of exclusion and rejection. Such a response is clear from subsequent translations and interpretations of this prophetic text.

When the Hebrew Bible was translated into Greek around B.C.E. 250–100 for the Jewish Diaspora[31]—immersed as it was in alien, Gentile, Hellenistic territory—the text of Isaiah 19:25 was rendered as follows:

> Blessed is my people who are *in* Egypt, and who are *in* Assyria and Israel which is my inheritance.
>
> (LXX of Isaiah 19:25; italics mine)

This translation "is characterized by a free approach to its Hebrew original. . . . [It] was used as a means of introducing some particular interpretation . . . Most of the differences between [the Hebrew text and the LXX] are not to be regarded as accidental ones, but as intentional ones."[32] Thus, a blessing that originally included Assyria and Egypt has been transmuted into a blessing for Diaspora Jews living *in* Assyria and *in* Egypt.[33]

To the audience of that era, the Assyrians and Egyptians—strangers, enemies, aliens, foreigners, culturally different, ritually unclean, religious infidels (i.e., the "other")—could not possibly be the objects of God's reconciling forgiveness and loving embrace.[34] And so they are placed outside the circle of acceptability, and another roll of barbed wire is installed on the wall separating them, keeping "others" out and the insiders safe.

This restriction of Isaiah's vision in the Greek OT is further seen in the Targum. These Aramaic interpretive translations of the books of the Hebrew Bible, intended for reading in the synagogue, reflect Jewish traditional thinking in the first century C.E. "But the Targum [of Isaiah] is not only an interpreted version of Isaiah because it is a translation from the Hebrew. The *metagurmen* [Aramaic for interpreter] actively departed from the Hebrew original."[35]

Thus, the Targum of Isaiah 19:25 represents a significant shift in meaning:

> Blessed be my people whom I have brought out of Egypt.
> Because they sinned before me, I carried them into exile in Assyria.
> But now that they have repented they shall be called my people,
> my inheritance, even Israel.

What clearly happened here is that Yahweh's designations (in the original Hebrew) of Egypt as "*my people*" and of Assyria as "*the work of my hands*" were stripped from these "others" and returned to their "rightful owners." Then, as now, translation was anything but "nonpolitical."

The ongoing tragedy of this emblematic tendency to make ethnocentric, exclusive claims on God—a tendency that very quickly and pervasively became also the *modus operandi* of the Christian and Muslim faith traditions—is that it represents a denial of the divine yearning to embrace "the other." It is a refusal to let God's embrace transform ethnocentric religionists into people who likewise reach out to embrace. This is the troubling story which Israel's prophets document, and that has repeated itself in numerous ways in the history of Christianity and Islam.

Called to be "a light to the nations" (Isaiah 42:6), God's servant people became preoccupied with protecting and preserving their national-ethnic identity and securing their special standing with God through ritual purity and legalistic performance. That "centripetal religiosity" is the reality—after the Babylonian exile—that stands under the strident criticism of the prophetic book of Jonah. Jonah resists the commission to proclaim God's word to Nineveh because

> I knew that you are a gracious God and merciful,
> slow to anger, and abounding in steadfast love,
> and ready to relent from punishing.

> (Jonah 4:4)

God desires the salvation of Nineveh? But they are the enemy. They worship at the shrines of other gods. They are Israel's former oppressor. They deserve judgment, not redemption. They are "the other." And Jonah cannot abide a God who loves the enemy and wants them to come home into his gracious, loving embrace (Jonah 4:11).

But that is precisely what God is about, according to Paul, the Jewish rabbi, follower of Jesus, several hundred years later. Writing to Gentile and Jewish followers of Jesus in Rome (Romans 5:8–10), he makes the astounding claim that in Jesus the Messiah "God demonstrated his love for us . . . while we were enemies."

God seeks to embrace the other; but those who claim that God for themselves seek to exclude the other. God's love reaches toward the enemy; but those who claim that God for themselves love to hate the enemy. God's mercy knows no boundaries; but those who claim that God for themselves are constantly building those boundaries.

The conflict between exclusion and embrace was at the very heart of the conflict between Jesus and the religious establishment of his day. He constantly crossed conventional boundaries in order to embrace: the Samaritan woman—despised member of another ethnoreligious group (John 4:1–30); the Roman centurion—feared representative of oppressive political power (Luke 7:2–10; John 4:46–54); the publicans—Caesar's despicable collaborators and tax collectors (Matthew 9:9–13; Luke 19:2–8); the Syro-Phoenician woman—a "gentile dog" (Mark 7:24–30); the ritually unclean (Luke 10:29–37; Mark 1:40–42); the morally defiled (John 8:1–11; Luke 7:36–50).

Jesus' earliest disciples followed his revolutionary model. Peter's vision of God's rejection of "clean/unclean" categories empowered him to cross the Jew-Gentile divide into the sphere of Cornelius, the Roman centurion (Acts 10). Philip crossed the barrier into the sphere of the Samaritans (Acts 8:4–8), a mixed-race people despised by Judeans (cf. John 4:9). And Paul, the ethnocentric rabbi (Acts 8:3) became the champion of the mission to the Gentiles (Acts 9). Yet, by the next century, these impulses toward the realization of a new humanity, where the separating walls are torn down (Ephesians 2:15), began to be thwarted by a spirit of exclusion.[36]

Just as Abraham wept over the exclusion and rejection—by his wife Sarah—of the Egyptian woman Hagar and their son Ishmael (Genesis 21:9–11), so Jesus wept over Jerusalem (Luke 19:41–44), because in the midst of its exclusion of all those whom God sought to embrace, Jerusalem failed to experience its own embrace.

I believe Jesus still weeps over the present-day inhabitants of "Jerusalem" (i.e., all the children of Abraham) who continue to thrive on the business of excluding. For when the children of Abraham claim the God of Abraham as their exclusive possession, they lose the God whose loving embrace transcends their myopic view. A religion of exclusion is "a maker of idols," not a living faith, because the God whom it claims to serve is not the living God in whose image all people are created, but a god created in our distorted human image in whose name we justify the demeaning, rejecting, hating, and excluding of "the other."

All three religious traditions have blood on their hands. The story of the Jewish tendency to exclude rather than to embrace stretches from Abraham to Jesus. But since then, the other two Abrahamic traditions have often excelled in the exclusion and demeaning of "the other" as well. From Constantine (in the fourth century) through the Crusades (in the eleventh to thirteenth centuries), from pogroms against Jewish communities to forced "Christianization" of native populations in the Americas, from inquisitions against dissenters to the justification and perpetuation of slavery, the Christian faith tradition has all too often succumbed to the demonic ideology of exclusion. And the history of Muslim violence, conquest, oppression, and persecution in the name of *jihad* reveals that this latest branch of the Abrahamic tradition has also found it difficult to hear the voices within that tradition that call for compassion, tolerance, forgiveness, and acceptance. All three traditions have tragically—and all too often—violated central values of their faith.

For their part, Christians recognize that virtues such as love, compassion, kindness, gentleness, peace, generosity, and self-control are, as the Apostle Paul said, evidences of the presence and work of the Spirit of God in individuals and in faith communities (Galatians 5:22). A reading of the Gospels in the Christian scriptures clearly reveals that Jesus embodied these divine values and lived them out in relationship with others—and most especially toward those who were excluded from the realm of God's kingly rule by the ethnocentric religiosity of many of his contemporaries. But these values are not the exclusive preserve of Christians; they are also high on the list of how people are to relate to and treat the other in the faith traditions of Judaism and Islam.

Therefore, in keeping with the vision of Isaiah, we must ask: could the abiding presence of these values—honored in the ideals of the children of Abraham and practiced by people of faith in all three traditions—also be in part a fulfillment of the promise that there will one day be a highway connecting Egypt and Assyria and Israel, uniting former enemies? Could it be that Assyria, Israel, and Egypt (and their descendants—Christians, Jews and Muslims) may truly become, in fulfillment of Isaiah's prophecy, an instrument of God's "blessing in the midst of the earth"?

The word of the Lord,

> *Blessed be Egypt my people,*
> *and Assyria the work of my hands,*
> *and Israel my inheritance,*

uttered in Isaiah's vision of God's future, is a powerful word. This word about the true identity of "the other" whom God claims as his own possession. This word about those whom we love to exclude. This word about the stranger whom we stereotype and reject. This word about the enemy whom we fear and hate. This word about the divine, loving embrace of all God's broken and distorted children. This word about God's yearning to reconcile his rebellious children to himself, and to each other.

This word calls all people of faith to be participants in the outworking of this divine purpose. It is not a religious ideology, nor is it a utopian vision. But it is an important parcel of theological common ground that it is imperative to reclaim. The challenge for religious leaders—including theologians—is therefore to cultivate this ground so that the diverse members of the Abrahamic family can coexist peacefully and with spiritual integrity. It is not about theological window dressing for naïve universalism or vacuous ecumenism, but about theological resources for a robust pluralism that works in the real world, enhancing security for all.

Notes

1. Miroslav Volf, *Exclusion and Embrace: A Theological Exploration of Identity, Otherness, and Reconciliation* (Nashville, TN: Abingdon, 1996), 9.

2. Sculpture by George Segal.

3. John L. Esposito, *Islam: The Straight Path* (New York: Oxford University Press, 1988), 24.

4. Marvin R. Wilson, *Our Father Abraham: Jewish Roots of the Christian Faith* (Grand Rapids, MI: Eerdmans, 1989), 4.

5. Wilson, *Our Father Abraham*, 4.

6. Esposito, *Islam*, 15.

7. John Kaltner, *Ishmael Instructs Isaac: An Introduction to the Qur'an for Bible Readers* (Collegeville, MN: The Liturgical Press, 1999), 87.

8. Translation by Ahmed Ali, *Al-Qur'an: A Contemporary Translation* (Princeton, NJ: Princeton University Press, 1984).

9. Esposito, *Islam*, 7.

10. Yaqub Zaki, "The Qur'an and Revelation," in *Islam in a World of Diverse Faiths*, ed. Dan Cohn-Sherbok (New York: St. Martin's Press, 1991), 41.

11. F. F. Bruce, "The Epistles to the Colossians, Philemon, and to the Ephesians," *The New International Commentary on the New Testament* (Grand Rapids, MI: Eerdmans, 1984), 229–33.

12. The following are as translated by Kenneth Cragg, *Readings in the Qur'an* (Portland, OR: Sussex Academic Press, 1988).

13. Esposito, *Islam*, 89.

14. Kaltner, *Ishmael Instructs Isaac*, 19–20.

15. See Peter C. Craigie, *The Problem of War in the Old Testament* (Grand Rapids, MI: Eerdmans, 1978).

16. Ralph P. Martin, *New Testament Foundations*, Vol. 1 (Grand Rapids, MI: Eerdmans, 1975), 58.

17. Wilson, *Our Father Abraham*, 64–84.

18. Wilson, *Our Father Abraham*, 87.

19. Esposito, *Islam*, 15.

20. Chawkat Moucarry, *The Prophet and the Messiah: An Arab Christian's Perspective on Islam and Christianity* (Downers Grove, IL: InterVarsity Press, 2001), 308–12.

21. Ovey N. Mohammed, *Muslim-Christian Relations: Past, Present, Future* (Maryknoll, NY: Orbis Books, 1999), 35.

22. Esposito, *Islam*, 64.

23. Moucarry, *The Prophet and the Messiah*, 312.

24. Mohammed, *Muslim-Christian Relations*, 37.

25. John D. W. Watts, "Isaiah 1–33," *Word Biblical Commentary*, vol. 24 (Nashville, TN: Nelson Reference, 1985), 261–62.

26. Otto Kaiser, *Isaiah 13–39: A Commentary* (Philadelphia: Westminster, 1974), 104–12.

27. Joseph Blenkinsopp, "Isaiah 1–39," *The Anchor Bible*, vol. 19 (New York: Doubleday, 2000), 317-20.

28. Walter Brueggemann, "Isaiah 1–39," *Westminster Bible Companion* (Philadelphia: John Knox, 1998), 165.

29. John N. Oswalt, *The Book of Isaiah Chapters 1–39* (Grand Rapids, MI: Eerdmans, 1986), 381.

30. Brueggemann, "Isaiah 1–39," 165–66.

31. W. Schwarz, "Discussions on the Origin of the Septuagint," in *Studies in the Septuagint: Origin, Recension and Interpretation*, ed. Sidney Jellico (Jersey City, NJ: Ktav Publishing House, 1974), 110ff.

32. Arie Van der Kooij, "The Old Greek of Isaiah 19:16–25: Translation and Interpretation," in *LXX: VI Congress of the International Organization for Septuagint and Other Cognate Studies, Jerusalem 1986*, ed. Claude E. Cox (Atlanta: Scholars Press, 1987), 127–28.

33. G. B. Gray, *A Critical and Exegetical Commentary on the Book of Isaiah*, vol. 1 (Edinburgh: Clark, 1956), 341.

34. H. Wildberger, *Jesaja* (Neukirchen Vluyn: Neukirchener Verlag, 1976), 729.

35. Bruce D. Chilton, "The Isaiah Targum" in *The Aramaic Bible*, vol. 2, The Targums (Wilmington, DE: Michael Glazier, Inc., 1987), xiii.

36. See Wilson, *Our Father Abraham*, 87ff, who documents the increasing anti-Semitism in the Christian community.

5

Truth, Pluralism, and Religious Diplomacy: A Christian Dialogical Perspective

Christopher A. Hall

ARGUMENTS ABOUT RELIGION are often explosive, particularly when they occur "within the family." And the Abrahamic family, for its part, has long been acutely argumentative. While some dissension is inevitable, perhaps even healthy, too often the casualty has been security. Indeed, the possibility surely exists, especially in light of recent events in Iraq and in the Israeli-Palestinian conflict, that the foreseeable future will be one of continued violence shaped in large part by religious differences. Rather than the heritage of Abraham leading to peace, freedom, and security, his descendents may well continue to war against one another throughout our lives and the lives of our children and grandchildren.

But is such conflict simply unavoidable? As Charles Kimball puts it, "Are religious people capable of building on the best in their respective traditions? Or are we doomed to live on religious islands, doomed to build contemporary versions of crusader castles until we find more effective ways to destroy one another in the name of God?"[1] Or is there a different path that can be charted, a new road map for the future that can be proposed, so that the descendents

Christopher A. Hall is dean of the Templeton Honors College and professor of biblical and theological studies at Eastern University. A specialist in Patristic theology and Christian spirituality, he is associate editor of the Ancient Christian Commentary on Scripture and editor-at-large for *Christianity Today* magazine, for which he has written numerous articles. He is the author of *Learning Theology with the Fathers* (InterVarsity, 2002) and *Reading Scripture with the Church Fathers* (InterVarsity, 1998), and has co-authored many books, including *Does God Have a Future?* (Baker Books, 2003) and *The Trinity* (Eerdmans, 2002).

of Abraham discover in their religious heritage the seeds of peace and security rather than conflict, fear, and disrespect?

There are, of course, many signposts that will be needed along such a path, all of which are likely to be contested. In this essay, I will address one of the most controversial, namely, the debate engendered by what, for lack of a better term, we might call religious "witnessing." Religious pluralism means, inescapably, plural understandings of religious truth. Thus it is not surprising that an increasing source of friction among religions is rooted in disagreements over the dialogical ground rules for communicating sincerely held views of religious truth. Pretending differences do not exist, or worse that they don't really mean anything, will not result in consensus "rules of the game" for pluralism; now more than ever, these norms of discourse are essential for linking religion positively to sustainable security.

The Advocacy of Religious Truth in the Global Public Square

In attempting to help create an arena in which freedom and security flourish, I will focus particularly on a significant supporting element in such a construction project, the pursuit and advocacy of religious truth in global public life. Judaism, Christianity, and Islam are all grounded in the Abrahamic tradition and each claims to possess the truth. How can these truth claims be reconciled with the need to create a secure environment for all religious traditions to freely practice their faith and express and advocate their own religious truth claims? In discussing this question, I want to propose the practice of a particular form of diplomacy, what in this essay I will call "religious diplomacy." This is a diplomacy in which advocates of religious traditions speak their understanding of religious truth in such a fashion that adherents of other religious traditions are enabled to hear, investigate, and safely accept or reject the religious claims offered.[2]

What requirements must be met if the religious claim to possess the truth is not to mutate into the dangerous and all-too-familiar attempt to impose that truth on others by means of force—political, military, or otherwise? More specifically, how can religious traditions rooted in the story of Abraham faithfully argue and advocate their truth claims, while simultaneously in love preserve the security of other religious traditions to communicate safely their own perspectives and practices? How can disciples of Moses, Muhammad, and Jesus learn to conduct more effectively the art and discipline of religious diplomacy? The command of Moses and Christ to love God and neighbor must, I believe, be wedded to the frank, open, and lively pursuit of truth. The union of love and truth is possible in a pluralistic religious environment, but it depends on the self-conscious cultivation of diplomatic virtues that are, sadly, too often honored only in the breach.

We must look carefully at what characterizes those people who wisely and lovingly inhabit an environment in which religious freedom and the pursuit of truth in love—and security—are protected and nourished. In this chapter I examine, from my own vantage point within the Christian tradition, the particular ambassadorial virtues and character traits that mark the religious diplomat operating within the Abrahamic tradition. To be sure, issues of methodologies and techniques within the various disciplines of security and human rights must be confronted if holistic security is to be achieved. Yet our best-laid methodologies will sooner or later short-circuit if we do not simultaneously address the question of dialogical virtues in interfaith relations.

We must acknowledge from the beginning that religious diplomacy is no panacea. It may fail. There are problems that will remain unresolved and intractable, simply because of the reality of human evil. As Jean Bethke Elshtain has astutely warned, the naïve assumption that rational discussion and negotiation can resolve every conflict and disagreement is a recipe for trouble. "Practicing a reasonableness based on the calculations of the 'humanist' world of infinite negotiation and 'logical' explanation is often of little use in helping us to face harsh evidence unfolding before our eyes. Moreover, naïveté—including the conviction that horrific events are momentary setbacks and will surely be brought to heel by 'reasonable' persons (who shrink from speaking of evil)—can get thousands of innocents killed."[3] Still, religious diplomacy, a diplomacy grounded in the skills and virtues the Abrahamic tradition applauds, will realistically acknowledge the reality of evil and consistently draw on the highest religious values to act decisively against evil's horrors when they raise their head.[4]

Religious Diplomacy

Think, for instance, of the roles and functions diplomats perform for nation-states. Among other things, effective diplomats represent the interests and concerns of their country to other nations. Diplomats have generally rooted themselves in the history, politics, language, and culture of their own country, but also possess a high level of cross-cultural expertise. An ambassador from the United States to France will no doubt have a deep grounding in French politics, language, culture, and history. In addition to a sound knowledge base, effective diplomats will possess a wide range of skills: the ability to listen well, to communicate effectively, to understand an opposing viewpoint, and so on.

It is somewhat questionable, however, whether the secular diplomat necessarily must possess a large range of virtues in addition to knowledge and skills, chiefly because the allegiance of political diplomats is fundamentally to the nation-state itself. Secular diplomats will be asked to veil the truth from their diplomatic counterparts as often as reveal it to them; mendacity plays a prominent role in relations between nation-states and is often used as a means to pursue and obtain national ends. A secular diplomat, then, might possess the skill of listening well to an opposing viewpoint, while being strikingly deficient in the virtue of truth-telling. Indeed, diplomats might be reprimanded or recalled by their home countries if they insisted on telling the truth or practicing love toward their neighbor.

I want to contend, however, that things change when we move into the context of religious diplomacy. Think, for a moment, about the issue of truth-telling and its relationship to religious traditions grounded in the story of Abraham. Jesus, the Lord of the Christian communion, was of course deeply concerned with issues of truth. Not only did Jesus claim that truth was incarnated in his own person (John 14:6), but he insisted that truthful words and a truthful life lead to and enhance human wholeness. "You shall know the truth and the truth will set you free" (John 8:32). Hence, Jesus likely would argue that if we are to live in a free, secure world, we must be willing to tell lovingly and clearly the truth to one another in a manner that can be heard and then received or rejected.

While political diplomacy between nation-states is often marked by suspicion and duplicity, is it a possibility or a pipe dream to think that the practice of religious diplomacy might be cultivated among faith traditions? Can we realistically hope for a diplomacy grounded in the basic presupposition that we will speak truthfully to one another and consciously work to create a safe environment in which truth-telling can occur? As Douglas Johnston and Cynthia Sampson have aptly described it, the role to be played by religious peacemakers and diplomats is "the missing dimension of statecraft." In fact, R. Scott Appleby comments that the "unique social location, institutional configuration, cultural power, and remarkable persistence of religions commend the cultivation of elements within them that foster harmonious and just relations among peoples and nurture the seeds of reconciliation when conflict threatens or after it occurs."[5] Among these elements is the willingness on the part of the religious diplomat to tell the truth.

We must acknowledge that at least for some within the Abrahamic tradition today, religious diplomacy is an oxymoron. Osama bin Laden, for instance, calls "on every Muslim who believes in Allah and wishes to be rewarded to comply with Allah's order to kill the Americans and plunder their money wherever and whenever they find it."[6] Once the other members of the Abrahamic family have been branded "infidels," the listening that plays such a key role in religious diplomacy has effectively ceased and caricatures multiply.

Only infidels "believe in separation of church and state. Infidels profess the wrong religion, or the wrong version of a religion, or no religion at all. Infidels believe in civic and personal freedom. Infidels educate women and give them a public presence and role. Infidels intermarry across lines of religion. Infidels have human rights."[7] Such religious hatred has left the truth far behind. Self-deception, individually and corporately, reigns supreme.

The antidote for the irrational hatred of the religious fanatic? An ever-deeper commitment to tell the truth as an essential aspect of religious diplomacy. For all who belong to the Abrahamic family this would mean, I think, a willingness to acknowledge sins of the past and present against other members of the Abrahamic tradition. Recent pronouncements by John Paul II are a hopeful step in this direction for the Christian community. In turn, Jews and Muslims should be encouraged to recognize the times they have sinned against other members of Abraham's heritage.[8]

Religious Diplomacy and the Dialogical Virtues

Not only does the issue of truth raise its head whenever one faces the critical issues of freedom and security, but a related question directly confronts us. What virtues characterize people who are willing to tell and receive the truth? The ability to speak and receive the truth in love does not arise in a vacuum. My primary thesis is that we can formulate methodologies and concrete strategies for cultivating security and religious freedom, methodologies grounded in the tradition of Abraham, and still fail to engender sustainable solutions if we do not simultaneously ponder a key question: what are the sine qua non human virtues that must be present and practiced if our policies, methodologies, and strategies are to be fruitfully achieved and sustained? If Christian, Muslim, and Jew are to live together in security and freedom in the years to come, we must learn to speak lovingly our understanding of truth to one another while yet avoiding the temptation to water things down to a vapid commonality.

Are there particular listening skills religious diplomats would do well to cultivate? For instance, when I encounter voices that are unfamiliar or foreign, does my attention lapse or my irritation increase? Do I fail to listen because I am unwilling to invest the time and energy necessary for listening to my religious neighbor well? Can I admit, if I am honest with myself, a tendency to prejudge my religious neighbors because they fall outside my own religious worldview and experience? Am I willing to enter into my religious neighbor's world, all the time cognizant of the differences between his culture and mine, in such a way that I receptively begin to hear what he is trying to say to me? Am I open to being taught?

A gifted listener is able to enter empathetically into another's world. While never able to leave her own world behind, the empathetic listener comes alongside another and asks the other to open a new world to her. She stands ready, receptive, open, eager to enter another's experience.

Good listening entails hard work. The insights and perspectives the empathetic listener seeks to receive from her religious counterpart offer themselves only to those willing to enter a new linguistic, symbolic, and cultural world. At first things will look terribly strange—indeed, a kind of religiocultural shock is likely to set in. Less empathetic listeners will soon retreat, deeply threatened by unfamiliar sights, sounds, symbols, expressions, perspectives, and actions.

The empathetic listener, though, because she is convinced that her religious neighbor has something valuable to offer, will resist the temptation to flee back to more comfortable and familiar surroundings. She will remain, struggling to hear and comprehend the mysterious world offered to her, patiently allowing herself the time and effort required to adjust to another's home. At heart she is utterly convinced that the convergence between two worlds is possible, that communication and mutual understanding can be accomplished, that two religious horizons can indeed meet without the need to merge. Gradually she will feel more and more at home with her new neighbors. And in time she will have earned the right to respond to her religious neighbor's perspective and even to criticize.[9]

I believe it does little good to tell the truth, whatever we perceive the truth to be, if we tell the truth in such a way that it cannot be heard and understood by our listeners. If so, a closer examination of the dialogical virtues is a must for all religious diplomats. What are the specific dialogical virtues that adherents of the Abrahamic traditions can recognize, embrace, cultivate, and practice? Nurturing these virtues enhances our ability to speak our perception of religious truth more clearly and listen more effectively, which in turn serves to aid us in the construction of a secure space in which to dwell freely and securely with members of other religious traditions. If we fail to construct a secure arena in which truth, respect, and love can be freely exchanged, the prospects for a mutual flourishing of religion and security appear bleak indeed.

As we all know and would acknowledge in our better moments, it is terribly difficult to tell the truth. In addition, if we do manage to tell the truth, we often do so in a self-righteous, self-deceived, mean-spirited fashion. Sadly, we are experts at proclaiming truths we ourselves have yet to embrace deeply. For instance, as a Christian I would like to be able to proclaim that the church has consistently lived out Christ's command to be as wise as serpents and as innocent as doves (Matthew 10:16). But while there are certainly examples of saints whose lives manifest both wisdom and innocence (Francis of Assisi comes to mind), Christian history is riddled with failures. Christians have occasionally persecuted those unwilling to accept Christian perspectives; during crucial junctures Christians have been more than willing to kill one another and those of other religious faiths, sometimes on a horrendously extravagant scale. Students of the church's history in the sixteenth century, for example, quickly encounter Catholics killing Protestants, Protestants killing Catholics, Protestants killing Protestants, and everybody ganging up on the Anabaptists. In earlier centuries we discover forced baptisms, the Inquisition, and the Crusades. What is especially striking to me is that in almost every case of abuse, persecution, and killing, the persecutors felt they were acting on behalf of God and the truth.

And so at the very beginning of our quest for truth we encounter a troubling paradox. Truth-telling appears to be an essential prerequisite for freedom and security. Yet the advocacy and embrace of "truth" have not infrequently undercut the security of others unwilling to acknowledge our own truth perspective. Therefore I want to propose that the conscientious and disciplined cultivation of specific dialogical virtues is an indispensable element in the creation of a secure environment in which religious claims to truth can be expressed, practiced, debated, received, and embraced or denied by others.

By way of background to a discussion of the dialogical virtues, I will first share a brief anecdote concerning an extended debate I have had in print with a Christian theologian by the name of John Sanders, who is also a close friend of mine. The details of the debate itself are unimportant, except to say that the theological position John has chosen to defend is provocative and controversial. As we engaged in theological debate John and I exchanged a series of e-mails, and in one of these John discussed a number of dialogical virtues, probably because many of the people arguing against John's position sorely lacked them.

Over the past few years John had interacted with a broad spectrum of American Christianity. Often he found himself the victim of name-calling and guilt by association. For instance, because John's theological position seemed to match up with heretical views from the past, many of his opponents immediately classed John's views as heretical. In one e-mail John writes of the

> great need for modeling how to carry on theological debate in irenic and loving ways with those who hold positions different from our own. This is especially needed in evangelicalism, where congregations split over minuscule points of difference.... Discussing issues is fine, but all too often evangelicals have resorted to power politics, name-calling, threats of exclusion, and other unseemly tactics in order to "win." Insecure people tend to want to short-circuit debate and get their way by other means. It is a sad testimony when a friend of ours, who is frequently asked to debate atheists and proponents of other religions on university campuses, says he would rather debate these folks because he finds much more honest wrestling with issues and even love among them than among fellow evangelicals.[10]

John experienced frustration, anger, discouragement, disillusionment, and deep sadness as a result of the purposeful caricature and demonization of his perspective. In much the same way, broad caricature and demonization too often occur within the larger religious marketplace, and they have scarred relations between Jews, Muslims, and Christians. This phenomenon, when taken to extremes, is not unrelated to security concerns. As Elshtain has observed, demonization plays a central role in the life of the religious terrorist: "Labeling their victims—calling them 'infidels,' the Islamist term for non-Muslims or Muslims who do not share their hatred; 'bacilli,' a Nazi term for Jews; or 'bourgeois reactionaries,' a Communist term for any who opposed their violent revolution—is but one way in which some human beings strip others of their protected status as noncombatants or, even more radically, of their very humanness."[11]

Mark Juergensmeyer reinforces Elshtain's point by turning to the example of Irish Protestant leader Ian Paisley. Paisley has frequently resorted to heated rhetoric in describing his political and religious enemies, once calling the pope a "black-coated bachelor." By doing so, Paisley was "insulting the religion of the community that he and other Protestants feared could eventually overwhelm them by their numbers in Ulster and by their strength in the adjacent Republic of Ireland." Further, Paisley "was also attempting to turn an ordinary opponent—a leader of a rival religious group—into a caricature and thus to dehumanize both him and the Catholics for whom he is an honored figure. On other occasions he not only denied that Catholics were Christian but also implied that they were subhuman. In these ways Paisley was doing what is commonly done to enemies: deny them personhood."[12]

There seems to be a universal, cross-cultural tendency—would Abraham have identified it with the fall of humanity into sin?—to name-call, employ guilt by association, bad-mouth, use words as rhetorical weapons, and to demonize those we are afraid of or with whom we are unfamiliar. Too often the result of the word as weapon is physical violence itself.[13] "All-out slaughter of one's opponents is made easier if one dehumanizes them, as happens when Jews are simultaneously depicted as subhuman (monkeys and pigs) and superhuman (they run everything and engineered the September 11 attacks themselves because they are diabolically, almost inhumanly, clever.)"[14] Violence in turn encourages further demonization and caricature. As John Paul Lederach observes, "Where there is deep, long-term fear and direct experiences of violence that sustain an image of the enemy, people are extremely vulnerable and easily manipulated."[15]

The cultivation of specific dialogical virtues would be a significant step toward a healthy religious diplomacy founded on the willingness to speak the truth with both integrity and grace. The disciplined nurture of character traits such as honesty, integrity, teachability, persistence, precision, articulateness, and foresight—traits the Abrahamic traditions admire and emulate—would help to create a secure space for the pursuit of truth and its attendant freedoms. Without the support of these virtues, Christ's admonition to his disciples to be simultaneously innocent as doves and shrewd as snakes cannot be carried out safely. Instead, less laudable snakelike behavior is likely to occur, often as truth itself is purposely undercut. Hannah Arendt, in fact, believed "that the first victim of totalitarian ideology is the truth. Totalitarianism obliterates the basic distinction between truth and falsehood; indeed . . . the ideal candidate for totalitarian rule is someone for whom truth and falsehood no longer exist as distinct categories."[16]

The following questions, as Sanders puts it, highlight characteristics of one rooted in the dialogical virtues:

- Am I willing to learn from others without being an intellectual pushover?
- Have I come to the point where I can understand why someone would take a different position from my own?
- Do I talk too much and listen too little?
- Do I reflect before I speak or am I more interested in making my next point?
- Am I using ideas to manipulate? To exploit? To pursue power over others?
- When we discuss issues around the table, is it the most aggressive or powerful person who "wins"?
- Do we possess the ability to state another person's view in such a way that the other person would say, "Yes, that is my position"?

There are, in short, a host of dialogical disciplines that are vital in our religious pluralistic world, and these virtues don't just drop out of the sky; they must be learned. Consider the advice of a great teacher, Yale philosopher Nicholas Wolterstorff. Once a week he would remind his students of the ground rules of constructive discussion: "Thou must not take cheap shots. Thou must not sit in judgment until thou has done thy best to understand. Thou must earn thy right to disagree. Thou must conduct thyself as if Plato or Augustine, Clement or Tertullian, [I would add Moses, Muhammad, and Jesus] were sitting across the table—the point being that it is much more difficult (I don't say impossible) to dishonor someone to his face."[17]

The Problem of the Passions

If we are to tell the truth well, it is worth taking a moment to mention the vices that so easily undercut the quest to tell the truth and the trust that truth-telling requires. Church fathers such as St. Augustine warned that inherent cracks in human nature cripple our ability to recognize the truth and speak the truth to our neighbor in love. The desert fathers branded these fault lines in human nature as the "passions." Exactly what is a passion? Roberta Bondi observes that in modern parlance, the word "passion" or "passions" "is used to refer to any very strong emotion, positive or negative. 'She has a passionate desire to serve the poor.' 'He was in a real passion when he killed the man.' 'She is a passionate lover.' 'He has a passion for chocolates.'"[18]

The ancients, Bondi notes, used the word "passions" in quite a different manner. She writes: "Our ancient monastic forebears are using the word 'passion' in a different way. They would not speak of a passion for life. As a word, 'passion' carries a negative meaning most of the time because for them a passion has as its chief characteristics the perversion of vision and the destruction of love. A passion may very well be a strong emotion, but it need not be. A passion can also be a state of mind, or even a habitual action."[19] Interestingly, the distorting effect of the passions leads to a loss of freedom. In Bondi's words, "The passions blind us so that we cannot love. They create for us interior lenses through which we see the world, lenses which we very often do not even know are there. When we are under the control of our passions, even when we think we are most objective, we cannot be—we are in the grip of emotions, states of mind, habits that distort everything we see."[20]

The distortion of the passions leads to the propagation of falsehood, though the propagator, because of the deeply self-deceiving effect of the passions, actually may believe he is speaking the truth. W. Jay Wood mentions how "passions and self-interest of various sorts prevent us from being intellectually honest with ourselves (in the form of self-deception) and with others (in the form of various kinds of lies and misrepresentation)."[21]

Out of the distorted, skewed, passionate soul bubbles a poisonous stream: the unwillingness "to feel the persuasive power of a colleague's criticism of our views and to pretend otherwise," "falsifying data or deliberately ignoring counterevidence," ignoring, inflating, discounting, or subtly shading "the meaning of information unfavorable to our cherished opinions," and "deliberately suppressing the truth."[22] The passions become a breeding ground for dishonesty as one lie births another. The result is that relations between persons are deeply damaged and human flourishing is undercut.

The individual and corporate self-deception fueled by the passions eviscerates freedom and the quest for a secure environment. As Wood observes, "one kind of intellectual dishonesty leads to another. . . . It is a common observation that people sometimes wind up believing lies when they repeat them often enough (or at least become incapable of distinguishing the lines separating the truth from exaggeration and plain prevarication)."[23] Or, as Jean Elshtain puts it, "If one says something long enough, and if it pops up on the

Internet and is repeated frequently enough, it comes to have the status of a given."[24] That is, if we lie to ourselves often enough about a given person, nation, religious tradition, culture, and so on, rancid falsehood appears to us as bedrock truth.

One wishes that disciples of Jesus, Moses, and Muhammad were somehow divinely freed from the dangers of dishonesty and self-deception, but obviously such is not the case. Merold Westphal, for instance, warns against a kind of religious "epistemological Phariseeism" that may particularly infect the mind of the religious believer. As the virus spreads the epistemological Pharisee is increasingly unable to empathetically enter into the world of another. Our "very religious convictions become instruments of invidious comparisons and discrimination."[25]

How might the Abrahamic tradition help us to speak the truth to our neighbor in a lively, engaging, approachable manner, while also guarding against the dangers of self-deception and its correlated vices? Jay Wood helpfully comments that all "three great monotheistic traditions of Judaism, Christianity, and Islam are unique in claiming not only that humans are dependent on God to show us the most important truths but that we are likewise dependent on him to assist us in understanding and desiring them."[26] The reality of our dependence upon God for wisdom in speaking and living the truth in relation to our neighbors, near and far, is a crucial aspect of creating a free and secure environment for believers of various religious traditions. In turn, dependence upon God is grounded in the virtue of humility, a realistic self-estimation in which we openly acknowledge our sinfulness and the distorting effect of sin upon our perceptions of the wider world.

At this juncture I think back on my extended theological debate with my friend John. As I verbally boxed with John, he reminded me that "none of us has the truth, the whole truth, and nothing but the truth." Or as the Apostle Paul reminded his Corinthian audience, at present we "see in a glass darkly," or only "know in part" (1 Cor. 13:12). John Calvin himself said that no theologian is more than 70 percent correct (a generous estimation). As Sanders expressed matters, "All of us are finite and we must never forget the noetic effects of sin on our research, reasoning, and theological formulations. We need epistemic humility and we need one another."[27]

The Modesty of Abraham

Humility does not demand that we timidly retreat from our advocacy of what we understand the truth to be. Rather, the self-perspective that humility provides helps to create a safe environment for debate and discussion. Instead of attempting to demonize, caricature, or kill our religious neighbor, we listen carefully, acknowledging that our neighbors might well have something to teach us. When we disagree, we speak what we believe the truth to be as intelligibly as possible, acknowledging that both we and those with whom we disagree have a right to exist and disagree with one another.

Perhaps because the humble person has so often been caricatured as a timid, withdrawn personality who has little to offer to the broader watching world, a different word—modesty—may more effectively communicate in a modern setting. I recall the words of Hanan Eschel to Bruce Feiler in Feiler's book, *Abraham: A Journey to the Heart of Three Faiths*. Feiler asked Eschel, "So what is the message of Genesis after September 11?" Eschel replied,

> If you ask me, it's a question of modesty. Why do religious people act the way they act? It's because of a lack of modesty. It's what happened in Jerusalem with Christian cults planning to blow up the Temple Mount to make way for the messiah. It's what happened in Israel with the murder of Prime Minister Yitzhak Rabin after he made peace with the Palestinians. Some people read the text and suffer from a lack of modesty. They really believed they had all the answers. I know that I don't have all the answers. I am trying to understand the text and the commentaries, and I know that somebody else will have more insights than I will.

"What I'm trying to do," Eschel added, "especially in this part of the world, is to teach people to be more modest. To explain to them that they don't have all the answers. If you'll be modest, you'll probably understand the text better, and there's much less chance that you'll do awful things in the name of God." Indeed, Eschel argues that the whole Abrahamic narrative is about the need for modesty. "The whole story is about modesty. Leave your family, leave what you know. Think of when God tells Abraham to follow what Sarah says in regard to Ishmael. We know Abraham felt bad about this; he had to send Ishmael away. But he knew he didn't know everything." Eschel concludes, "You can take the story of Abraham and teach people they don't have all the answers, because we *are* Abraham . . . and we don't have all the answers."[28]

To be sure, Abrahamic modesty is no excuse for shoddy thinking, oversimplification, theological shallowness, or naïve sentimentalism.[29] But what better way to nurture the shrewdness of a serpent and the innocence of a dove than to imitate the humble modesty of Abraham himself, a modesty that can serve well as the cornerstone of the dialogical virtues and the benchmark of an effective and sensitive religious diplomacy? In an ever more globalized world that is deeply pluralistic in religious confession, we must name, celebrate, and indeed, demand the dialogical virtues for candid yet peaceful interfaith relations.

Notes

1. Charles Kimball, *When Religion Becomes Evil* (San Francisco: Harper/San Francisco, 2002), 25–26.

2. John Paul Lederach comments that traditional "statist diplomacy" must be supplemented in the contemporary world by new models for resolving conflict. "I have a rather modest thesis," Lederach writes. "I believe that the nature and characteristics of contemporary conflict suggest the need for a set of concepts and approaches that go beyond traditional statist diplomacy . . . away from a concern with the resolution of issues and toward a frame of reference that provides focus on the restoration and rebuilding of relationships." John Paul Lederach, *Building Peace: Sustainable Reconciliation in Divided Societies* (Washington, DC: United States Institute of Peace Press, 1997), ix. Reconciliation, Lederach believes, is grounded in relationships. "Reconciliation is promoted by providing space and opportunity for encounters at various levels, bringing together people from opposing sides and encouraging them to articulate their past pain and to envision an interdependent future." Lederach, *Building Peace*, 150.

3. Jean Bethke Elshtain, *Just War Against Terror: The Burden of American Power in a Violent World* (New York: Basic Books, 2003), 2.

4. Dietrich Bonhoeffer, Elshtain notes, "criticized a 'naïve lack of realism' on the part of the 'reasonable' people whose failure, he argued, is obvious, since they believe, with the 'best of intentions . . . that with a little reason they can bend back into position the framework that has got out of joint.'" Cited in Elshtain, *Just War Against Terror*, 25. The religious diplomat will readily acknowledge that dialogue itself, while valuable, must be supplanted by a constellation of insights and pressures if conflicts are to be avoided or resolved. Indeed, it is very difficult for religious diplomacy to function effectively in an atmosphere of terror, violence, and intimidation. Ideological fundamentalism makes the practice of religious diplomacy precariously difficult, if not impossible. Why? The fundamentalist has already decided he has nothing to learn from those with whom he disagrees. Regardless of what his religious neighbors may attempt to say to him, he has nothing to learn. Cf. Elshtain, *Just War Against Terror*, 44–45.

5. R. Scott Appleby, *The Ambivalence of the Sacred: Religion, Violence, and Reconciliation*, (Lanham, MD: Rowman & Littlefield, 2000), 8. The Johnson and Sampson citation is also found in Appleby, *The Ambivalence of the Sacred*, 8.

6. Cited in Elshtain, *Just War Against Terror*, 3.

7. Elshtain, *Just War Against Terror*, 4.

8. Muslims will face particular challenges, it appears, when it comes to acknowledging possible mistakes and engaging in genuine dialogue. Elshtain comments that when

Saudi religious scholars and academics issued a statement in response to "What We're Fighting For" and, in the mildest possible terms . . . suggested there were possible grounds for dialogue between Muslims and the West, the reaction in Saudi Arabia, according to the *New York Times*, was immediate, negative and severe. Subsequently, the Saudi regime banned the distribution of *Al-Hayat*, the Arab-language newspaper of record, which had published in full our response to the letter from Saudi scholars. Apparently such an exchange is regarded as too dangerous by those in charge in Riyadh. They are unwilling to accord their intellectuals the preconditions for genuine debate, namely, an open and public forum. For every voice calling publicly for tolerance or at least for dialogue, or condemning attacks on innocent civilians, there are other, often official, voices eschewing the possibility of dialogue altogether. (Elshtain, *Just War Against Terror*, 141–42)

Mark Juergensmeyer writes of the comments made by Rabbi Yitzhak Ginsburgh at the funeral of Dr. Baruch Goldstein, the murderer of more than thirty Arab Muslims as they worshiped in Hebron. Ginsburgh "comforted the assembled followers of Goldstein by explaining that Gentile blood was worth less than Jewish blood. Followers of Kahane's Kach group, on the bus en route to Goldstein's funeral, passed around newspaper pictures showing Arabs who were killed in Goldstein's slaughter." Mark Juergensmeyer, *Terror in the Mind of God: The Global Rise of Religious Violence* (Berkeley, CA: University of California Press, 2000), 174. More positively, Lederach mentions "grassroots cases from within war-torn Bosnia, where efforts by local Franciscan and Muslim clerics led to communities joining together across the lines of conflict to pursue and sustain local cease fires." Lederach, *Building Peace*, 31–32.

9. Adapted from Christopher A. Hall, *Reading Scripture with the Church Fathers* (Downers Grove, IL: InterVarsity Press, 1998), 180–83.

10. Christopher A. Hall and John Sanders, *Does God Have a Future? A Debate on Divine Providence* (Grand Rapids, MI: Baker Academic, 2003), 198.

11. Elshtain, *Just War Against Terror*, 10.

12. Juergensmeyer, *Terror in the Mind of God*, 173.

13. Lederach describes common characteristics of contemporary conflict: "Conflicting groups live in close geographic proximity. They have their direct experience of violent trauma that they associate with their perceived enemies and that is sometimes tied to a history of grievance and enmity that has accumulated over generations. Paradoxically, they live as neighbors and yet are locked into long-standing cycles of hostile interaction. The conflicts are characterized by deep-rooted, intense animosity; fear; and *severe stereotyping*" (*Building Peace*, 23; my emphasis). Juergensmeyer agrees:

[The] blanket characterizations of a people make the process of dehumanizing an enemy easier. It is difficult to belittle and kill a person whom one knows and for whom one has no personal antipathy. As most Jews are aware from centuries of experience at the receiving end of anti-Semitism, it is much easier to stereotype and categorize a whole people as collective enemies than to hate individuals. The Christian Identity activists still regard Jews this way. . . . [S]ome Jewish extremists collectively brand Arabs in such a manner. To many Muslim activists, America and Americans are collective enemies, with the particulars of how and why they threaten Muslim people and their culture left unspecified. (*Terror in the Mind of God*, 174–75)

14. Elshtain, *Just War Against Terror*, 64. Appleby observes that Israelis are depicted in Hamas literature as "dogs, rats, strangling octopi, pigs, monkeys, dragons, ghouls, Evil Eyes, and bug-eyed creatures to be crushed underfoot" (*The Ambivalence of the Sacred*, 26).

15. Lederach, *Building Peace*, 15.

16. Elshtain, *Just War Against Terror*, 79.

17. Hall and Sanders, *Does God Have a Future?* 192.

18. Roberta Bondi, *To Love as God Loves: Conversations with the Early Church* (Philadelphia: Fortress Press, 1987), 57.

19. Bondi, *To Love as God Loves*, 58.

20. Bondi, *To Love as God Loves*, 65.

21. W. Jay Wood, *Epistemology: Becoming Intellectually Virtuous* (Downers Grove, IL: InterVarsity Press, 1998), 61.

22. Wood, *Epistemology*, 61–62.

23. Wood, *Epistemology*, 62.

24. Elshtain, *Just War Against Terror*, 91.

25. Quoted in Wood, *Epistemology*, 65.

26. Wood, *Epistemology*, 67–68.

27. Hall and Sanders, *Does God Have a Future?* 199.

28. Bruce Feiler, *Abraham: A Journey to the Heart of Three Faiths* (New York: William Morrow, 2002), 134–35.

29. Elshtain particularly faults religious communities for the "weak arguments and strong rhetoric" employed by them after the September 11 attacks. Of particular concern for Elshtain are "a tendency to traffic in utopianism and sentimentality concerning politics; easy criticism, if not condemnation, of America and her leaders; and the loss or distortion of central theological categories" (*Just War Against Terror*, 113).

6

Pluralism and the "People of the Book": An Islamic Faith Perspective

Osman bin Bakar

T O MANY WESTERN EARS, the phrase "Islam and religious pluralism" has come, tragically, to have an oxymoronic ring. But in fact, so important has been the subject of religious pluralism and freedom to Muslim faith and thought that Muslims have been discoursing on it throughout the fifteen centuries of their history, beginning with Prophet Muhammad in the seventh century right through to today.[1] Given the varied Muslim historical experiences with issues of religious pluralism, I will first approach the subject by presenting the history of Muslim discourse and scholarly treatments. I will then review exegeses of the relevant passages in the Qur'an and utterances of Prophet Muhammad written during those centuries from a wide range of viewpoints. In both volume and variety, we will be encountering in these exegeses alone a body of traditional and modern Muslim writings on freedom and pluralism that is no less significant than the Western contribution. And, far from projecting a monolithic Islam, these writings actually tend to reflect Islam's pluralistic character.

Osman bin Bakar is Malaysia Chair of Islam in Southeast Asia, Center for Muslim-Christian Understanding, Edmund A. Walsh School of Foreign Service, Georgetown University. He has served as deputy vice chancellor/vice president (academic) of the University of Malaya, Kuala Lumpur (1995–2000), where he was also professor of philosophy of science (1992–2001). His research interests include Malaysian-Indonesian Islam, contemporary Islamic thought, and religion and science in the Islamic context, both classical and modern. His publications include *Islam and Civilizational Dialogue* (University of Malaya Press, 1997).

Added to this is the large volume of writings resulting from Muslim discourse on the ethical-legal dimension of pluralism. This particular type of discourse is very important to Islam, because both the Qur'an and Prophet Muhammad, the two most important sources of the religion, not only affirm the desirability of religious freedom as a matter of principle but also seek to concretize its meaning in the form of basic rights to be granted to individuals and religious groups, and in the form of duties and responsibilities that they have to honor. Since it is the sacred law, the shari'ah, of Islam that deals with problems arising from the concrete cases of pluralism and human rights (in a religious context or otherwise), and this law occupies a central place in the organization and regulation of Muslim societies (internally and in relation to other religious communities), the richness of Islamic ethical-legal discourse on freedom and pluralism should not be surprising.

Islamic legal and political thought, for example, deals with freedom implied and necessitated by interreligious and intra-Islamic pluralisms. It has to concern itself with the practical questions of religious freedom that Muslims and believers in other religions face in their attempts to live together in the same society, be it a Muslim-majority one or otherwise. The traditional Muslim response to the practical demands of religious freedom in a multireligious world is to advance the idea of *ahl al-kitab* (the "People of the Book") mentioned in the Qur'an. The main significance and goal of this idea is inclusiveness. In regarding believers in other religions as "People of the Book" who have received different messages from the same God and who therefore have to worship God differently, Muslims acknowledge not just grudging acceptance but sacred commitment to religious freedom.

What's more, in the past Muslims have shown willingness to adapt themselves to new realities in the religious environment by extending the idea of *ahl al-kitab* to include more religious groups into this Abrahamic category, and hence realizing a greater sense of inclusiveness. Initially, the "People of the Book" were confined to Jews and Christians, precisely because they were the first followers of other revealed religions the early Muslims had encountered. This was then followed by other smaller and older religious groups in the Middle East region such as the Sabeans mentioned in the Qur'an. Later when Muslims began to have a presence in places like China and India, encountering respectively adherents of the Chinese religions and Hinduism, the meaning of *ahl al-kitab* was revised and the "People of the Book" club enlarged still further to include certain schools and sects in those religions. Lately, it is encouraging to hear of a growing number of American public leaders who have been invoking the idea of *ahl al-kitab* as a clear testimony to the Muslim commitment to inclusiveness, no doubt out of concern over the tense relationships that exist between the Muslim community and other religious communities in the United States.

The historical Muslim treatment of the subject of religious pluralism and freedom has been impressive, and scholars have yet to map this complex terrain. Now that the issue of religious freedom in Muslim countries has become a major concern in the West, it is especially incumbent on Muslims to present their perspectives on the issue, being honest about Islam's successes and failures in dealing with it, presently and in the past.

It is important to stipulate at the outset that this chapter does not pretend to represent the views of all schools of thought in Islam on the meaning of religious pluralism and freedom. However, as far as possible, I will try to present views that to my mind represent mainstream Islam. There have been others in the past who have approached the relevant passages in the Qur'an very much under the influence of the social conditions of their times. I am quite sure my own understanding of the same passages has been influenced by factors peculiar to our contemporary world. Nonetheless my focus here is articulating my understanding of what a comprehensive, good-faith reading of the Qur'an can teach us regarding pluralism in religion and implications for security.

What the Qur'an teaches represents the ideals to which all Muslims should aspire. There may be many failings on the part of present-day Muslims to live up to the expectations embodied in those ideals, just as there are failings on the part of many non-Muslim countries, including Christian ones, in guaranteeing justice for their religious minorities. But it is my view that part of the contemporary Muslim problem in dealing with peaceful coexistence among religions has to do with the failure of many Muslims to understand correctly those very ideals and their demands in practical life. Nor do we have many people in the West who are adequately informed about the Qur'anic ideals on religious freedom. As a result, in the minds of many Westerners, Muslim failings are to be attributed to the teachings of Islam, indeed to the Qur'an itself. Given this unhealthy situation, this essay focuses on the actual teachings of the Qur'an on the meaning and significance of religious freedom, pluralism, and interreligious understanding. In the long run it is by appealing to the authority of the Qur'an that Muslims have the best chance of being corrected for their beliefs and practices that are contrary to its teachings.

The Meaning of Religious Freedom

Religious freedom may be described as one of the various kinds of freedom with which we humans are all familiar. For most people it is easily the most important kind of freedom. But what is freedom? Perhaps before going ahead with a discussion of the meaning of religious freedom we need to discuss briefly what we mean by freedom itself. All religions, not just Judaism, Christianity, and

Islam, generally agree that, metaphysically speaking, freedom is both a divine and a human attribute. It is this metaphysical fact that explains why humans have a natural love for freedom and yearn for it. But there is a big difference between divine freedom and human freedom, the former absolute and the latter relative. God alone is absolute freedom. If it also occurs to the human mind to seek freedom in an absolute sense it is because in seeking that freedom, probably without knowing it, he or she is actually seeking God. We then understand why, from the viewpoint of religion, the freedom to believe in God, the core of religious freedom, is of utmost importance to humans.

Religions also acknowledge the nature of human freedom as a kind of "double-edged sword." The sword of freedom carries with it both risks of "damnation," or what the Qur'an terms "falling to the state of the lowest of the low," and opportunities to attain "salvation in God." Although human freedom is relative, it is very real at its own level. So real—but also risky—is human freedom that in exercising it in ignorance humans may fall into the danger of denying God, who is the ultimate source of that freedom itself. But antireligionists seek to affirm their right to deny God and religion in the name of freedom of religion itself, although from the point of view of religion the kind of freedom embraced by the antireligionists is nothing more than freedom from religion. Indeed, freedom of religion is not the same as freedom from religion.

Contrary to the standpoint of antireligionists, who insist that religion stifles and kills freedom, religion teaches us that human freedom has no meaning and no value if it does not lead to the recognition of God alone as the absolute freedom and as the source of all human freedom. For Muslims and most other religionists, true freedom is freedom in God, and it is in this true freedom that we find our true humanity. It may be asserted that to be free is to be human and to be truly human is to be truly free. Muslims express this essential relationship between humanity and freedom by saying that humans have been endowed with free will, or in Arabic, *iradah*, which is a precious gift from God.

As asserted earlier, there are many types of freedom, and it is the view of Islam that religious freedom is by far the most important. Islam would add that so central is religious freedom that all other freedoms are viewed and judged in the light of the former. One could even say that from a Muslim point of view freedom is synonymous with religious freedom itself. Seyyed Hossein Nasr, currently University Professor of Islamic studies at George Washington University and arguably the world's leading Muslim scholar of Islam alive today, has this to say about Muslim attitudes toward freedom:

> If one asks if Muslims want freedom, the answer is definitely yes. But the vast majority of Muslims would add that, first of all, for them freedom does not mean freedom from God and religion; they would embrace other freedoms, provided

they do not destroy their faith and what gives meaning to their lives. Second, they would point out that to be free means also to be free to understand what one means by freedom. They certainly do not want "freedom" to be imposed on them as an ideology by a more powerful West that knows better than they do what is good for them. Coercion under the guise of freedom is still coercion. What Muslims would like most of all is to be allowed the freedom to confront their own problems and find their own solutions.[2]

Most Muslims would find little disagreement with Nasr in his description of Muslim general attitudes toward freedom. What Muslims want most is the freedom to believe in their religion and practice it. But if Islam wants Muslims to enjoy religious freedom it insists also on them ensuring the same kind of freedom for followers of other faiths. A short chapter in the Qur'an reads: "Say, O you who do not believe [in the Qur'an]. I do not worship what you worship. And you do not worship what I worship. To you your religion and to me mine."[3] This passage is a Muslim cry for freedom of worship for all religions, not just for their own religion. Even in the face of irreconcilable differences among religions—and these are real and not to be underestimated or ignored—Muslims are called upon to observe peaceful coexistence among the various religions.

Religious freedom is to be understood at two levels. One is at the individual level, the other at the societal level. In the former case each person must have the freedom to choose his or her own religion. A person's acceptance of religious faith, if it is to be sincere and genuine, has to be the result of an exercise of free choice. The Qur'an is emphatic on this individual freedom of choice: "Let there be no compulsion in religion: Truth stands out clear from Error."[4] In explaining the meaning of this verse and its importance as a basis of individual freedom in matters of religious faith, the late Indian-born Yusuf Ali, perhaps the most well-known modern exegete on the Qur'an in the English language, maintains that compulsion would be incompatible with the nature of religious faith. He gives three fundamental reasons for the incompatibility, were coercion to be used.[5] First, religion depends upon faith and will, and these would be meaningless if induced by force. Second, Truth and Error have been so clearly shown up by the mercy of God that there should be no doubt in the minds of any persons of good will as to the fundamentals of faith. Third, God's protection is continuous, and the divine plan is always to lead us from the depths of darkness into the clearest light. On the basis of Yusuf Ali's very reasonable explanation, we may say that religion in its true spirit demands sincerity of faith. Coercion in religion is counterproductive as it would only give rise, among other things, to hypocrisy.

Islam as a religion is as deeply concerned with freedom for religious pluralism at the societal level as with individual religious freedom. What is meant by

religious freedom at the societal level is the collective right of followers of a religion to exist and function as a community in the society or nation-state of
which it is a part. The Qur'an recognizes the right of such a community to
exist with its distinctive identity, rights, and responsibilities in the promotion
of the common good. It terms such a community *ummah*. For example, in one
verse the Qur'an claims that "to every people [*ummah*] was sent an apostle,"[6]
meaning, God has given guidance to every branch of the human tree. Again
what the Qur'an seeks to emphasize here is the idea of inclusiveness and spiritual sharing which is extremely important as a basis for a healthy pursuit of
religious freedom.

One may also understand the verse as conveying the meaning of divine justice and spiritual democracy, clearly two of the main recurring themes in the
Qur'an. In the light of this understanding, the idea of inclusiveness and spiritual sharing then appears as something central to Islam's vision of a spiritual
democracy. In conformity with the idea of divine justice and spiritual democracy envisioned in the Qur'an, no nation or *ummah* has been deprived of spiritual benefits from heaven or exempted or barred from participating in the
race for spiritual salvation. Indeed, this imagery of a race among people of the
different *ummahs* is to be found in the Qur'an itself. A passage reads: "To each
among you, We [i.e., God speaking in the plural] have prescribed a set of rules
of practical conduct and a spiritual way. If God has so willed, He would have
made you a single community, but (His Plan is) to test you in what He has
given you: so strive as in a race in all virtues. The goal of you all is God."[7]

Americans are used to hearing the phrase "freedom, justice, and democracy" from their political leaders in the earthly context of secular politics. But
these two Qur'anic verses suggest that in the spiritual realm as well, freedom,
justice, and democracy are all closely interrelated. With the amount of discussion going on right now in both the West and the Muslim world on the issue
of compatibility between Islam and democracy, as well as on the issue of
human rights in Islam, it is advisable to reflect on the Qur'an's conceptions of
spiritual freedom, justice, and democracy.

Likewise, it is important to note from such verses that the identity of an
ummah is closely linked to the personality of a particular apostle God has sent
to guide that community, as well as to the nature and content of the divine
message he has received. These determining factors of an *ummah*'s religious
identity guarantee that there will be many *ummahs* with their own moral laws
and spiritual paths, since each divine message is said to be composed of a
moral law and a spiritual system. Consequently, diversity and pluralism have
come to characterize the world's moral and spiritual systems. Naturally, the
Qur'an's first and primary concern is with the foundation and growth of the
Muslim community, more popularly known among the Muslims themselves,

before modern times, as the Muhammadan *ummah*. Its next concern is with the *ummahs* of different people of the book, followed by those of the polytheists. From the societal point of view, Islam recognizes the collective rights of all religious communities to exist and their equality before the law. However, the ultimate context and the ultimate goal of this societal pluralism are spiritual in nature. The Qur'an has prescribed religious freedom for human societies because it wants to see a free and yet healthy competition among the various religious groups to be among the best in the cultivation of all kinds of virtues for the sake of God.

On the basis of the Qur'an, furthermore, Islam does not restrict itself to providing merely a theological and philosophical framework for thinking about pluralism. Islam also provides a legal framework, the shari'ah, for the concrete practical realization of it in society, and the regulation of its societal expressions in the interests of the common good. The shari'ah is supposed to guarantee religious freedom for all, Muslims and non-Muslims alike. Indeed, in the perspective of the Qur'an, every religion contains a kind of sacred law or "shari'ah." Where the shari'ah of the Qur'an differs from all the previous shari'ahs is in its scope and comprehensiveness. From the point of view of the Qur'an (little understood in the West, and missed even by many Muslims), Islamic shari'ah has to be necessarily broad and comprehensive in its treatment of societal laws and ethics since it is the last sacred law to be revealed to humankind. In this sense it must always be "contemporary" and even modern; it has to address itself to the needs of a world that is increasingly complex in its cultural makeup and societal organizations.

The shari'ah of the Qur'an is both universal and particular in its nature and content. The particularist dimension deals with societal laws and ethics that are specific either to the Muslim community or to a particular religious community such as the Jewish or the Christian community. As for the universal dimension, it deals with societal laws that are common to all groups and communities, Muslims included. In the context of our contemporary world of nation-states, we would be identifying this universal dimension of the shari'ah with societal laws and ethics that are binding on all citizens irrespective of their color and creed. In short, the sacred law of the Qur'an constitutes Islam's formula for solving the tricky problem of diversity and pluralism within the context of religious freedom.

In Islamic history, Muslim rulers have played the role of the guardian of the shari'ah in both its dimensions. A very important issue is involved here, particularly from the point of view of non-Muslim communities. To be guardian of the shari'ah in its entirety is to be the guardian and defender of all faiths. Indeed as articulated by philosophers of the shari'ah in the classical period, one of the primary aims of the shari'ah is the protection and defense of religion (*din*) as such, meaning not only Islam but all religions. How have the Muslim rulers fared in their role of guardian and defender of all faiths in the past and in our present period? From the general Muslim viewpoint there has been a decline in the quality of their performance in that role, only to be arrested from time to time by sparks of quality leadership in some parts of the Muslim world that inspired interreligious tolerance and peace. For Muslims it is Prophet Muhammad himself and to a lesser extent the first four caliphs who succeeded him as rulers of the expanding Muslim state, affectionately referred to by Muslims as "the rightly guided" (*al-rashidun*), who provide positive examples for Muslim rulers of succeeding generations.

A notable example in the later period of a region of interreligious tolerance and peace under Muslim rule was Spain, which presents itself as a classic case of the shari'ah of the Qur'an finding its practical expression in a European Abrahamic setting. Lately there has understandably been renewed interest in, and much nostalgia about, that era in the Middle Ages when Jews, Christians, and Muslims lived together to create a culture of tolerance in Spain. In his foreword to Maria Rosa Menocal's *The Ornament of the World: How Muslims, Jews, and Christians Created a Culture of Tolerance in Medieval Spain*, Harold Bloom highlights the following point: "The Jews and Christians of Muslim Andalusia flourished economically and culturally under the Umayyads, whose dynasty had been transplanted from Damascus to Cordoba by the audacious Abd al-Rahman. Indeed, of the Jewish exile cultures, from Babylon to the United States, the three later summits are Alexandria (from the second century B.C.E. to the second century C.E.), Muslim Andalusia, and Austria-Germany (from the 1890s through 1933)."[8]

In the postcolonial period we see many cases of Muslim nation-states failing to live up to the expectations of the shari'ah of the Qur'an, even if some of them are being ruled in the name of Islam and more particularly in the name of the shari'ah. It is with justification that non-Muslim religious minorities in a number of Muslim countries have complained of a lack of freedoms, such as freedom to build their places of worship and to carry out other legitimate religious activities. Many Muslim rulers today hardly merit to be considered as the guardians of the faiths in their respective states, regardless of whether or not they rule in the name of the shari'ah. Some of them have failed to guarantee religious freedom even for their own Muslim community, let alone for the non-Muslim communities. No less serious an issue is those cases of Muslim states ruled in the name of the shari'ah and yet failing to grant their non-Muslim communities the kind of religious freedom and human rights enjoined by the shari'ah of the Qur'an. Non-Muslims, especially in the West, need to know that there are many Muslims who are critical of such inconsistencies in contemporary Muslim practice. However, in the light of Muslim failings in the exercise of religious freedom in a number of countries, doubts have been created in the West concerning the ability of Islam or the shari'ah to respect the legitimate rights of non-Muslim communities.

Seeing that there has been much misuse and abuse of the shari'ah in the Muslim world, including its exploitation by political forces for sectarian goals that often run counter to the real teachings of the shari'ah and opposition from many non-Muslims based on their own understanding of it, it would be a difficult task to convince people that the shari'ah of the Qur'an has something precious to offer to the contemporary world. But sooner or later Muslims have to confront the issue of the need for an enlightened Muslim political leadership that is fit to play the role of guardian and defender of all faiths, understood in societal terms. In my view, the future belongs to the shari'ah of the Qur'an (more specifically, its universal dimension that has been discussed), though this may be formulated in different ways and using different terminologies to suit different political and cultural climates. For the sake of interreligious peace and tolerance there is really no other alternative that makes sense. None of this is easy, to be sure. It is of interest to note, for instance, that with the increased presence and impact of Muslim communities in America and Europe, the issue of a Christian ruler as the defender of all faiths has also surfaced and caused controversy. In England, Prince Charles raised hackles a few years back when he openly expressed his desire to become "the figurehead for all religions in Britain, including Catholics, Muslims, and Hindus" and "as defender of faiths" rather than as the defender of the Church of England alone.[9] The fact that the Prince received a public rebuke from then–Prime Minister John Major and the Church of England for his wish only goes to show how sensitive and controversial is the issue of defending a faith other than one's own to both Muslims and Christians.

To remind ourselves of the universal goals of the shari'ah of the Qur'an, let me refer here to Ibn Khaldun's discussion in his famous work *The Muqaddimah*.[10] Ibn Khaldun, regarded by many in the West as the father of modern sociology, had lent an intellectual support to the traditional argument that the sacred law of Islam exists to ensure the preservation of five fundamental things, namely religion, life, intellect and reason, progeny, and property. But Ibn Khaldun gave universal meaning and application to these goals, just as, in my view, the Qur'an wants them to be understood. These goals are not just those of Islam and Muslim societies but of all human societies. Befitting the larger context of his discussion, in which he sought to advance his universal science of human civilization, Ibn Khaldun had maintained that in protecting and preserving those five fundamental things insisted on by the shari'ah of the Qur'an, societies are in effect ensuring the preservation of the human species and human civilization.

Pluralism, Religious Freedom, and Security

It is very significant indeed that the first aim of the shari'ah is the protection of religion as such, meaning in universal terms the freedom of all faiths to believe in God. Freedom of faith would be the real source of safety and security for all faiths. If it has been presented as the first aim of the shari'ah it is because it is not unrelated to its four other aims. From the point of view of safety and security, understood in both physical and spiritual senses, religious freedom is no doubt extremely important. But so are the respect for human life and dignity, human reason, marriage and family, and the protection of property. Human security is paramount in the consideration of the shari'ah. Moreover, the Qur'an has provided an inseparable link between the issue of religious freedom and that of human safety and security.

The idea of religious freedom is also closely related to the issue of pluralism.[11] I have already made a few brief references to that relationship. Now, I wish to present a more detailed discussion of the issue that I believe is important to the advancement of the cause of religious freedom. Religious freedom entails a genuine appreciation of pluralism and a deep respect for it. Accordingly, let me highlight some of the most important teachings of Islam on the subject of pluralism, both ethnic and religious.

Ethnic Pluralism

The first fundamental fact about human pluralism that the Qur'an seeks to impress upon the human mind is that our world is by nature multiethnic and multilingual. Says the Qur'an: "O humankind! We created you from a single pair of a male and a female, and made you into nations and tribes that you may know each other. Verily the most honored of you in the sight of God is the most righteous of you. And God has full knowledge and is well acquainted with all things."[12] This verse carries meanings that have several implications for our understanding of humanity and our diverse and pluralistic world. Here I intend to give only three of them. First, humankind has a common origin. We are all descendents from the first human couple identified in the Abrahamic religious tradition as Adam and Eve. Our common human origin means that we should always be mindful of our status as members of a single human family. It also means that we should always believe in the universal ideal of the unity of humankind and human brotherhood. The actual state of affairs and the practical conduct of the human family may be far removed from the ideals the Qur'an has envisaged, but the Qur'an does demand that humankind give a lasting commitment to that ideal. It enjoins Muslims to believe not only in the unity and brotherhood of fellow Muslims but also in the unity and brotherhood of all human beings. Further, it is in conformity with the Qur'an's universal outlook that, in appealing to the ideal, it is not just addressing the Muslims but the whole of humankind.

The second implication is that the evolution of humankind into many different tribes, races, and nations is not due to pure chance. It is not the product of a natural process that is devoid of purposes of cosmic proportion and significance. On the contrary, the Qur'an maintains that there is a definite purpose to this diversity and pluralism in the ethnic composition of humankind. This purpose constitutes an integral component of the divine universal plan. There is an inherent wisdom in the natural division of humankind into so many ethnic groups. Its immediate purpose is so that humans may know one another. This means the Qur'an recognizes the legitimacy of ethnic identity.

The Qur'anic idea of "mutual acquaintance and understanding" between people of different ethnic groups is of course to be understood at various levels of knowledge, from knowledge of physical characteristics to knowledge of psychological traits, and from knowledge of manners and customs to knowledge of the higher aspects of culture and civilization.[13] One practical implication is that, in the Qur'anic perspective, intercultural and intercivilizational dialogues are very much encouraged. Such dialogues can serve as a very useful instrument for achieving the goal of "mutual acquaintance and understanding" that we have in mind. We may even claim that dialogue is the best method of realizing this Qur'anic goal. Our mutual acquaintance and understanding, if progressively pursued, will lead us to a better appreciation of our similarities and differences as well as to a better appreciation of the oneness of the human family. The higher purpose of ethnic diversity and pluralism is so that all ethnic and racial groups will come to recognize and acknowledge their common humanity. Only then can there be human solidarity and human brotherhood on earth. But the ultimate purpose of ethnic pluralism is so that man will acknowledge its reality as one of the many signs of divine wisdom in creation. From the Qur'anic point of view, in making that acknowledgment, a human person has succeeded in attaining the highest level of knowledge possible, which is spiritual in nature.

The third implication of the verse concerns the meaning of human dignity that we earlier saw was a primary concern of the shari'ah. In the final analysis, what matters most is the moral and spiritual worth of the human individual. The real worth of a person does not reside in his or her social status, his or her blood and color, his or her race or ethnicity, his or her wealth, and not even his or her creed. The divine criteria of judging the quality of human beings are spiritual in nature and also the most objective and the most universal, since these transcend subjective and sectarian considerations. This conception of human dignity means that in our world of ethnic pluralism, the correct approach to intercultural and intercivilizational understanding and to the unity of humankind is based on spiritual principles. Intercivilizational dialogues must therefore incorporate spiritual ideas—otherwise these dialogues will lack depth and seriousness which are so essential to their success and lasting impact.

Religious Pluralism

The second fundamental fact about human pluralism stressed by the Qur'an concerns the multireligious character of our world. Again, it is in conformity with the divine universal plan that we have religious pluralism. Muslims faithful to the real meaning of the Qur'an have a positive view of interreligious dialogues, because their consciousness of religious pluralism is rooted in the very fundamental beliefs of Islam. The Qur'an's teachings on religious pluralism are emphasized in many of its verses, perhaps the most powerful of which—in terms of conveying the meaning and significance of religious pluralism—is a part of a verse cited earlier, which I now present in full:

> To thee (O Mohammed) We [i.e., God] sent the Scripture in truth, confirming the scriptures that came before it, and guarding it in safety. So judge between them by what God has revealed, and follow not their vain desires, diverging from the truth that has come to thee. To each among you, We have prescribed a set of rules of practical conduct and spiritual way. If God has so willed, He would have made you a single community, but (His Plan is) to test you in what He has given you: So strive as in a race in all virtues. The goal of you all is God. It is He that will show you the truth of the matters in which you dispute.[14]

Religious diversity and pluralism in human society is thus recognized in the Qur'an as a social fact and as a permanent reality in the global human community. Muslims are called upon to accept this reality and to confront it in a practically realistic manner in accordance with the divine guide in that book. According to the Qur'anic verse just cited, it is not God's plan to make us human beings a single religious community. Rather than harboring the illusion that one day the whole world will embrace their religion, Muslims should instead try to comprehend the meaning and significance of other religions and strive to learn the art of peaceful coexistence, mutual respect, and fruitful interaction among followers of different religious beliefs.

Conclusion

For religious freedom to be fully meaningful in a civilized human society it has to concern itself with the practice of tolerance and the advancement of human dignity. Guided by the Qur'anic injunction "there is no compulsion in religion," Muslims are duty-bound to respect the beliefs of those who of their own free will do not wish to live within the fold of Muslim brotherhood. Respect for human dignity is a universal principle that is to be applied to all individuals, regardless of whether they are fellow Muslims or nonbelievers in Islam. Muslims who are expected to model their lives after Prophet Muhammad should take heed of his practical observances of this important principle.

Genuine respect for human dignity has to be grounded on solid principles. For Muslim believers prepared to plumb the true depths of the Qur'an, one principle should be simple and clear: God is one but the paths to God are many. This principle is the source and the fundamental basis of religious pluralism and diversity in the world. The Qur'an has attributed diversity and pluralism in the world's religious creeds ultimately to God Himself. It is He who has "prescribed a set of rules of practical conduct and spiritual way" to every nation and religious community. In the light of this inclusivistic spirit that the Qur'an is apparently seeking to inculcate in the global human community, Muslims and likewise people of other creeds are enjoined to learn three fundamental things in the art of peaceful, principled coexistence among religions. These are:

(1) Each community should remain faithful to the tenets of its own religion because God wanted "to test you in what He has given you."
(2) The different religions should strive as in a race in all virtues. Each religion in its own way seeks to enjoin its followers to do good works and to practice virtues. It would be a good thing for the world community if religions see themselves as being in a healthy competition with each other in pursuing virtues in human societies.
(3) In trying to live with other religions, each religion should respect differences that set themselves apart. They are discouraged from passing ultimate judgment on others because in the hereafter God will show us "the truth of the matters in which you dispute."

If only the art of peaceful coexistence among religions as stipulated above can be practiced well, our world may yet be more rather than less secure for its pluralism.

Notes

1. For a contemporary Muslim discussion, but from the traditional point of view of the place of freedom in relation to the Islamic faith, see Seyyed Hossein Nasr, *The Heart of Islam: Enduring Values for Humanity* (New York: Harper/San Francisco, 2002), 290–99.

2. Nasr, *The Heart of Islam*, 294.

3. The Qur'an, Sura 108.

4. The Qur'an, Sura 2:256.

5. Abdullah Yusuf Ali, *The Holy Qur'an: Text, Translation and Commentary* (Beirut: Dar Al Arabia, 1968), 103.

6. The Qur'an, Sura 5:47.

7. The Qur'an, Sura 5:51.

8. Harold Bloom, introduction to *The Ornament of the World: How Muslims, Jews, and Christians Created a Culture of Tolerance in Medieval Spain*, by Maria Roas Menocal (Boston, New York, London: Little, Brown and Company, 2002), xxii.

9. See *Sunday Times*, May 26, 1996.

10. See Ibn Khaldun, *The Muqaddimah: An Introduction to History*, trans. Franz Rosenthal (London: Routledge & Kegan Paul, 1986).

11. For discussions of Islamic views of pluralism, see Abdulaziz Sachedina, *The Islamic Roots of Democratic Pluralism* (New York: Oxford University Press, 2001); Osman bin Bakar, "Inter-Civilizational Dialogue: Theory and Practice in Islam," in *Islam and Civil Society in Southeast Asia*, eds. Nakamura Mitsuo, Sharon Siddique, and Omar Farouk Bajunid (Singapore: Institute of Southeast Asian Studies, 2001), 164–76; and Nasr, *The Heart of Islam*, 46–54.

12. The Qur'an, Sura 49:13.

13. Bakar, "Inter-Civilizational Dialogue," 170.

14. The Qur'an, Sura 5:51.

INTO THE BREACH:
RESTORING SUSTAINABLE SECURITY

7

Military Intervention and Justice as Equal Regard[1]

Jean Bethke Elshtain

IN RECENT YEARS, arguments about how to achieve a greater measure of justice in international affairs have often focused on certain moral ideals, such as distributive fairness in a globalizing economy (a topic emphasized strongly by religious progressives) and religious freedom (a favorite of religious conservatives). While such causes are perfectly valid as far as they go, their advocates too often ignore the prior question of political stability and order. In failed or failing states, the intervention that suffering people need most may well be that of establishing a basic system of political power, order, and accountability—and this is the kind of intervention that may well require use of military force.

Security and political stability are not, therefore, somehow irrelevant to moral imperatives of justice and human rights. The exigent matter that now lies before the international community is how to bring about the political stability—the minimal civic peace—necessary to attain and to secure fundamental human goods, including distributive justice and political and religious liberty. It is a preeminently political question that involves, inescapably, the good or ill use of power, including military power. Of course, the danger in the

Jean Bethke Elshtain is the Laura Spelman Rockefeller Professor of Social and Political Ethics at the University of Chicago. She lectures widely and has written more than 400 published essays and more than twenty books, including *Just War Against Terror* (Basic Books, 2003), *Jane Addams and the Dream of American Democracy* (Basic Books, 2002), *Who Are We? Critical Reflections, Hopeful Possibilities* (Eerdmans, 2001), *Augustine and the Limits of Politics* (Notre Dame, 1998), and *Democracy on Trial* (Basic Books, 1995).

politics of military power is that force can be so easily abused. Amoral Machiavellian "realists" rush to use military force in crass service of national interests, while Kantian "idealists" rush from crisis to crisis demanding that someone *do something*. In this debate, the complexity of factors that are actually involved in principled statecraft is frequently underestimated.

By far the most significant casualty of analysis in this regard is religion. Typically, in the conventional discourse of international affairs, religion is seen in simplistic alternatives. It is either a source of sanctimonious aspirations to "peace and love" that are politely ignored in "real" statecraft, or it is seen as the source of all the terrorist extremism that now threatens the developed world's vital interests. In this chapter I will contend, by contrast, that sustainable security will become possible only if military intervention is guided, not by narrow realpolitik nor by naïve humanitarianism, but by a religiously grounded philosophy of *justice as equal regard*. This philosophy emerges from the rich and venerable tradition of moral reflection known as just war theory. It is a tradition that is associated with Christian (especially Roman Catholic) social ethics, but in its development and practice it has been far from "denominationally" exclusive. Indeed, it has wide resonance within and without the Abrahamic traditions, and its central ethos of "equal regard" should be taken seriously by those who seek to make military intervention principled and effective in securing a just and stable peace.

The Preeminence of "The Political"

The political question must precede any discussion of justice. Why? Because absent political stability, every attempt to prop up impoverished countries must fail.[2] Justice demands accountability and there is no political accountability where there is no structure of power and laws. Instead one sees disasters like the current unrest in the Congo where human beings are prey to the ruthless, the inflamed, and the irresponsible. Absent such a structure, culminating in some form of political sovereignty, the likelihood of what we now routinely call "humanitarian catastrophes" is magnified manyfold. A paradigm example of the ills attendant upon political instability absent a central, legitimate locus of power and authority is the disaster of so-called failed states. It is, of course, the case that states themselves, whose raison d'etre is maintaining stability and civic peace, may become disturbers of civic peace, hence agents of injustice. An ossified, dictatorial order also qualifies as a violator of minimal civic peace given the horrors of a state—like the Iraq of Saddam Hussein—in which fear reigns supreme. This latter, however, is a bit off to the side of the question on which I intend to focus. What follows is an argument for international justice construed as an equal claim to the use of coercive force, deployed in your behalf, if you are a victim of one of the many horrors attendant upon radical political instability. Most often this instability is instigated by ruthless ideologues or presided over by feckless profiteers.[3] The force to be brought to bear in such cases is lodged within a structure of restraints that I will spell out. Equal regard backed up, if need be, by coercive force, is an ideal of international justice whose time has come.

If you are a political theorist, as am I, your starting point is almost invariably the ancient Greeks. Most often political theorists look to how the Athenians understood the life of the citizen in the polis. But what happens if you explore the contrast between the rules that applied to citizens within the polis to the norms and practices that governed dealings with foreigners? An ideal of to whom justice is owed lies at the heart of the matter. According to Athenian thinking—and it is this thinking that lies at the basis of what became known as realism or realpolitik in international relations—different spheres set the boundaries for norms of right and wrong, the just and the unjust. Justice governed relations among citizens within the polis. Force came into play between Athenians and others. What would be counted a wrong against a citizen was not so adjudged if it pertained to an external political entity or a foreigner.

The locus classicus of this rule in its most extreme form is the so-called Melian dialogue familiar to all readers of Thucydides's great work, *The Peloponnesian War*. When the citizens of the island of Melos refused to give up their seven-hundred-year-old tradition of civic liberty, the Athenian generals proclaimed that the strong do what they will and the weak suffer what they must. The Athenians attacked the island, slew the men, young and old, and sold the women and children into slavery.[4] To be sure, diplomacy and arbitration might be called upon to mediate this norm of force in relations with external others, but the presumptive divide—justice as internal norm, force as external rule—held, with acts of generosity toward the foreigner embodying an exception.

To Whom is Justice Owed?

Political and conceptual debate surrounding the concept of justice since the ancient Greeks concerns to whom justice is owed, as well as in what justice consists. Over the centuries, there were challenges to the sharp "us" (citizens) versus "them" (foreigners) rule. One was embodied in Christian teaching. Christianity put pressure on the notion that good or ill treatment should be meted out differently, depending on whether or not a human being was or was not a member of one's particular tribe or polity. Instead, hospitality extended to all without exception. One of the most famous of the parables of Jesus of Nazareth illustrating this claim is the story of the Good Samaritan. If a Samaritan, with whom the Jews of Jesus' day had only hostile relations, could treat a beaten and robbed Jew with tenderness and mercy, was it not possible for a Samaritan to be good and for the normative presumptions to be reversed? Hospitality—*caritas*—obliged believers, whether the one to whom aid was proffered or from whom aid was received was a family or tribal member or a stranger.

In many ways, this melting down of the neighbor-stranger divide where moral obligation is concerned is counterintuitive. It is unsurprising that we feel most deeply obligated first and foremost to family and friends, and second, to members of our own culture, clan, or society, with foreigners and strangers coming in a distant third. An injustice meted out against one of our own pains us more keenly than does injustice perpetrated against those far removed from us by language, custom, and belief and separated from us by borders and geographic distance. This is only human and the fact that this "only human" intuition got solidified into enforced practice should not surprise us.

More surprising by far is the insistence that all human beings without distinction deserve consideration and should not be subjected to arbitrary abuse, a claim I have associated with Christian theology, whatever the lamentable shortcomings of Christian practice over the centuries. The ancient Greek distinction between justice and force never disappeared, of course. It made a powerful comeback in the writings of Machiavelli and other so-called civic republicans. It was reencoded by the Peace of Augsburg (1555) and, most tellingly, the Treaty of Westphalia (1648). With Westphalia, the norm of justice as pertaining to members of a particular territorial entity was given official sanction in its recognizably modern form, marking the beginning of the international state system.

The presumption of state sovereignty held that the state alone was the arbiter of what counted as justice, law, freedom, and everything else within its bounded territory. The alternative—a world with multiple centers of contending self-help and incessant warfare—came to be seen as much less desirable than the alternative, despite the obvious excesses to which sovereigns might be drawn. Efforts at softening sovereign autonomy (associated with Hugo Grotius and the notion of international law) were only partially successful, and were observed most often when hewing to international norms and state self-interest could be reconciled.

Just War as Comparative Justice

At the same time, Christian universalism remained alive not only in theological and moral arguments, but present as well in several traditions of theologically grounded political practice. Where the matter of international justice is concerned, the most important of these is the just or justified war tradition. Many will find this a surprising claim. How can a method of assessing whether a resort to war is justified and evaluating the means used to fight it bear directly on contemporary debates about international justice and security? The argument, simply put, is this: the just war tradition is not just about war. It is a theory of *comparative justice* applied to considerations of war and intervention. Among other things, this means that the post–World War II universalization of human rights deepens and enhances the importance and reach of the just war perspective rather than running counter to it. Just war argument and universal human rights are not only not incompatible, they can and should be placed within the same frame. In what, then, does the notion of justice with universal applicability, embedded within the just war tradition, consist?

To answer this question, a précis of the basics of just war doctrine is required. Following that, I will argue that the just war tradition helps to secure a *citizenship model* for international justice—this by contrast to the model of victim/victimizer that underlies the humanitarian intervention model, one that invites the use of force as a form of rescue, even welfare, rather than the use of force as a way to strengthen or to secure a polity within which accountable officials are responsible for securing civic security, order, and minimal decency.

Just war argument insists that no unbridgeable conceptual and political divide be opened up between domestic and international politics, precisely the cleavage central to the ancient Greek world and, as well, to realpolitik with its insistence that the rules that govern domestic moral conduct and obligation apply to the body politic internally but are inapplicable to relations between states, who function in an international arena construed as a zone of anarchic self-help. Just war politics, by contrast, insists that while it would be utopian to presume that relations between states can be governed by the premises and care apposite in our dealings with family, friends, and fellow-citizens, this does not mean that the international arena is a war of all against all.

Here it must also be noted that just war thinkers worry as well that appeals to a cosmopolitan order that minimizes or even aims to eliminate the distinction between the thick moral obligations we owe to those nearest and dearest and the thinner obligations that oblige us where strangers are concerned, cut so powerfully against ordinary human moral intuitions that they are either unrealizable in principle or unsustainable in practice. The universalism flowing from the obligation of neighbor-regard in the just war tradition, by contrast, *begins* with the concrete, then goes on to embrace members of one's faith community as "brothers and sisters," and then extends to a wider circle from this humble beginning. This expanded ideal obliges those who are members of a particular community in relation to others outside their community. The obligation is a concrete one compelled by one's profession of faith that works from basic human experience outward, so to speak: this by contrast to the notion of universal categories and norms that descend from a great height and are supposedly untainted by particular interests or communal experiences.

The typical contrast—either the particular *or* the universal, at least as these are cast philosophically—is an artificial antinomy when assessed from the perspective of the theology that underlies the just war tradition. Within that theology, the world is one of *both . . . and.*

From Just War to Equal Regard

Just war thinking is best known as a cluster of concrete injunctions: what it is permissible to do; what it is not permissible to do, where the resort to, and the use of, force is concerned. For example, a war must be openly and legally pursued; a war must be a response to a specific instance of unjust aggression or the certain threat of such aggression; a war may be triggered by an obligation to protect the innocent (noncombatants), including those who are not members of one's polity, from certain harm; a war should be the last resort. These are the so-called *ad bellum* criteria.

As a set of strictures about war fighting, just war insists that means must be proportionate to ends (the rule of proportionality), and that a war be waged in such a way as to distinguish combatants from noncombatants (the principle of discrimination and the most important *in bello* criterion). Note that one harm that justifies a forceful response, if other criteria such as last resort are also met, is sparing the innocent from certain harm (the innocent being those in no position to defend themselves). A response to a direct attack is similarly exigent. Acts of aggression, whether against one's own people or against those who cannot defend themselves, are stipulated as cases of injustice that warrant the use of force. This does not mean one *must* respond with force. It does mean that a justice claim has been triggered and a resort to force is justifiable without being automatic.

Herein lies the rub, the point at which just war and international justice as equal regard make contact. Because the origins of just war thinking lie in Christian theology, a view about human beings as equal in the eyes of God underscores what is at stake when persons are unjustly assaulted, namely, that human beings qua human beings deserve equal moral regard. Equal regard means one possesses an inalienable dignity that is not given by governments and cannot be revoked arbitrarily by governments or other political bodies or actors. It follows that the spectacle of people being harried, deported, slaughtered, tortured, or starved en masse constitutes a prima facie justice claim. Depending on the circumstances on the ground as well as the relative scales of power—who can bring force effectively to bear—an equal regard claim may trigger a movement toward armed intervention in behalf of the hounded, tortured, murdered, and aggrieved.

There are times when the claims of justice may override the reluctance to take up arms. This is a principle sanctified over the centuries in the case of aggrieved *states* that are the victims of aggression. As a principle applying to all *peoples* without distinction, however, this claim is by no means universally affirmed. What I am calling for is controversial, namely, the use of force as a remedy under a justice claim based on *equal regard and inviolable human dignity.* This principle takes a political form rather than the inviolable form of a Kantian categorical imperative that leaves no room for the operation of prudential and consequential concerns. Prudential considerations enter into *all* political decisions, including those based on an equal regard justice claim, an issue I say more about below. For now, the basic point is a presumptive case in favor of the use of armed force by a powerful state or alliance of states who have the means to intervene, to interdict, and to punish in behalf of those under assault.

If the claim is universal, some might cavil, ought not an international body respond? Perhaps, but all too often United Nations "peacekeepers"—and they are tagged peacekeepers, not soldiers—are obliged by their rules of engagement (rules of disengagement would be more like it) to stand by as people are being rounded up and slaughtered. International bodies have defaulted on the use of coercive force in behalf of justice as equal regard. Joseph Nye points out that the "power of the veto in the Security Council has prevented it from authorizing the use of force for collective-security operations in all but three cases in the past half-century."[5] This makes the insistence that there are grievances and horrors to which "we" must respond provided "we" can do so in a manner that avoids, to the extent that this is humanly possible, either deepening the injustice already present or creating new instances of injustice, doubly difficult to sort out.

Equal Regard: What It Means, What It Does Not Mean

Let us tackle the first difficulty, what it means to make a claim under the equal regard norm, before turning to the second vexation, namely, who can be called upon to use coercive force on behalf of justice.

Defining and defending international justice as the equal right to have force deployed in your behalf means that an aggrieved group has the obligation to make the case that theirs is a *just cause* of substantial gravity. Genocide or ethnic cleansing is the most obvious case in point. But there are others, including many man-made disasters that are now the occasion for "humanitarian intervention." Devastating famine is also a case in point. As Amartya Sen has demonstrated, famine on a catastrophic scale is most often the coming together of natural factors with manipulated starvation engineered by ruthless political actors to further their own ends. In such circumstances, it makes more sense to speak of intervention in a just cause, and to call it justified war, than to fog matters with the term "humanitarian relief." If attack helicopters, armored personnel carriers, automatic weapons, and the like are involved, it is a war of one sort or another. If famine is the casus belli, one interdicts and punishes those responsible for preventing food from reaching starving people.[6] Calling these situations "humanitarian intervention" only clouds the issue. The real problem is a political one and coercive force remains an extension of politics by other means.

Let us now unpack further an equal regard claim to the deployment of armed force in one's behalf. An implication of this claim is that a third party may be justified in intervening with force in order to defend those unable to defend themselves, to fight those who are engaged in unjust acts of harming, and to punish those who have engaged in unjust harm in order to diminish if not destroy their capacity to continue on a path of egregious and limitless violence of the sort embodied in Osama bin Laden's infamous *fatwas*—an example of the limitlessness of so-called holy wars—calling on all Muslims everywhere to kill all Americans wherever they may be found. Force that observes limits is frequently called upon to fight force without limits.

Here it is worth noting that the obligations of *caritas* in Christian theology are defining features of the just war thinking of such theologians as St. Augustine and St. Thomas Aquinas. Each was working and thinking in a pre-Westphalian world. The secularization of just war thinking and its insertion, so to speak, within a Westphalian model—especially if sovereignty becomes something akin to the highest political good—diminishes the neighbor-regard features of the just war tradition. Interestingly enough, scratch the post–World War II universalization of human rights that serves as a background to the neighbor-regard issue, and you will find lurking underneath a theological claim.

Because I advance this argument as a form of comparative justice, it is important to note what the equal regard argument does *not* mean. It does not mean that any one nation or group of nations can or should respond to every instance of violation of the innocent, including that most horrific of all violations—genocide. The just war tradition incorporates a cautionary note: Be as certain as you can, before you intervene in a just cause, that you have a reasonable chance of success; don't barge in and make a bad situation worse. Considerations such as these take us to the heart of the *in bello* rules, those restraints on the means deployed even in a just cause. Means must be proportionate to ends. The damage must not be greater than the offenses one aims to halt. Above all, noncombatant immunity must be protected, even as one recognizes that, in any armed conflict, noncombatants will fall in harm's way.

A prudential warning that intervention in a just cause might exacerbate the harm, or that the only means available in a given situation will themselves create unacceptable injustice—like massive damage to the civilian population of a country or group being harmed by another country or group—must be addressed within the equal regard–just war framework.[7] In such sad situations, those called upon to intervene are obliged to affirm the equal regard norm even as they spell out explicitly how and why they are unable or unwilling to undertake the risks attendant upon intervention with force. The reasons for standing down must themselves be grounded in the equal regard norm: for example, the high probability that more victims would die as a result of armed intervention in their behalf than would likely suffer if such intervention is not mounted.

This approach is better than the strategies of evasion and denial of the sort visible in the 1994 slaughter by Rwandan Hutus of Rwandan Tutsis, to take one example. Exculpatory strategies at the time included claiming that the full extent of the slaughter was unknown. Or that, as bad as the slaughter was, it wasn't *as* bad as other cases of genocide, so action that might put American (or other) soldiers in harm's way wasn't warranted. In this and other well-known cases, one is confronted frequently with the spectacle of officials speaking boldly about universal human rights and going on to revert to a narrow doctrine of national self-interest in order to evade the implications of embracing these rights. This tension is lodged in the heart of the United Nations itself—a universal body whose members are *sovereign* states, hence the final judges of their own interest. The moral candor and requisite decision making within the just war tradition make it more difficult to slide into evasive maneuvers vis-à-vis the word "genocide," for example, or minimizing the problem in other ways because one has chosen not to act and would rather not discuss this openly. Killing of the innocent needn't rise to the level of genocide—although Rwanda was, in fact, a case of attempted genocide—to trigger an equal regard claim.

Accounts of the Bosnian war illustrate both evasion and ineptitude. Safe havens under a United Nations umbrella were declared for beleaguered Bosnian Muslims. People flowed into these safe havens and were there shot to pieces as United Nations peacekeepers stood by. Why? Because United Nations peacekeepers were impotent under standing rules of engagement. The United States, fearing unfavorable domestic political reaction, temporized, making promise after promise it never kept. Indeed, according to Samantha Power, word was sent down that administration spokespersons were to avoid using the word "genocide" because that word triggers a reaction of horror and might create pressure to act. She writes: "First, they [administration officials] wanted to avoid engagement in conflicts that posed little threat to American interests, narrowly defined. And second, they hoped to contain the political costs and avoid the moral stigma associated with allowing genocide."[8]

By turning the issue into one of *international peacekeeping* rather than *just war making*, ethnic cleansing proceeded apace. Refusing to name horrors correctly—calling genocide genocide, for example—is a strategy of evasion that becomes more difficult to mount if a clear commitment to international justice as equal regard attains a status akin to that now enjoyed by the right for a state to defend itself and, further, if the assumption is that the use of coercive force to interdict such violence—to stop its perpetrators—is a reasonable expectation rather than an act akin to moral supererogation.

Humanitarian Intervention or Equal Regard?

Suppose one state, or a coalition of states, intervenes in behalf of a victimized state or people. Does this in and of itself mean that the principle of equal regard is being honored in full? Not necessarily. Take, for example, U.S. intervention in Kosovo under the rubric of NATO authority.[9] The rules of NATO engagement in Kosovo are an example of a deflection of one central norm of *jus in bello* requirements, namely, that it is morally preferable, albeit politically excruciating, to risk the lives of one's own combatants than those of enemy noncombatants. With its political determination to keep American combatants out of harm's way—to enjoy a zero-casualty war—the Clinton administration embraced a principle I tagged *combatant immunity*, not only for our own combatants but, ironically, for Serbian soldiers, too, as no attempt was made to interdict the Serbian forces on the ground where the damage to Kosovar civilians continued and even escalated with NATO bombing. The Serbian Army operated with impunity for weeks even as plenty of infrastructural damage, harmful to civilian life, was going on.

In a hard-hitting piece on "War and Sacrifice in Kosovo," Paul W. Kahn scored this violation of the equal regard/just war norm. His comments are worth quoting at some length:

> If the decision to intervene is morally compelling, it cannot be conditioned on political considerations *that assume an asymmetrical valuing of human life* [emphasis mine]. This contradiction will be felt more and more as we move into an era that is simultaneously characterized by a global legal and moral order, on the one hand, and the continuing presence of nation-states, on the other. What are the conditions under which states will be willing to commit their forces to advance international standards, when their own interests are not threatened? Riskless warfare by the state in pursuit of global values may be a perfect expression of this structural contradiction within which we find ourselves. In part,

then, our uneasiness about a policy of riskless intervention in Kosovo arises out of an incompatibility between the morality of the ends, which are universal, and the morality of the means, which seem to privilege a particular community. There was talk during the campaign of a crude moral-military calculus in which the life of one NATO combatant was thought to be equivalent to the lives of 20,000 Kosovars. Such talk meant that those who supported the intervention could not know the depth of our commitment to overcoming humanitarian disasters. Is it conditioned upon the absence of risk to our own troops? If so, are such interventions merely moral disasters—like that in Somalia—waiting to happen? If the Serbs had discovered a way to inflict real costs, would there have been an abandonment of the Kosovars?

It is my contention that the humanitarian intervention doctrine animating the Kosovo war, triggered by the sight of Kosovars fleeing by the thousands, being shoved into trains and expelled, together with eyewitness reports of hundreds if not thousands simply "disappearing," not only built in no barriers to the kind of calculus Kahn condemns, but it tacitly encouraged a situation of unequal regard.[10] I will say more about just why this is but, first, it is important to acknowledge the attractiveness and moral power of the humanitarian relief model. It taps many of our deepest human reactions and sympathies. For some, the cry of pity is natural (Rousseau made such an argument); it is simply part of our human makeup. For others, a complex capacity for empathy that emerges developmentally is involved. Certainly the backdrop of Christianity and the insistence that one offer the shirt off one's back to one in need; that one give even though one has little oneself; that one sacrifice for those less fortunate—all come into play here. The problem emerges when such potent human sentiments are refracted as state policy. How so?

The state's primary task is maintaining civic peace. Constitutive of civic peace is justice, especially in its retributive form as punishment for those who prey on others, who violate civic order, whether one construes this order as emerging from a social contract or in some other way. None of the other goods human beings cherish can flourish if one lives in a world in which, in St. Augustine's mordant phrase, people are "devoured like fishes." Beyond order, the state is also the instrument of justice in the sense of just desert. For a variety of complex cultural reasons, citizens in the modern West, shaped as it is by centuries of Christian belief and practice, feel more "comfortable"—in current parlance—with the compassion end of politics rather than with the punitive or coercive end required to make possible the free flow of *caritas* in the first place.[11]

Humanitarian intervention relies on a model of international victimization. Those victimized are represented as in need of relief. We—the more powerful—come to their assistance as an act of pity or, at best, empathy, rather than as a requirement of justice for those perceived as our equals in moral regard. The humanitarian relief model in such circumstances is somewhat analogous to the bureaucratic welfare model of a needy client dependent upon the largesse of a powerful and remote provider. This invites situations in which American soldiers, the best equipped and trained in the world, are deployed as relief workers—tasks that could be undertaken by others, including nonmilitary American personnel. To the extent that stopping violent activities prevents relief from going to victims, to that same extent just war principles come into play. Even here, however, the model that ought to pertain in the use of force *and* in the provision of life is a civic and political one—the model of equal regard.

The equal regard doctrine as an elementary requirement of international justice sets up a *citizenship model.* We—the more powerful—respond to attacks against persons who cannot defend themselves because they, like us, are human beings, hence equal in regard to us, and because they, like us, are members of nations, states, or would-be states whose primary obligation is to protect the lives of those citizens who inhabit their polities. Thus, *all* states or would-be states have a stake in building up an international civic culture in which fewer horrors such as Rwanda or Kosovo take place and in which those that do take place trigger a level of concern that warrants the use of armed force, *unless* grave and compelling reasons preclude such intervention. We intervene by sending in soldiers who fight under rules of engagement that abide by just war norms, most importantly noncombatant immunity.

If we cannot intervene, other means must be resorted to immediately. People should not be slaughtered because powerful nations are dithering, hoping the whole thing will soon be over, and using domestic political considerations as a trump card in refusing to do the right thing. Doing the right thing is frequently, if not uniformly, consistent with the interest *all* states have in preventing the emergence of deadly cycles of violence. As Samantha Power notes: "People victimized by genocide or abandoned by the international community do not make good neighbors, as their thirst for vengeance, their irredentism, and their acceptance of violence as a means of generating change can turn them into future threats."[12]

I have long argued in my work that moral imperatives are not so many nice-sounding nostrums that we can simply ignore when the chips are down in favor of hard-headed evocations of national interest. Instead, I have held that ethical considerations are a core feature of national interest. For the United States, it is in the nation's long-term interest to foster and to sustain an international society of equal regard. An equal regard standard is central to a well-functioning international system composed of decent, if not perfect, states. These states may or may not be democratic in our constitutional and representational sense. But some form of what we usually call "democracy" is essential in the sense that avenues for public involvement and engagement in the life of a polity must be available. This is no "imposition" of some alien "Western" ideal, nor is it a holdover from colonialism. The discourse of human rights and democratic decency is now worldwide: witness the student protests against the Islamic Republic of Iran, with its theocratic stringencies. Stopping brutality and arbitrary violence, including terrorism of international reach, is both a strategic necessity and a moral requirement of the highest priority. There will always be moral heroes who challenge tyrannical regimes, even at the risk of their lives. But for the overwhelming majority of people in any society, the development of genuine political freedom becomes a salient issue when freedom from fear is largely won.

The politics of equal regard, hence the right to make a claim for armed intervention rather than simply humanitarian assistance, establishes a framework for the achievement of a decent, stable international order as the necessary prelude to freedom and to international justice. Many states are capable of responding to local situations indigenous to a region, even if that means sending their soldiers into a neighboring country. But if you come from a country whose nationals comprise a minority population within a country at some remove, and they are being destroyed, or threats are made to destroy them, your obligation under the equal regard rule is clear. You are obliged to make your case on the grounds of justice rather than mere humanitarian relief as you call upon those with the means to intervene.

Conclusion: Who Enforces Equal Regard?

I argued above that *all* states or would-be states have a stake in creating and sustaining an international system of equal regard. This is not, of course, entirely true as an empirical fact. It is a normative claim derived from principles that are part of the universal armamentarium of states at present (whether they like it or not), if they are members of the United Nations and signatories of various international conventions. Not all states, however, have the capacity to act to enforce a model of equal regard. Given my argument, the more powerful have greater responsibilities. One might call this the Spider-Man ethic: with great power comes great responsibility.[13] Despite all the clamor about U.S. power, and the resentment it engenders in some quarters, the "we" likely to be called upon to intervene to protect the innocent from harm, the "we" to whom a country without the means to intervene should likely make its case, is the United States. The United Nations cannot be ignored, of course, but nor has it proved to be effective in this regard. Once a measure of order is restored, a United Nations peacekeeping force may indeed be the best body to enforce a fragile peace, at least in some situations. But the United Nations habitually temporizes, sends radically mixed signals, and takes too long to gear itself up and put peacekeepers on the ground; its unreliability in this respect needn't be argued at great length. I have already noted that a Security Council veto is the predictable outcome when a "collective security" matter is brought before that body.

The upshot is that the likeliest "we" at present with both the means to enforce international justice as an equal regard norm and a strong motive to do so is the United States. The United States is capable of projecting its power as no other state can. The United States is itself premised on a set of universal propositions concerning human dignity and equality. There is no conflict in principle between our national identity and universal claims and commitments. The conflict lies elsewhere—between what we affirm and aspire to, what we can effectively do, and what we can responsibly do. Here fundamental human moral intuitions will inevitably and invariably come into play. I described these as a powerfully felt human urgency to protect, to care for, and, yes, to seek justice in behalf of those nearest and dearest to us—our families and friends. Second, we feel these obligations keenly toward our fellow countrymen and women and, third, toward a more universal category of all persons without distinction.

If the case can be made—and it is not just an exculpatory strategy to avoid acting under the equal regard principle—that those nearest and dearest will be directly imperiled if one acts, the obligation to act under equal regard may be affirmed even as exigent prudential reasons for why one cannot act in this case are proffered. A reasonable and justifiable departure from the equal regard norm (e.g., a claim that substantial harm will come to one's fellow citizens if one acts, not as a remote possibility but as a nigh-certain probability) does not apply to the anticipated harm to military men and women. It is their job to go into harm's way. It is also their honor to fight as just warriors rather than as terrorists unleashed like the Athenians at Melos, determined to slay young and old alike or to take them into slavery.

It is extraordinarily difficult to articulate a strong universal justice claim and to assign a particular state and its people a disproportionate burden to enforce that claim.[14] But international justice as coercive force in behalf of equal regard does precisely this. We arrive, therefore, at a clear conclusion: At this critical juncture in human history, the United States is a polity that acknowledges on a foundational level universal premises *and* is sufficiently powerful to act (or to put pressure on others to act) when and where no other state or states can. The brutal Melian rule is thereby reversed: The strong do what they must in order that the weak not suffer what they too often will.

Notes

1. An earlier version of this chapter was published in article form as "International Justice as Equal Regard and the Use of Force," *Ethics and International Affairs* 17, no. 2 (Fall 2003): 63–75.

2. It is, of course, true that conflict over resources may exacerbate political tension and invite unrest. That said, without a structure of law, a mailing address and phone number for what could reasonably be called a "state," tensions over economic maldistribution are likely to erupt into the anomic violence from which so many human beings now suffer.

3. It should be obvious from my description of the problem that the instability to which I refer is not the disturbance to civic peace attendant upon social and political contestation. In such cases, including those involving widespread civil disobedience, a structure of laws and accountability is in place—and it is precisely this structure that becomes a target for protesters to the extent that they believe the law encodes specific injustices. I am referring to lawless situations of cruelty, arbitrariness, violence, and caprice; these abound at present.

4. Thucydides, it must be noted, did not lift up the Melian dialogue as a depiction of exemplary behavior on the part of the Athenian generals; indeed, it presaged disaster for Athens. Oddly enough, however, this extreme case of the use of force is often located by contemporary realists as a case in point for their perspective.

5. Joseph S. Nye, Jr., "U.S. Power and Strategy after Iraq," *Foreign Affairs* 82, no. 4 (July/August 2003): 60–73. As Nye points out, "the UN is torn between the strict Westphalian interpretation of state sovereignty and the rise of international humanitarian and human rights law that sets limits on what leaders can do to their citizens. To complicate matters further, politics has made the UN Charter virtually impossible to amend." (68)

6. I would not use U.S. military personnel to respond to authentic natural disasters, such as flood relief. International humanitarian relief agencies, including nonmilitary U.S. personnel and NGOs, should be deployed in such instances. In light of the current war on terror, deploying our military to respond to the aftermath of hurricanes and the like will stretch us too thin. Humanitarian relief and coercive force must be kept distinct, in part in order to limit coercive force rather than to bury it under the humanitarian rubric. At the same time, deploying U.S. military personnel in the aftermath of a coercive military operation to help restore civic order, repair or build up an infrastructure, police chaotic situations, and the like, makes enormous good sense.

7. Here precision guided weaponry has rolled back many arguments that modern war and the just war tradition are by definition incompatible. This is surely true of a total war absent restraint. It is not true of a limited war with restraint and fought in order to punish egregious aggression, to interdict terrible violence, to prevent further harm.

8. Samantha Power, "Genocide and America," *New York Review of Books*, 14 March 2002, 15–18.

9. It is fascinating that the decision by the Clinton administration to act outside the United Nations passed by largely without notice—certainly without the denunciations

that were routine fare in op-eds and anti-war arguments in the run-up to Persian Gulf War II. It is as if the Bush administration and its allies were punished for *attempting* to act through the UN and finding their way blocked, this despite the fact that Iraq was in material breach of the terms of the 1991 truce concluding Persian Gulf War I.

10. Let me be clear that this was not in any way an explicit policy aim; rather, it is one attendant upon what is now the tradition of so-called "humanitarian intervention."

11. This is a complex cultural development. But something has happened over the past four decades that drains the Judeo-Christian tradition, for Christians or "post-Christians," at least, of the powerful images of God as sovereign, as the instigator and enforcer of justice, central to the Old Testament and absorbed, therefore, into New Testament teaching. I grapple with this issue in my book, *Just War Against Terror: The Burden of American Power in a Violent World* (New York: Basic Books, 2003). See especially chapters 7 and 8.

12. Power, "Genocide and America," 18.

13. One of my grandsons is a Marvel and DC comic addict, so I am very well acquainted with superheroes at the moment.

14. This does *not* mean that the United States should "go it alone." Coalitions of the willing based on issue-specific concerns are one possibility, already part of our repertoire. Surely there are other avenues for multilateral action, perhaps a series of regional security alliances. The United States will have to demonstrate its reliability to the skeptical, of course, by showing that, in a post–Cold War world, principled concerns of equal regard are not going to play second fiddle to geopolitical issues that lead, or have led in the past, to a whole series of unsavory alliances between the United States and some very unpleasant people and polities. While understandable contextually, such alliances are now less and less defensible. This means that the United States may frequently find itself in some very delicate situations indeed as we need allies to combat international terrorism and many of those allies (such as Saudi Arabia) are not paragons of equal regard. At the same time, the Saudis are not rounding up, "disappearing," and hounding portions of their population. Minimal decency is the criterion for working with other states and all states should be put on notice that the United States will vigorously enforce the principle of equal moral regard as a guiding, normative principle even though this may wind up putting pressure on the internal arrangements of many states, including regimes with which the United States cooperates. What persons within their respective polities do with this principle—one central to human rights—is up to them. The United States can applaud those who "fight the good fight" without actively intervening, something the moral regard principle does *not* require or strongly suggest—unless a regime slides into the abyss of mass murder (e.g., Iraq under Saddam Hussein).

8

When the Fighting Stops: Healing Hearts with Spiritual Peacemaking

Marc Gopin

IN OUR PRESENT ERA of dramatically heightened sensitivity to security issues (terrorism, the "war on terrorism," pre-emptive war, arguments over American "imperial" power, and so on) there has been a necessary and sometimes productive discussion about faith-based contributions to security policy. Not surprisingly, the emphasis has been on theological and ethical criteria for evaluating when and under what authority military force can be used for exacting international justice and restoring security and a lasting peace. Too often left out of this discussion, however, are the spiritual and emotional dimensions of securing a sustainable peace. Regrettably, "healing the heart" has not figured prominently in leading approaches to conflict theory.[1] For example, distributive justice theorists maintain that the more even the distribution of resources the deeper the resolution of conflict. It does not seem to matter how little or how much there is to be distributed as long as it is distributed with a certain measure of fairness, so that no group sees the other group as having a systematic and consistent advantage.[2] Others prefer less structural solutions, along the lines of equal opportunity. According to theorists of democratic capitalism and libertarianism, for example, if only we could establish genuine

Marc Gopin is the James Laue Professor at the Institute for Conflict Analysis and Resolution of George Mason University and is the director of the Center on World Religions, Diplomacy, and Conflict Resolution. A rabbi, scholar, and consultant, he has conducted extensive training seminars in conflict resolution and has made many media appearances. His publications include *Healing the Heart of Conflict* (Rodale, 2004), *Holy War, Holy Peace* (Oxford, 2002), and *Between Eden and Armageddon: The Future of World Religions, Violence and Peacemaking* (Oxford, 2000).

equality of opportunity (though not necessarily equality of outcomes) we could turn intergroup conflict into a long-term social justice struggle that would run in parallel to individual initiative and self-improvement strategies for communities.[3]

Approaches such as these fail to account adequately for the subjective experience and interpretation of supposedly "objective" social conditions. The condition of the heart either circumscribes or empowers real-world possibilities; as the adage goes, perception is reality, but even in conflict resolution and social change circles, there is often disregard of and opposition to the notion that healing the heart should be a priority. This attitude is typically encapsulated in the vantage point of the social scientific reduction of conflict analysis to the issue of structural violence. Many political scientists argue that a focus on the emotional life will often serve as a cover for unjust systems that will remain intact.[4] "Healing the hearts" of the masses, on this view, may merely be feeding them opiates, following along the lines of the old Marxist approach to religion. In a curious way, a proper attention to emotional life and proper attention to religious life suffer the same fate in political analysis of conflict—both are seen as a distraction from the "true" material struggles at stake.

This perspective, of course, must be taken seriously, but the inherent problem with it is the inseparability of the rational mind and the emotional/spiritual mind: they are one in all of us. There is nothing rational about the "rational distribution of resources" that is the vaunted bedrock of "peace and justice" political culture. Distribution of scarce resources is and always has been profoundly conditioned by emotions, some positive and some negative. Some may argue for rationalist distribution strategies out of fear of the alternatives, while some may argue for rational distribution out of a sense of generosity to those who may not be able to stand up for their own interests. One cannot escape the role of antisocial and prosocial emotions in a variety of political positions with regard to scarce resources.

Our state of nature is not one of rational constructs buffeted constantly by emotional barbarism waiting at the wings.[5] It is rather that our state of nature is an emotional maelstrom that mixes noble feelings and ignoble ones, hope and despair, security and fear, love and hate, trust and paranoia. They mix at such a fantastic rate, and they are so easily affected by rapidly changing circumstances and the unpredictable effects of groupthink, that rationality appears more and more the pretense of minds desperately in search of an escape from passions. But emotions and spirituality cannot be escaped, nor should they be, for the simple reason that they can be every bit as much a source of solutions to our deepest problems as they can be sources of destruction. It is therefore patently irrational for theories of conflict and peacemaking to ignore the prosocial resources of the spiritual and emotional life.

Our passions are our life, our spirit. They embody our most noble dreams, and our most sacred visions, not just our worst nightmares. We human beings work with our passions as a potter with clay, and we grow over the course of a lifetime. Of course some philosophers, both religious ones as well as rationalists from the Enlightenment, would argue that that we must work with emotions as a taskmaster driving a slave. But this is not empirically true—that is, it isn't true unless we will it to be true, unless we convince ourselves that emotions are inherently destructive to civil society.

Good and bad impulses are constantly in conflict. They provoke internal conflict that is expressed through the confusion of our emotions as well as the inconsistency of our analyses and rational ideas. But our best passions, those of love, empathy, forgiveness, pity, remorse, and hope, are not emotional excesses to be tolerated. Rather, they are the jewels of reconciliation. They must be cultivated in each generation as the building blocks of human survival just as surely as we nourish the children of the earth with potable water and healthy food. "Security" that is achieved via only grudging acceptance is no security at all. The cycle of violence will re-engage immediately, on whatever pretense of the moment, if hearts are not healed.

We must of course admire efforts at peacemaking that put justice issues at the front and center. Who can argue with this from a theoretical view of moral balance? But the basic problem with such efforts is that justice is completely perspectival in the heat of conflict. There are injustices on all sides, at every turn—everyone lives in fear, abused by the situation on many levels. The "haves" are as filled with fear as the "have-nots," assuming we can even determine who are the "haves" and who are the "have-nots" (or at what point in time we are even positioned to try to sort this out, the haves of one generation being the have-nots of the next).

The deepest problem of all, however, is that justice alone is unable to move the human being out of a place of injustice without the use of military or police force. Throughout history, every attempt to restore civil society through justice and retribution alone has necessitated the use of force, whether military or police. Only empathy and other prosocial emotions, such as generosity and forgiveness, have the capacity to move human beings out of a place of injustice to one of equality without the use of force, and only these emotions can break the violent cycle of hatred in ultraviolent situations. How these emotions should be evoked from the heart, then, is the essential question of healing. For once empathy, for example, is evoked in a sufficient number of people of all classes, on both sides of a conflict, and among the witnesses of third parties, the mind begins to discover its genius for reason, compromise, and justice.

In many approaches to conflict resolution, the emotional and spiritual passions of the individual or community are merely tolerated, and redirected where possible toward more "constructive" strategies of conflict resolution, such as crime tribunals and financial reparations.[6] But many of us who work at peacemaking have come to discover that "indulgence" of emotions and spiritual needs and resources, even the seemingly peculiar, is sometimes the best way to move the human heart away from violence. In fact, the seemingly crazy responses to conflict are the most interesting, the most revealing, and the most instructive as to what needs to be said and done. The acceptance and cultivation of emotions and spirituality is a crucial aspect of making peace and security. It is a matter not just of theory but of practical results; peacemaking that ignores the spiritual does so at its own peril.[7]

How then can we bring someone scarred by violent conflict (including conflict that, by conventional criteria, may be ethically "just") to a state of mind in which he can see the pain of the other, recognize faults in himself or in his group, envision a better future, and properly mourn the past without hatred or the need for revenge? How can he travel to a place of practical reason and justice? By nurturing all his senses, with good food and a welcoming environment; by honoring him; by finding what is unique in him and his group and exalting its value; by acknowledging with dignity his existence and that of his group; by mourning with him and sharing sorrow in its entirety no matter how long it takes, no matter how many years; by listening, often silently, with infinite patience; by sharing in the daily chores of life and the cyclical experiences of life and death; by experiencing the insanity of conflict together, across enemy lines, by whatever means possible; and by the intimacy of friendship and even love. I have seen this between enemies, from time to time, and it heals like nothing else. Open acceptance and cultivation of the emotions can sometimes bring about true healing in ways that seem rationally impossible, and I have seen it with my own eyes on the grounds of conflict, else I would scarcely believe it possible.

The vast majority of human beings are governed by reason only when their emotions tell them to be governed that way. There are endless resources at work in the world today that incite people's *destructive* emotions, filling them with rage and hatred. We can compete against this; we can fight such manipulations of the human heart and mind, and we can fight to cultivate the very best of human emotions in the very worst of situations. But we cannot pretend that emotions do not exist, or that we can conquer destructive emotions with conferences and papers. On a global scale, the implications are clear. The competition for hearts and minds is the order of the day; the rescuing of the human heart from its darkest expression and the infusion of the heart with its best potential is our massive task, and we dare not desist.

Healing the heart requires great internal discipline as well considerable ingenuity in one's engagement with the unique circumstances of all relationships and conflicts. It requires intuition and experimentation. It is challenging to classify all the different ways in which healing hearts contributes to peacemaking; so many approaches overlap and convene inside spectacular exemplars of peacemaking, whose ways of interacting with others give rise to healing and rethinking of enemy systems. Let us try, nevertheless, to isolate a number of these ways, through the use of examples from experience.

Before we continue, however, we must deal with the problem of labels. What do we call these wonderful ways of interacting? One could call them "moral principles," "paths of friendship," "discovering the divine spark," or "seeing God in all people." Alternatively, one could refer to the same phenomena as "methods" or "strategies" of peace building or conflict resolution. But the latter embraces an instrumentalist approach to human relations, engaging in certain patterns of behavior for the sake of some practical end. The problem with the instrumentalist phraseology typical of secular conflict resolution is that it misses the compelling and sustainable nature of moral relationships and uncalculating gestures. These relationships and gestures are not pragmatic or strategy-driven. Rather, they are *a way of being* as one stands before one's highest principles, before one's path to Enlightenment—or as one stands before one's God.

A way of being is not a method or a strategy. It is a cognitive and emotional construct that is reinforced regularly by a certain way of viewing oneself, one's community, and the world itself. It is spiritual in essence. As such, it has great power over both the cognitive and emotional components of human character. It has a deep solidity to it inside the human heart and thus it translates into a heart-to-heart encounter as it is engaged in peacemaking. Its greatest strength is its depth and enduring reliability, but its greatest disadvantage is the difficulty of its replicability as a practice to be taught to others. It requires therefore apprenticeship and the adoption of a vocation rather than the simple learning of a series of strategies or techniques.

Its other great disadvantage is that it is emotion-driven and thus can easily be swayed from the central requirement of peacemaking—the capacity to empathize with all sides of a conflict. It can also distract from the driving necessity of all peacemaking, which is ultimately to bring combatants to a space of rational compromise. The depths of emotions engaged can often lead its practitioners to "go native," diminish their capacity as mediators, and thus lose their place between enemies. Thus, both the secular and religious characterizations of peacemaking have strengths and weaknesses and we should keep in mind their respective shortcomings as we search for the best paths of peacemaking. Let's begin with a study of Caux.

The Example of Caux

I will first discuss these issues by way of personal experience at Mountain House, an international retreat center of Initiatives of Change that is found in a small village of the Swiss Alps named Caux. Through these stories we can illustrate a series of moral and spiritual paths to healing the hearts and souls of conflict.

In 1944, in the heat of the Second World War, the Palace of Caux, known as Hotel Esplanade, opened its doors to escaped prisoners of war from Italy, as well as Jewish refugees from Hungary. Over the next several years Hotel Esplanade housed over 1,600 Jewish refugees. Two years later, following the end of the war, the palace was purchased by Moral Re-Armament (MRA), Initiatives of Change (IC), a program dedicated to the moral and spiritual reconstruction of former enemies. Since then, IC has been dedicated to the vision of intergroup reconciliation, emphasizing the importance of individual healing and interpersonal reconciliation at its international retreat center. Ironically, although its history is significantly linked to the struggle of the Jewish people during the Second World War, Jews have been relatively absent from this interfaith conference center since its inception. In fact, the site's long history with the Jewish people has only recently become part of the official history of the place.

In 1997 a tree overlooking Lake Geneva was planted in acknowledgment of refugees who made it over the border, as well as of those who were not permitted to enter. A plaque erected in 1999 reads, "In remembrance of the Jewish refugees who stayed here, and of those who were not admitted to enter Switzerland during World War II. We shall not forget."[8] Planting that tree, surrounded by new friends, was one of the most powerful experiences of homecoming that I was privileged to have at Caux. Let's back up a bit, though.

My experience at Caux began with what may seem to be a trite matter— keeping kosher. Food consumption is one of the deepest things we do as human beings. It speaks to the essence of human survival and embodies symbols of psychological and spiritual nourishment, especially in terms of home and security. Food keeps people separate if they have peculiar needs and requirements, but food is also one of the most powerful bonds between human beings. Feeling safe enough to eat with others is a fundamental crux of conflict and peace.[9] Dietary laws often serve as a way of bringing people who share the same guidelines together. They comprise a very special bond. They also constitute a ritual path to draw closer to God and to discipline oneself before unbridled gluttony. Indeed, they are a way to purify oneself (though they can also be a way to declare others impure).

Hinduism, Judaism, and Islam are three major religions that make eating rituals a basic test of one's commitment to sacred pursuits, although most religions contain this component to one degree or another. In our day and age, however, there is a wide degree of variation in observance of these practices. Indeed, the observance of these practices and interpretation thereof are as diverse as the people who observe them. We also live in an age in which people have discovered the value of holding fast to that which is peculiar and unique, such as dietary restrictions, as they resist the bland onslaught of modern life.

Observing the dietary laws of Judaism, "keeping kosher," is one of the most peculiar elements of Judaism. It is a practice that has survived over three thousand years of Jewish history and has developed in the last 1,500 years or so into a rather arcane and complex set of rules and regulations regarding the consumption of food. Kashrut has put me personally in an odd, yet interesting position for many years now. More often than not, I find myself traveling well beyond the confines of my own small subgroup of Jews who appreciate, respect, and share my Kashrut standards. I travel beyond them to engage sometimes with those who are more strict in Kashrut, less strict, not Jewish at all, or even antireligious. I have even encountered people from Ireland to Africa who think Jews are some kind of Christian sect. I have traveled beyond my cultural comfort zone because I have come to see the driving force of peacemaking as a religious endeavor of the highest order, something that is front and center in a legitimate religious experience.[10] Inevitably, since I left the cocoon of smaller universes nearly twenty years ago, I have endured countless inconveniences and serious embarrassments as I tried to negotiate a reasonable observance of Kashrut in the most difficult of circumstances.

Kashrut, with all its challenges, however, has given me a lens through which to observe the world around me—a device to evaluate others in their degree of commitment to tolerance and respect for difference. What a revelation it has been that tolerance and liberalism in word have nothing whatsoever to do with tolerance in deed, and that religious intolerance or conservatism in principle has sometimes nothing to do with personal respect in practice for religious differences.

I came to Initiatives of Change on the heels of its complicated transition from a very conservative, mostly Christian society to a more diverse, interfaith organization. I had some difficulties, and I had some amazing experiences. What amazed me the most, however, was the degree to which a number of members of the society understood that my dietary needs were my most private place of vulnerability as well as my barometer of acceptance, fear, and trust.

Food has been an important part of Caux for fifty years. Meals, their preparation, their service, their cleaning, and their sharing are a central opportunity for spiritual and moral bonding to take place between members and guests.

People from all over the world come and partake in meals: people of all races, religions, and income brackets, each serving the other in ways that fly in the face of their fame, their fortune, or place of privilege—or lack thereof—outside of Caux. It is an astounding experience.

It should not have come as a surprise that members of a group that has valued meals as an opportunity for reconciliation would take my needs seriously. It is the lengths to which some of them went that astonished and taught me, and the degree to which they were prepared to defy traditions and establish new ones. With each passing encounter, with each year, it became clearer to me that they understood what perhaps I myself did not even acknowledge— that my unique guidelines for food consumption were reflective of the deepest part of my person. The most peculiar aspect of who I am as a Jew was what they wanted to welcome the most. They understood that the injuries of being deliberately left out required the healing essence of being deliberately ushered in. They understood that nothing accomplishes this more than honoring what makes a person unique, even peculiar.

Those who understood this, these very special members of the society, bought utensils for me. They bought special food for me in more than one Swiss city—every year. They eventually made a special kitchen section for me and other religious Jews, in many cases even going beyond my own Kashrut requirements. They insisted on celebrating special meals for special days of my religion, especially the Sabbath. I think what astonished me most is the way some of them listened for special needs as if they were secrets, as if they were keys to open up doors. And somehow they knew that through all my travels far and wide, through all my engagements with the outside world, I had had many painful experiences with regard to my private observances, ranging from gross intolerance to insensitivity, ignorance, and the benign cultural imperialism of majorities, secular and religious. They knew my injured heart, and they knew the way in. They changed me forever in ways that are hard to describe, and for which I will be eternally grateful. As time went on they also began to make special accommodations for vegetarians and other people of various dietary needs. In effect, my case began to open up a kaleidoscope of accepted dietary differences and, consequently, a parade of inclusions.

These friends have shattered for me a known world of exclusion and thrust me into a new and uncertain world in which there are no absolutes about humanity. There are no more consistent assumptions of assured alienation, no guarantees that genocide will always come in the end for a Jew in Europe. Instead there is the reality of a world of free men and free women who create either hell on earth or heaven on earth with their each and every gesture to a stranger. That is truly a strange world, but better than a world circumscribed by Holocaust certainties.

A Personal Encounter

One beautiful Friday night at Caux, sixty-five years after the Nuremberg rallies of the Nazis that were blessed and attended by bishops, I sat huddled with a Christian bishop at our Sabbath table in the large dining room, along with over thirty friends. We sat late into the night with the dark expanse of Lake Geneva beneath us and the shadow of the Alps just beyond the window. So as not to spoil the Sabbath of the others, he and I spoke in hushed words.

With a translator between us, we spoke about concentration camps and went through the exact images and corridors of torture. We indulged memory as if it were the only thing we could do for the tortured and the dead. We saw before our eyes the victims who could not be helped; we heard their cries as we drove past the walls of the camp and as we tried to reason with the guards to no avail. We felt the anguish, guilt, defiance, and nightmares of broken souls that continue to try to observe ancient religious rituals in a strange and unredeemed world.

But these memories and images were not mine; the victims were not my people. They were his people and his memories. They were not from Poland in 1942 but from Bosnia in the 1990s. The Jewish rabbi was not the victim and the bishop was not the bystander, but the Jew was the bystander feebly attempting to console the Christian. It was the bishop who pleaded with the guards for the sake of his people inside, and it was the Jew who tried to understand the unspeakable.

The healing of Caux's legacy on that night, at least for me, was complete; for it had turned the Jew from a victim who had stayed in Caux as a desperate refugee in 1942, into a responsible healer in the twenty-first century. Hope springs in my heart when I imagine that perhaps the bishop's students will comfort others some day, a half century from now, in the same place, so that even if the forces of destruction continue to hold sway in history, the force of compassion for strangers will not yield its place in history.

Here we were, a conservative and broken bishop, a survivor, sitting in close intimacy with a rabbi, at a traditional Sabbath table, with the bread and wine before our eyes, receiving comfort and comforting each other, embracing with tears, speaking of God's eternal love. Were we in the depths of hell together or were we in heaven? I was in both that night.

There is much that is mundane about Caux, but then mystery seeps in, and you question who else or what else is inhabiting such moments that you cannot see or touch. You look at the darkened mountains over Lake Geneva, you look up at the thick bed of stars at three in the morning, you see the bishop's mournful eyes before you, emblazoned in your own mind's eye, and despite your ingrained skepticism, you feel accompanied, and on an inescapable journey not of your own choosing.

Thousands of encounters such as this have occurred in Caux over the years. There are many different venues for these encounters; at meals, on the veranda at tea time, in private talks, on walks in the woods, in highly dramatic moments of public confession, through the media of arts and music, even on kitchen duty. It is the complete experience of living together, from early morning to late at night, in the context of such a beautiful, contemplative, isolated world that generates new possibilities for healing. It is also in the context of the best talents of individual members at work as they facilitate or orchestrate special, often private encounters between one or two people that such healing is made possible. Much thought goes into these encounters, and often the best work takes place inside the hearts of individual members of IC.

How Healing Hearts Leads to Peacemaking

What then can we derive from these and many other stories to help us understand what healing hearts entails, and how it can become a part of peacemaking on a broader scale, beyond one venue in Caux, Switzerland? There is more to be said on this score than can be fitted within the constraints of this essay, but here I will underscore nine dimensions of an emotionally and spiritually "realistic" approach to securing a holistic peace.

Respectful Peacemaking

Respectful acknowledgement of identity is an imperative of peacemaking, for it is directly related to the emotional power of honor as an antidote to the humiliations that are part and parcel of human conflict. The more the acknowledgment and honor speak specifically and surprisingly to the uniqueness of the group or the person, the more effective they will be in true peacemaking. As Nancy Fraser has rightly argued, "recognition" is a unique form of justice—distinct from both retributive and distributive justice.[11] Expanding on her words, Elizabeth Kiss writes, "The practices of a victim-centered justice seek to recognize the dignity and voice of those who have suffered. . . . Justice as recognition entails acknowledging the distinctive identity of the other, striving to repair damage done to him or her through violence, stigmatization, and disrespect, and including his or her stories in our collective histories."[12] Without the acknowledgment and honor of identity, the heart is unable to heal from the pain and alienation that others' rejection of this identity has caused it.

Symbolic Peacemaking

Symbolic peacemaking can take on many forms, including honoring of another's rituals, the joint partaking of a meal, or a public handshake. The type of symbol used will of course depend on the cultural traditions of the victims and offenders. Regardless of which forms it takes, however, the assumption of symbolic peacemaking is that the deepest things in life go beyond words, and that deeds—symbolic deeds—evoke trust and change in ways that sometimes words cannot accomplish.[13]

Confessional Peacemaking

The value of confessional peacemaking cannot be overestimated. Those rare moments in which people publicly acknowledge some wrong that they or their group has committed open an abundance of opportunities for healing and for individual and social transformation. This public acknowledgment of wrongdoing acts as a kind of participatory drama that often evokes counter-responses and dynamics of its own. Sometimes the response to such a confession is immediate, sometimes years later, but the effect on the human psyche is unmistakable. Confession entails a certain degree of self-humiliation, even though it can and should be buttressed by a group that honors such gestures. Nevertheless, that moment of deliberate self-humiliation is a partial restoration of honor to the recipient of such a confession, reestablishing a sense of moral equality between the victim and the offender.[14]

Visionary Peacemaking

Visionary peacemaking entails the creation of an atmosphere that encourages hope by virtue of examples of success and survival. It requires a quiet confidence, patience, and faith that people eventually learn the futility of violence. For some it induces healing through trust in Providence or trust in historical turns; for others, trust in becoming an instrument of God's plan. This is a kind of simultaneous surrender to and empowerment by the forces of history, or the power of God's guidance. It has features of childhood and adulthood that interlace, mixing freely, as do our moods and emotional states. It appeals to the hope and innocence of our childhood—the part of us that believes everything is possible, and believes in the inherent goodness of man. And it appeals to the rationality of our adulthood—the part of us that can look back on history and see positive examples of changed persons and redeemed situations. Visionary peacemaking is concerned with the cultivation of trust and hope in the possibilities of the future.

Narrative Peacemaking

For half a century Caux has used the well-known elements of story and narrative in its peacemaking initiatives. Indeed, Caux is a living example that there is no substitute for the truth of story in conflicts where we continually despair of knowing the truth. A parade of honest stories from war zones always brings people closer to effective peacemaking and further away from fruitless political slogans.[15] Alex Boraine, Deputy Chairperson of South Africa's Truth and Reconciliation Commission (TRC), writes that "By facilitating the telling of 'stories,' the TRC not only helped to uncover the existing facts about past abuses but also assisted in the creation of 'narrative truth.' The TRC contributed to the process of reconciliation by giving voice to individual subjective experiences. The TRC was about the task of 'restored' memory and humanity."[16] The diversity of stories, in particular, is what deepens understanding. Personal stories skewer platitudes of blame, and expose unexpected heroes and saints on all sides. At first such knowledge yields some despair as we face the absence of simple solutions, but in the end it brings us closer to individual people and their needs—and this is the essence of peacemaking.

Psychodramatic Peacemaking

Drama, in all of its manifestations, has always played a critical role at Caux. Both the staged productions and the unexpected drama of public meetings between enemies who are ready to apologize or forgive are important components of the healing process that takes place. Drama has a way of inculcating vision in ways that abstract conversations cannot. It reaches a deeper place in us. Of course, its message can be manipulative depending on one's point of view or the intentions of those who have authored the message. Therefore, as we encourage the use of the dramatic we must always be aware of its implied messages and whether those messages are inclusive and realistic, whether they enlighten or manipulate. Drama, however, both planned and spontaneous, has a great potential for healing and restoration in the lives of both victims and offenders.

Humble Peacemaking

Humility plays a crucial role in successful peacemaking, for without humility there can be no forgiveness. Philosopher Joram Graf Haber argues that forgiveness is inextricably linked to the virtue of humility. Using the Christian parable of the unforgiving servant (Matthew 18:23–25) as an illustration, he explains that human beings consider offering forgiveness to others because "we ourselves are in need of forgiveness." Thus, forgiveness is only offered when the victim realizes his or her own need for forgiveness—in essence embodying the virtue of humility.[17] Likewise, humility is both the moral and spiritual foundation of listening skills and the active display of compassion for both sides even when one's bias is to side with one group. Humility is critical in the process of working with others in groups—whether they are groups as small as two people or as large as an entire organization. Humility is not a skill, and not even a way of being. Rather it is a struggle with our desire to pursue what we think is right versus what others think is right.

Agreeing with what other people think is right is not always beneficial, however. Humility must be distinguished from self-deprecation and under-confidence, which are never helpful to the process of peacemaking. Most of the great peacemakers I know walk a fine line between pride in some of their work and silence about work that they have done (for which others will no doubt take credit). Walking this line is a kind of discipline that shuns the kind of pride that destroys the objective of the peacemaker, but also shuns the kind of self-deprecation that is destructive to the human spirit and to the sustainability of the peacemaker. Balance, therefore, is key to the heart of the peacemaker. Ideally if we, as peacemakers, remain humble but are praised for who we are by our colleagues then the balance we seek will satisfy all hearts. Since this ideal is rarely fully achieved we must aim for an Aristotelian mean between humility and self-appreciation in order to help others find balance and inner healing.[18]

Devotional Peacemaking

Participants at Caux deliberately and consciously cultivate the kind of anticipatory meditation and prayer that awaits a voice within, a kind of self-instruction that is believed to be from God. (In some ways this is a classic Protestant style of engagement with the spiritual life.) It is only natural to ask: Why would it have a salutary effect on peacemaking? Why would it be proper to encourage enemies to engage in such behavior? These are difficult questions that in some ways only have existential or personal answers. In my experience, the inner voice is the voice of intuition. It is the voice of clarity that rises above the cacophony of external information as well as the cacophony of conflicting cognitive analyses and internal emotions. There is no greater characteristic of deadly conflict than the pervasive and enervating reality of chaos and complexity. Intuition that seems to be outside of ourselves—and perhaps it is—touches on a higher capacity in human beings that we do not fully understand. But it is undoubtedly the case that those who do not at least try to do this often become tricked by their own basest instincts. Self-reflection is a chance to liberate oneself from confusion and place a bright light upon one's darkest instincts, see them for what they are, and then try to see something else.

Scaling Up Spiritual Peacemaking

The single greatest tragedy of most peace work is its limited effect. Even when its programs are excellent and its representatives are the best, their work cannot match the overwhelming power of violence to destroy what they do. Most people are ten times more conscious of the violence that surrounds them than the peace that surrounds them. Why? Put simply, peace is quiet and violence is loud—peacemakers do things in quiet ways for the few, whereas war instigators do things loudly and appeal to the many.

And it is the latter that modern technology has so dangerously amplified, at the expense of the former. If the twentieth century teaches nothing else, it is that the media and technology—the airwaves, the microchip, the website—are like a latter-day sacred trust. As with all things sacred they have great power, a power that, at times, can be demonic. There would have been no mass murder quick enough to be successful in the previous century without the wonders of technology. It is a sacred trust that has been violated and usurped by killers and predators of many different kinds in a number of different cultures.

We can no longer afford to ignore its captivating power over the human heart, and we can no longer afford the kind of peacemaking and healing of hearts that is exclusively private. Yes, peacemaking in person is more real, more authentic. But the power of the virtual has shifted our reality for the worse. We must compete on the global stage for the billions of hearts and minds that are daily being infiltrated by evil, and we must find more creative ways to do this. The media must become a place in which many of the aforementioned categories of healing the heart can be realized. This is the direction of the future.

In many ways, the power of the media represents a complete shift in privileges. The media are more individualistic—less subject to traditional hierarchies of religion, for example—and yet more dependent than ever on astonishingly large sums of money. It is no surprise, then, that religions can be shifted dramatically by whoever controls the message.

That is not to say that poverty or social injustices do not play a major role in the kind of message made and received. But it is also the case that suffering people make vastly different choices in history depending on the message they hear and the power of its delivery. Some riot and kill, others proclaim a messianic arrival, others retreat to mysticism, and others strive for wealth as testimony to their "chosenness" or better destiny. Still others hear the message of nonviolent social struggle and democracy. Some hear the message of revolution and others of evolution. Some are told that love is the answer and others are told that hate is the answer. Thus, despite the poverty and desperation of a people's situation, it is the message that matters. It always has been. The message of healing hearts as a way to peace and security needs to see the light of day in the virtual reality of every teenager, not just in the private reality of retreat centers and conferences. This is our great task.

The Complexity and Simplicity of Love

It is a tradition at Caux that at least several people, sometimes many, accompany you to the train station near the retreat center as you depart. I remember in the summer of 2000, as my family departed, the good-byes were long and heartfelt. As the train pulled out of the station and slowly started down the mountain I told my daughter Ruthie, who was four, to take one last look at the house and the gardens surrounding Caux. As she looked she began to wail in a way that I had never heard before; it felt ancient. We had left family before, many times, but I had never seen this kind of reaction from her. I believe to this day that my daughter was expressing a feeling that we were all experiencing. The one word that comes to mind is "beloved." So many people embraced her presence at Caux. So many made her feel safe and wanted. She craves that like one craves water in a desert.

When all is said and done, there is nothing simpler nor more profound that we can do for each other in war and in conflict than give the gift of love. It is a rare gift and not everyone can or should give love to everyone else. If it is given away too lightly it becomes disingenuous. But if we can find an enemy to love, then we have changed the world. We have changed the world because, at a minimum, we have changed ourselves.

I know all the books and papers I have written and the speeches I have delivered for peace, and the back channels that I have sought. But little of it really matters in the end. What matters is the Sheikh in Palestine to whom I became a beloved brother, as we mourned together, as his voice and face became implanted in my heart, and mine in his, and as we wept together for the sacred family of Abraham. One day, at the end of one of a thousand fruitless phone calls to the West Bank, my Jewish rabbi and friend asked me to send a message to a Muslim Palestinian officer with whom he had worked for years to create peace. Direct contact was too dangerous for the Palestinian, but the message he passed back to my rabbi through me, as the bombs were falling like rain, was "Tell him that I love him." I broke as I heard those words. I broke because "love" was the word that surrounded all of my frenetic behavior, a word that I could not utter for fear that it would crush me with its weight. "How can one fall in love with these people precisely when they are dying?" I would think to myself. And yet I did. Not with many—I have also been filled with much rage at people on both sides. But love is a gift in the worst of times that we dare not squander, and we dare not desist from it, for it is often the one last bridge that has not been destroyed. The Talmud said thousands of years ago, "Who is a true hero? He who can make those who hate him into those who love him."[19] Love is a victory in the midst of war that no one can take away, and it is sometimes the only font of hope.

The best jewels of our inner lives, our generous emotions, are untapped resources of conflict resolution, and in an era when so many resources have been marshaled to kill we must not squander them. Like all jewels they can be easily damaged and misused; they can easily become an excuse to ignore the necessary rational constructs of conflict management, de-escalation, diplomacy, and settlement. Denying their reality, however, is the *least* realistic path to take for those who want to turn a violent, injured world less violent, for those who are serious about undermining prevailing constructs of hatred. Armed with the power of both a rational mind and a creative heart, we stand a far better chance of constructing bridges across the barriers of religions and civilizations.

Notes

1. I would like to thank Rebecca Miller, Research Associate at the Institute for Global Engagement, for her assistance in the preparation of this chapter.

2. John Arthur and William H. Shaw, eds., *Justice and Economic Distribution* (Englewood Cliffs, NJ: Prentice-Hall Inc., 1991).

3. See Robert Nozick, "Distributive Justice," in Arthur and Shaw, *Justice and Economic Distribution*, 57–102. This has been largely the experience of immigrant groups in the United States, for example, with the exception being any minority group that consistently lacked equal opportunity due to ingrained prejudice, such as was the experience of African Americans.

4. See David A. Crocker, "Retribution and Reconciliation," *Report from the Institute for Philosophy and Public Policy* (winter/spring 2002).

5. For a further exploration of this point, see Thomas Hobbes, *Leviathan*, and the political theories drawn from Hobbes's basic picture of the "state of nature."

6. See Martha Minow, *Between Vengeance and Forgiveness: Facing History after Genocide and Mass Violence* (Boston: Beacon Press, 1998), 65–70, 91–117.

7. See Minow, *Between Vengeance and Forgiveness*, and Robert I. Rotberg and Dennis Thompson, *Truth v. Justice: The Morality of Truth Commissions* (Princeton, NJ: Princeton University Press, 2000).

8. For more information about Caux and Initiatives of Change, visit their website at www.caux.ch/en/.

9. Witness, by contrast, the pervasive tales and beliefs regarding poisoning and cannibalism that permeate centuries of distrust in some cultures. Deliberate food poisoning and cannibalism are the exact antithesis of food's general effects in creating comfort and trust.

10. For a further exploration of the role of religion in conflict resolution, see Marc Gopin, *Holy War, Holy Peace: How Religion Can Bring Peace to the Middle East* (New York: Oxford University Press, 2002).

11. Nancy Fraser, "From Redistribution to Recognition? Dilemmas of Justice in a 'Postsocialist' Age," in her collection of essays, *Justice Interruptus: Critical Reflections on the "Postsocialist" Condition* (New York: Routledge, 1997), 11–39.

12. Elizabeth Kiss, "Moral Ambition Within and Beyond Political Constraints: Reflections on Restorative Justice," in *Truth v. Justice*, ed. Rotberg and Thompson, 73.

13. For a discussion of the need for symbolic peacemaking in the Israeli-Palestinian conflict through the use of the traditional *teshuva* and *sulh* rituals, see Marc Gopin, "Forgiveness as an Element of Conflict Resolution in Religious Cultures: Walking the Tightrope of Reconciliation and Justice," in *Reconciliation, Coexistence, and Justice in Interethnic Conflicts: Theory and Practice*, ed. Mohamed Abu-Nimer (Lanham, MD: Lexington Books, 2001).

14. Jean Hampton, "The Retributive Idea," in *Forgiveness and Mercy*, ed. Jeffrie G. Murphy and Jean Hampton (New York: Cambridge University Press, 1988), 95.

15. See Minow, *Between Vengeance and Forgiveness*.

16. Alex Boraine, "Truth and Reconciliation in South Africa: The Third Way," in *Truth v. Justice*, ed. Rotberg and Thompson, 152.

17. Joram Graf Haber, *Forgiveness* (Savage, MD: Rowman & Littlefield, 1991).

18. See Minow, *Between Vengeance and Forgiveness*, and Rotberg and Thompson, *Truth v. Justice*.

19. *Avot of Rabbi Nathan* 23:1.

RELIGIOUS FREEDOM AND SECURITY: THE CIVIL SOCIETY NEXUS

9

Neither Sacred Nor Secular: A Public Anthropology of Human Dignity, Religious Freedom, and Security

Kevin J. Hasson

O N PAPER, EVERYBODY AGREES. Countries as varied as Cuba, Egypt, and France all profess their belief in religious liberty. What is more, they all profess their agreement that religious liberty is not just a legal right; it is also a basic human one.[1]

But they do profess too much.

Cuba, for its part, is lying. That it bothers to lie is eloquent testimony, though, to the widespread consensus that there are such things as human rights to which even a thuggish regime like Cuba must at least pay lip service. It seems that even a pariah state cannot afford to admit to the world community that it actually opposes religious liberty. It would be like publicly opposing motherhood. And France and Egypt, while they don't appear to be lying, exactly, couldn't possibly be farther apart on what religious liberty means. It is one thing to agree that there are human rights, or moral constraints on power that follow from human nature. It is quite another to agree on what that nature is.

Every society has its answer to that question. Put differently, every civil society is suffused with a public philosophy of some kind, whether articulated

Kevin J. Hasson is the founder and president of the Becket Fund for Religious Liberty, a public interest legal and educational institute that protects the free expression of all religious traditions. He has specialized in religious freedom cases for fifteen years. Before founding the Becket Fund in 1994, Hasson was an attorney at Williams & Connolly in Washington, D.C., where he focused on religious liberty litigation. From 1986 to 1987 he served as Attorney-Advisor for the U.S. Department of Justice's Office of Legal Counsel.

or not. It is made up of the predominant assumptions about the great ideas—ideas about God and man, the nature of society and the state, freedom and responsibility, and so forth. We don't recall when or where we learned them, they are just presumed to be true. For example, few Americans have read Einstein. But every McDonald's clerk can tell you that "all things are relative." Most people don't read Kierkegaard, but many still remark on the need for "a leap of faith." These sorts of assumptions compose the lens through which we view the issues of the day. A critical aspect of a society's public philosophy is its anthropology, its implicit understanding of who human beings are and what makes them tick. To take a simple example, in the same way that any McDonald's clerk will tell you that "all things are relative," any American will tell you that "all men and women are created equal." This is a particularly important facet of America's public philosophy, and one that differs significantly from, say, Saudi Arabia's or even England's public philosophy.

What place does public anthropology have in an essay on religious liberty and security? A very important one. The most serious security threats of the modern era have emanated from various forms of totalitarianism and its disregard for human rights, especially religious human rights. A robust, stable understanding of religion as a human right is thus a bulwark against security breakdowns. And this understanding is best understood as a manifestation of a kind of public anthropology in international civil society—that is, a diffused consensus on the nature of human dignity.

Indeed, the foundational document integrating religious freedom into the international human rights consensus, the Universal Declaration of Human Rights, proceeds on that basis. While the Universal Declaration does not lay out a systematic grounding for human rights, it nevertheless hints at one. Its preamble implies that the fundamental error behind totalitarianism is not firstly an error of political theory, but an error about the human person. Because it was precisely a "disregard and contempt for human rights" which lay behind those "barbarous acts which have outraged the conscience of mankind," the preamble says, it was necessary to insist that it is "the inherent dignity and . . . the equal and inalienable rights of all members of the human family [that] is the foundation of freedom, justice and peace in the world."

This focus on dignity was not accidental. When the delegates from the fifty-eight nations of the Human Rights Commission surveyed world leaders as diverse as Mahatma Gandhi, Pierre Teilhard de Chardin, and Aldous Huxley, they found surprising agreement on a basic enumeration of rights. Yet when the Commission began its debates, the wide range of members' philosophies and religious backgrounds precluded consensus on recognizing divine revelation or natural law as the source for human rights. However, human dignity was the one foundation *all* participants could agree on, even countries with poor human rights records. It was the one notion that bridged the widest ideological divides and made possible international agreement on the protection of important human rights.[2]

But why did the Universal Declaration signers insist that the foundation for "peace in the world" lies in recognizing and protecting inherent human dignity? While it is impossible to divine the reasoning of every signer, we can look to context to hazard a guess. It is agreed that the modern human rights movement was a direct response to the nightmarish experiences of the Second World War. The belligerent regimes of the time can be likened to illegitimate surgeons that promised radical cures for the human condition. These human rights offenders fraudulently diagnosed humanity's ailments and thereby switched healthy tissue for cancer. Their attempts at social cures, pretextual as they were, in actuality did extraordinary violence to the human person and for too long the world allowed it to occur. Although this analogy is admittedly a coarse oversimplification, the basic point endures—doctors as well as nations must first do no harm. While much of the world now agrees with this principle, it remains manifestly impossible to apply if we fail to recognize the patient for what he or she truly is and seeks to be.

Simply put, the question of human rights in general, and of religious liberty in particular, all boils down to one basic (and anthropological) question: who are we? As the renowned historian of religion, Mircea Eliade, famously described human beings, we are members of the species "*homo religiosus.*"[3] Human beings typically come with a built-in thirst for the transcendent. They may not know who, or even if, God is, but they have a natural desire to find out. It is a desire that may be repressed or even ignored. But nevertheless it is natural to human beings to wonder about and search out the possibility that there is a God. In the words of Abraham Maslow, "spiritual life is . . . part of the human essence. It is a defining characteristic of human nature . . . without which human nature is not full human nature."[4]

This is not a new idea. It is a common point of all world religions, and is also firmly rooted in the classical Western tradition. It is, for example, vintage Aristotle. But if it is not merely new, it is also not merely old. It is a prominent feature of personalist philosophy, as well as of Vatican II and the Universal Declaration on Human Rights. And if the Gallup polls year after year are to be believed, it is the anthropology accepted by the vast majority of Americans.

What is more, the human religious impulse is intimately bound up with a social impulse. We are born with the desire for community. While each of us is unique, we humans are nevertheless social creatures, eager to form families, gather in clans and tribes, display our arts, and commemorate with ritual the great events of life. This, once again, is vintage Aristotle—book one of the Politics. (In fact, the English word "idiot" derives from the Greek, *idiotes*, meaning a private person, i.e., one who does not participate in the life of the *polis*. Aristotle, in other words, wouldn't hesitate to describe postmodern, autonomous, self-seeking loners as idiots. And, as usual, he would be right.) Although authentic religious expression is often intensely personal, it is never as radically "privatized" as current fashion would have it. Religious experience deals with transcendent questions and so, when one finds even a hint of truth about the matter, that knowledge is rarely bottled up—at least not voluntarily. Across cultures people cannot resist publicly commenting about the weather; should we not expect even greater interest when the topic turns to the weather *maker*? Knowledge remains one of the few resources that enrich both the receiver and the giver. The receiver, of course, learns something not known before and grows in wisdom. Yet the giver also gains as not one bit of the imparted knowledge is lost but rather it is tested and refined and the giver soon becomes the teacher. In this manner knowledge of the transcendent spreads through society, organically.

These human phenomena, moreover, are not mere brute facts without moral consequence. These aspects of our nature are so central to who we are as persons that they make it immoral for anyone to coerce our belief or our unbelief, our religious observance and celebration or our lack of them. Indeed, hunger for the divine and thirst for community are so fundamental that they warrant legal protection as a matter of foundational law. They are, in other words, the source of our religious liberty.

The religious impulse holds the potential for the highest form of human flourishing and is thus a wellspring of our universal dignity. It is among those characteristics unique to human beings that give each and every person inestimable value. That potential, however, can only be achieved in freedom. Religious belief or expression undertaken under coercion or duress can hardly be described as religious at all.

Free cultivation of human religious potential is also essential to social harmony. Not only does religious repression give rise to civil strife and insecurity seemingly as durable as the religious impulse itself, but social cohesion depends on the transmission of those virtues typically fostered by religious participation. In the words of George Washington, "Reason and experience both forbid us to expect that national morality can prevail in exclusion of religious principle."[5]

Accordingly, governments at all levels should acknowledge human religious potential, avoid interference with its full expression, and actively promote its voluntary cultivation. In short, we humans come with a built-in thirst for the transcendent and a built-in desire to live in community. We therefore require freedom to do two things: first, to search with authenticity for the transcendent; and second, to express in the full measure of our humanity—in the arts, in public worship, and in political discourse—what it is we believe we've found. Because the religious impulse is natural to human beings, religious expression is natural to human culture. Thus, religious liberty acts as the great stabilizing force of society because it provides the opportunity for fulfillment that all persons instinctively yearn for. Religious freedom is at once a release valve and a common ground. Even when starkly separated by creed, religious believers share a common understanding; much like two hikers, though carrying differing maps, still share a bond as travelers.

When a culture's public philosophy accords with this understanding of the human person (i.e., when it accords with this anthropology), the culture will at least aspire to authentic religious freedom. When it does not, however—when it holds some other anthropology—it will recognize only a correspondingly deformed vision of that right and must suffer the consequences.

Let us follow the *via negativa* and examine three examples of what authentic religious freedom is *not*, ways in which governments often *fail* to respect the religious impulses and institutions of their people. Specifically, those failures are: state-imposed atheism; state-imposed religion; and state-imposed secularism. Each phenomenon is useful to study because each demonstrates the importance and precise contours of the particular facet of religious liberty that it offends. Since religious liberty acts as a moderating agent between extreme (and erroneous) views of human nature, every attack on this liberty has profound implications for global security.

In the case of state-imposed atheism, the religious impulse is targeted for repression because it is considered both a source of illusion and a threat to the hegemony of the state. In an atheistic regime, religion is condemned, first of all, because it is thought to be false. (It is ironic that "truth" and "falsity" could even be meaningful categories in an atheistic regime.) Perhaps more importantly, religious expression, especially in institutional form, is considered dangerous because it represents a source of authority that does not originate in, or otherwise depend upon, the state. The spiritual authority of religion, moreover, claims *superiority* to the temporal authority of the state.[6] Thus, religion offers a competing vantage point from which citizens may effectively critique and oppose government action.

Although this anthropology does not deny the religious nature of humanity, it errs in evaluating that nature by condemning it rather than exalting it. On this view, the religious impulse certainly exists (or else there would be nothing systematically to repress), but that impulse *ought* to be repressed because it has no object in reality and precludes totalitarianism.

The most concrete example of state-imposed atheism was the frightening Soviet experiment in global social engineering. From Karl Marx's condemnation of religion as the "opium of the people"[7] came the pseudoscientific efforts to eliminate all traces of religion from public and private life. Religion in the Soviet bloc, though never completely eliminated, was systematically ripped out of the ancient fabric of society and unraveled in the name of utopian progress. The Communist experiment was that of a mad scientist. With such a great stabilizing force removed, the resultant social upheaval was as predictable as it was brutal. The extent of Soviet cruelty arose from the gnawing fear that someone, somewhere, was putting God ahead of the state. The consequences for global security could not have been more profound.

By the latest dependable reckoning, over 100 million have died under Communist oppression.[8] 100 million. The destabilizing effect of such carnage needs no elaboration—*res ipsa loquitur*. Unfortunately, this great lesson has been too little publicized or too quickly discounted. The fact remains: it is no mere coincidence that the ideology that most thoroughly oppressed religious liberty also presented the greatest threat to world peace in a generation (if we consider nuclear weapons, it arguably posed the greatest threat in human history). God and religion were literally seen as a disorder that the Soviets attempted to "cure" in an ideological quest to alleviate human alienation. But that is likely too charitable a characterization. Soviet communism was so obsessed with achieving a future utopia that the sacrifice of the present, even if it meant armed conflict and oppression, was deemed a price well worth paying. The Communist worldview drafted the human person into the service of an abusive and all-encompassing state precisely because there was no religious freedom (and thereby no religious adherents) to act as an external check on Communist designs. That the Communist enterprise was by nature globally destabilizing is not surprising; state-imposed atheism unleashed an appetite that knew no bounds, and country after country quickly fell.

By contrast, where a state imposes one religion (or, less commonly, more than one), it affirms both the existence and value of the universal craving for God. Indeed, in a theocracy, satisfying that human need is deemed so urgent that the state will employ any means to that end. The stakes are so high—whether the fate of citizens' immortal souls, or the protection of society from corrosive forces—that the state considers itself justified in using force to exact religious observance.

But the conception of human nature implicit in this approach misunderstands the religious impulse. There is no exigency—spiritual, social, or otherwise—that warrants coercing religious belief or observance, by the sword or even by more subtle means. This is not because spiritual and social problems are unimportant, but because mandating religious adherence is not an effective remedy. In fact, enforced religion will only worsen those problems. Religion at gunpoint is merely the semblance of religion, not the real thing. Exacting such empty conformity does nothing either to vindicate our humanity or to promote social harmony; even the overzealous state would be disappointed with this result. Indeed, theocracies *preclude* genuine adherence to whatever religion they enforce, because they squelch that freedom that is a necessary condition for authentic embrace of *any* religion. Religious coercion also commonly meets intense resistance, risking civil strife that would tatter the fabric of civil society. In short, if a government seeks to maximize the religious flourishing of its people, as well as the individual and collective goods attendant to that flourishing, mandatory observance will not achieve that result—freedom will.

A recent example of the failed theocratic model is the shameful experience of the Taliban regime in Afghanistan. Throughout the 1980s, a particularly strong religious motivation helped the Afghan mujahideen, or "holy warriors," to confront and eventually repel the Soviet invasion of Afghanistan. However, in the ensuing power vacuum, it was the Taliban that consolidated control over most of the country after much bloody conflict with competing factions. Once in power, the Taliban regime proceeded to go off the proverbial deep end. Women were barred from schools and work, apostasy was punished by death, and even something as seemingly innocuous as beard length was strictly regulated. It was as if the Taliban were saying "if religion is good for the people then by God they shall have it!" The Taliban's mistaken anthropology placed violence at the service of superficial religious conformity.

In March 2001, the world held its collective breath as it learned that the Taliban was about to shell two majestic Buddha statues carved into the remote cliffs of Bamiyan, Afghanistan. The ancient Buddhas, among the tallest in the world, had withstood the ravages of 1,800 years, but crumbled before the Taliban's intolerance. The destruction was instantly condemned by countries around the world, including Muslim nations. These cultural treasures, ironically coming from a generally nonproselytizing religion, were obliterated in a stunning display of fear, fear of religious liberty. But the Taliban did not stop with statues. Once such fear is actualized it is notoriously difficult to contain, and having hijacked the good name of Islam, the Taliban quickly became the world's greatest exporter of terror.

Beyond state-imposed atheism and state-imposed religion, there is yet a third problem: even in contemporary democracies, where religious freedom is affirmed by the state, there remains the risk of state-imposed secularism. Although this is typically the result of well-intentioned but overzealous opposition to state-imposed religion, it is occasionally based on the same contempt for religion that animates state-imposed atheism. In either case, the nominal goal is government "neutrality" with respect to religion, but the actual effect is the banishment of religion from public life. The laudable institutional separation of church and state becomes the unworkable separation of anything religious from anything political. Thus, religious values must not inform any public moral debate, much less any legislative action that might issue from such a debate. Though the state may not specifically target religion for suppression, the state remains free to act in callous disregard of it. Indeed, the "neutrality" of the state may be called into question if the state accommodates, or otherwise acts with sensitivity toward, religious expression.

Even if forced to acknowledge that human beings are religious by nature, and that their religiosity bears implications for all aspects of their lives, including the political, the secularist might respond that the role of religion in politics should still be minimized. But this view reflects yet another anthropological mistake, one implicit in state-imposed atheism: the notion that cultivation of human religious potential is harmful to society and the state, rather than essential to their well-being. By treating religious contributions to public debate as out of bounds or merely tolerable, the state needlessly deprives itself (and, in turn, the people it exists to serve) of the rich moral and political resources that so many religious traditions hold in stewardship for the benefit of all. In the same way, by failing to affirm the singular importance of religious observance in the lives of its citizens, and by insisting instead on regulating extraordinary and mundane behavior on the same terms, the state harms those religious communities and institutions that serve as the seedbeds of virtue. Thus, democracies that embrace religious freedom can avoid lapsing into state-imposed secularism by acknowledging that the presence of religion in public life is not merely inevitable, but invaluable.

Eastern Europe is a good example of all three sorts of lapse. Virtually from its founding in the late tenth century, the Jewish community in Prague fell victim to the acts and omissions of theocratic governments. Prague Jews were confined to the ghetto for over seven hundred years, were prohibited from holding public office, and were temporarily expelled from the city on several occasions. With little or no recourse to the law, thousands of Jews were killed by angry mobs incited by pernicious rumors. These crimes are obvious sins against religious freedom. Nevertheless they are worth recalling—in large part because they were not always held to be obvious. And in some places they still aren't.

It has been the atheist states in the twentieth century, however, that have committed the most horrific offenses against the peoples of Eastern Europe and especially the Jews. The crimes of the Nazis were followed by the official atheism and brutal religious repression of communism—also obvious, never to be forgotten.

And most recently, the problem of secularization has emerged along with democracy. Notwithstanding the long history of governmental repression of religion in Eastern Europe, many people, and especially religious adherents, view the prospect of Western-style democracy with more fear than hope. As Czech President Vaclav Havel has put it:

The main source of objections would seem to be what many societies see as the inevitable product or by-product of these [democratic] values: moral relativism, materialism, the denial of any kind of spirituality, a proud disdain for everything supra-personal, a profound crisis of authority and the resulting general decay, a frenzied consumerism, a lack of solidarity, the selfish cult of material success, the absence of faith in a higher order of things or simply in eternity, an expansionist mentality that holds in contempt everything that in any way resists the dreary standardization and rationalism of technical civilization.[9]

France trumpets its secular government, working hard to erect a high wall between religion and the state. But that high wall comes at a price. Every year, several French public schools expel Muslim girls for wearing the hijab, or head scarf.[10] France wants to take this practice nationwide, and has introduced legislation that bans hijabs, yarmulkes, large crosses, and all other "conspicuous" religious items from public schools. It fears that such symbols will corrode the secularity of the state.[11] (In a nationally televised speech on the subject, President Chirac put it succinctly: "Secularism is not negotiable."[12]) In characteristic French form, schoolgirls will be allowed to wear any scarves that stylishly pay homage to the god of fashion, but none that reverently honor the God of Abraham. The French objection is to anyone who would dare to be openly religious in the public square. (At the other end of the spectrum lie the religious authorities of Saudi Arabia, who infamously locked girls inside a burning campus when they didn't take the time to put on their hijabs before fleeing the fire.[13])

Again, the problem with this approach is anthropological: "neutrality," or what the French call "secularism," is understood to require the state to ignore the religious nature of humanity, to pretend it does not exist, rather than to acknowledge, accommodate, and promote it in an evenhanded way. But the human desire to seek the truth, and especially religious truth, cannot be overlooked, much less eliminated. Moreover, convictions derived from religious inquiry unavoidably inform moral decision-making, which, in turn, unavoidably informs political decision-making. It is mere fiction (alas, happy and useful to some) that these intimately entwined aspects of human thought and social action can somehow be extricated from one another. Similarly, human beings will never cease to distinguish the sacred from the profane, and so will always require, to varying degrees, exceptions to generalized rules of behavior for purposes of religious observance. In short, it is quite simply impossible to ignore or eliminate these hard-wired patterns of human being, whether for the sake of drawing a neat-and-tidy distinction between religion and politics, or for any other purpose.

Muslim countries, too, are less than edified by French-style secularism. It quite literally doesn't translate well. When the English word "secular" is translated into Arabic, it translates as "almehni." The problem? "Almehni" is more equivalent to the English word "godless." So rather than a wall of separation, we get active hostility. And therein lies the danger. Secularism by its very nature has a hard edge. When secularism accommodates and encourages all but the religious viewpoint, we should expect religious believers to feel targeted and discriminated against. Indeed, the growing unrest in countries like France may soon escalate as the secular pressure becomes too much to bear. When large segments of society are officially branded outsiders because of their religious identity, there is a real risk of radicalization. Every civil rights movement known to history has had radical factions, though usually small, that eventually reject nonviolence as ineffective or unjust. This is a lesson from history that should not be overlooked when considering secularism's implications for security.

Religious communities, of course, have an essential role to play in addressing these problems, because they have singular access to hearts and minds of their people. By forming their own in the virtues that make for good souls and good citizens, strong religious communities assure that their traditions persist and thrive. But they also assure that the public square will remain clothed with the values of which it is so often stripped in Western democracies, and which are necessary for the acceptance and longevity of democracy.

So if French-style secularism is inconsistent with human dignity, and so are theocracy and official atheism, what does a state that understands the human person look like? The answer is that such a state is neither "godless" nor "religious" per se. Rather it welcomes religious expression—from all traditions—into culture just as it does ethnic expression from all traditions. It affirms its citizens' thirst for transcendence (e.g., with moments of silence and similar observances), but it keeps its thumb scrupulously off the scales, taking no position in theological debates. It is not secular, as "secular" government implies something adverse to religion, but neither is it sacred. A better fit would be the Arabic word "dunyawi," best translated into English as "temporal." It's not hostile to religion; it's just not unduly concerned with it. Such a state understands that healthy citizens naturally require room for religious expression—space to breathe religion on their own, if you will. Thus a healthy state will neither suffocate nor forcibly intubate their citizens on matters religious. A state that accommodates the religious aspirations of its citizenry promotes stability and security for a very simple reason: such a state accurately recognizes who its citizens are.

Notes

1. I would like to thank Roger T. Severino for his assistance in the preparation of this essay.

2. See generally, Mary Ann Glendon, "Propter Honoris Respectum: Knowing the Universal Declaration of Human Rights," *Notre Dame Law Review* 73, no. 5 (1998): 1153, 1155–56.

3. See Eliade Mircea, *The Sacred and the Profane: The Nature of Religion* (New York: Harcourt, 1959).

4. A. H. Maslow, *The Farther Reaches of Human Nature* (Harmondsworth, Middlesex: Penguin Books, 1973), 341.

5. Farewell Address by George Washington (September 17, 1796), in *A Compilation of the Messages and Papers of the Presidents, 1789–1908*, ed. I. J. Richardson (Washington, DC: Bureau of National Literature and Art, 1908), 220.

6. Jacques Maritain, *Man and the State* (Chicago: University of Chicago Press, 1951), 153.

7. Karl Marx, introduction to *A Contribution to the Critique of Hegel's Philosophy of Right. Deutsch-Französische Jahrbücher* (February 1844).

8. See Stéphane Courtois, Nicolas Werth, Jean-Louis Panné, Andrzej Paczkowski, Karel Bartosek, and Jean-Louis Margolin, *The Black Book of Communism: Crimes, Terror, Repression* (Cambridge, MA: Harvard University Press, 1999).

9. Vaclav Havel, "Forgetting We Are Not God," *First Things* 59 (January 1996): 37.

10. Keith B. Richburg, "French President Urges Ban On Head Scarves in Schools; Chirac Confronts Spread of Islam," *Washington Post*, 18 December 2003, A1.

11. Christopher Marquis, "U.S. Chides France on Effort to Bar Religious Garb in Schools," *New York Times*, 18 December 2003, A8.

12. Richburg, "French President Urges Ban," A1.

13. Mona Eltahawy, "They Died for Lack of a Head Scarf," *Washington Post*, 19 March 2003, Editorial, A21.

10

Relational Realism: Toward a New Political Paradigm for Security

Harold H. Saunders

R ELIGIOUS DIFFERENCE has long been a focus of conflict. In the post–Cold War world it has replaced political ideology as the focus of conflict in significant parts of the world. Deep human grievances are widely expressed in the language of religious extremism. How, then, can security and religious freedom coexist? There are, of course, tensions and trade-offs, but the positive meeting ground between religious freedom and security is ultimately to be found in the dynamic of *inclusion*. The dialogical openness of a civil society that respects religious freedom while agreeing on limits to its excesses provides an effective avenue of inclusion to those who otherwise would feel excluded and alienated. Religious freedom defined in open dialogue can offer citizens an opportunity to express their convictions freely in ways that do not harm others. However, in those cases when religious "freedom" is manipulated into a harmful agenda toward others under the auspices of divine sanction, limits will have to be defined. This is neither avoidable nor illegitimate.

While religious freedom must be defended, like all other aspects of freedom it must be balanced with the interests of the greater body politic. The key is to ensure that this balancing process is itself characterized by the inclusive ethic

Harold H. Saunders is director of international affairs at the Charles F. Kettering Foundation. He worked for twenty years at the National Security Council in the White House and the State Department. He was a key member of the U.S. team that mediated five Arab-Israeli agreements, and he helped negotiate the release of U.S. hostages from Tehran in 1981. His awards include the President's Award for Distinguished Federal Civilian Service, and his publications include *A Public Peace Process: Sustained Dialogue to Transform Racial and Ethnic Conflicts* (St. Martin's Press, 1999).

of a participatory dialogue in civil society. Religiously inspired violence is usually conducted by private citizens without government sanction. For this reason, governmental solutions may not be effective. Harsh repression only
breeds resentment among the silenced group, and violence is often the language of the voiceless. Any solution to religious violence, then, must come
from citizens.

Here I offer an alternative security paradigm that builds on sustained dialogue among citizens to form relationships of peace: relational realism. I believe
that citizens in sustained dialogical encounter can become a microcosm of their
communities, experiencing a change in relationships, and then learning to design political actions and interactions that can change their larger societies.
Using my experience with the Inter-Tajik Dialogue within the framework of the
Dartmouth Conference as a model, I want to present the advantages of approaching security through a relational, instead of a "realist," paradigm.[1]

Getting "Real"

There is an essential real-world connection between religious freedom and national security. It is practical, and it must be worked out by each society
through its own political processes. It is not simply a matter of principle to be
accepted or rejected. It must be negotiated and established by thoughtful citizens as they struggle for their own social balance on the issue. Yet principles
and practices are inextricably intertwined, and we will not be able to effectively nurture the nexus between religious freedom and security unless we first
change the reigning conceptual framework of realpolitik.

Four decades of experience have taught me that the so-called realpolitik or
"realist" paradigm is not, in fact, realistic. It does not define a workable policy
option in a complex world, nor does it embrace the politics of whole bodies
politic. It does not provide a realistic prescription for establishing a workable
connection between the practice of religious freedom and national security.
Why? Because it is state-centered. It does not provide adequate conceptual
space or tools for the inclusion in our analysis of the full complex of human
interactions that contribute to (or subvert) security. Relationships—within
and between whole societies, among citizens in and out of government—are
as concrete a "reality" as bricks and mortar shells. Any paradigm that leaves
human beings, with all of their spiritual and emotional needs and aspirations,
out of the picture is unrealistic indeed. It is at this human, relational level
where real security and religion meet.

Our first step must be to replace the realist paradigm with a paradigm more
richly realistic for the twenty-first century. I would substitute what I call the

relational paradigm. The relational paradigm starts from the premise that politics is not only about power. It is about relationship, of which power is only one—and not always the most important—component. A simplified statement of the relational paradigm would focus on politics as a process of continuous interactions across permeable borders among citizens on multiple levels. "Politics," rightly understood, is about relationships of identity, interests, and power (the latter defined not as control but as the capacity to influence the course of events), perceptions, and patterns of interaction.

This contrasts to the realist paradigm, which focuses on leaders of states amassing economic and military power to confront other states in zero-sum confrontations for control. To be sure, there are important and enduring elements of truth in the emphases of realpolitik, but the paradigm has numerous weaknesses. Most important is that its state-centered focus does not provide space for inclusion in our analysis of the full array of relevant interactions and relationships among citizens in civil society as well as in government. The realist paradigm leaves human beings out of the picture and provides no space for religion—an especially problematic omission in our current international context. Religion shapes and is shaped by all the dimensions of politics, and in today's geopolitical struggles the relevance of religion—both as part of the security problem and part of the security solution—is clear.

We must find a way of treating religion and religious freedom not just as "soft" culture but "hard" geopolitics. It is an urgent task for practitioners as well as scholars, and it is primarily from the perspective of the former that I write. Experience working with five presidents of the United States, other world leaders, and people in deep-rooted human conflict has taught me that the conceptual lenses we use to bring into focus the world around us and to give meaning to events largely determine how we act. Until we get our basic assumptions about how the world works—our paradigm—straight, we will not meet the challenges of this new century. We will have no space for talking about religious freedom and national security because we will have no space for defining national security in holistically human terms.

It is from that perspective that I address the political realities that shape our discussion of religious freedom and national security. In this charge I am working from two propositions. First is the familiar statement that freedom defined in a religious context is qualified by the fact that it is exercised within a discipline of service to the believer's God. For instance, the God of the Old Testament told Pharaoh not simply, "Let my people go," but "Let my people go that they may serve me" (Exodus 7:16; 8:1, 20; 9:1, 13; 10:3).[2] In the New Testament, as Richard Bauckman has noted, the principle of "mutual service" reflects the thought that those in authority "are to exercise their authority in such a way that it is just as much service to their slaves as the slave's work is service to them."[3] Those in the early church "did not attempt to abolish [the existing structures of political and social subjection in their contemporary society] in the name of freedom, but they did attempt to transform them from within by turning them into relationships of voluntary and (where possible) *mutual* subjection."[4] In short, freedom defined in a religious context is defined in relationship—relationship to God and to fellow human beings.

Second, when we put the concepts of religious freedom and national security together we add to disciplined freedom the further requirements of common social-political life. Consider the example of the United States. There religious freedom is defined in specific terms that (1) recognize a basic human right to determine one's own relationship to God and (2) restrict the power of state and government to intrude on that relationship. The concept of national security, on the other hand, introduces the right of the state, not to intrude on a person's right to choose his or her way of relating (or not relating) to God, but to define limits on the *practice* of religion. Freedom in secular terms has long been defined with the limitation that its exercise not impinge on the freedom of others. The concept of national security may cause government itself, or religious organizations and other citizens outside government, to define specific further limits to the exercise of freedom to protect the interests of the larger society.

The challenging question in any society is how those further limits on religious freedom will be defined. It is my thesis that they can only be defined properly by citizens in a political process—that is, "politics" in its richest, relational sense. What limits will citizens accept on their exercise of religious freedom? If governments, elite international organizations, or authoritarian leaders alone attempt that definition, they risk creating grounds for a challenge to national security, rather than creating a politically acceptable balance between religious freedom and national security.

A Case Study of Tajikistan

My thoughts about these political realities are formulated from ten years of personal experience in the former Soviet republic of Tajikistan, located on the southernmost Soviet borders, next to Afghanistan. The 5.5 million Tajikistanis live this problem every day, and I know firsthand that their experience is a valuable case study, a microcosm of the challenge and opportunity we must face in international affairs today.

It should come as no surprise that Tajikistan has a history of excluding a vast majority of its citizens from the political process. Throughout the Soviet era, political power was held by Communist party members who comprised an elite minority. Tajikistan, however, is a diverse land with many linguistic, regional, and ethnic differences. When communism started to crumble, the stage was set for the formation of new opposition groups, hungry for political participation.[5]

Gorbachev's *perestroika* opened the door for the formation of *Rastokhez*, a movement that advocated religious freedom and the return of traditional Tajiki language in schools. In 1990, however, the government blamed *Rastokhez* for inducing violent riots in the capital two weeks prior to Tajikistan's first parliamentary elections. The government's response was predictably heavy-handed; it banned all opposition parties from participating in the elections. Tajikistan's first parliamentary elections produced a largely old-line Communist parliament.

After the 1990 election, several new opposition parties—including the Democratic Party of Tajikistan and the Islamic Renaissance Party—united to back an opposition presidential candidate in the November 1991 elections. The opposition candidate was defeated in an election most observers described as rigged. The new regime—consisting mostly of former Communist officials—passed a series of repressive measures to prevent the opposition parties from gaining any role in government.

The opposition parties, now excluded from the political process, resorted to violence. The year 1992 saw violent clashes between the opposition forces and the government forces (the latter were reinforced by the Russian army). In hopes of ending the violence, then-President Rahmon Nabiyev formed a coalition government involving the opposition parties. This upset the extremist elements in the governing structure, who declared the new government invalid, since the parliament, which failed to reach a quorum, did not approve it. The result: more violence.

In September 1992, President Nabiyev was forced to resign at gunpoint and opposition forces made Akbarsho Iskandarov president of a government of "national reconciliation." By December 1992, however, Iskandarov resigned and government forces regained power. In order to consolidate power, progovernment forces conducted a campaign of executions, looting, and terror against anyone affiliated with opposition parties. The government also imposed a ban on all opposition parties, as well as their media. This resulted in mass displacement of refugees into Afghanistan. From 1993 sporadic fighting continued along the Tajikistan-Afghanistan border as well as inside Tajikistan. Finally, in 1997 a three-year United Nations mediation produced a peace treaty.

Since then, Tajikistan has begun the long, hard work of reconciliation—a process that has been challenging, but also hopeful and instructive. The point that the Tajikistani case underscores for our purposes here is that the nexus between religious freedom and national security, along with crucial political relationships, must be shaped and reshaped through a continuous political process of dialogue among citizens in and out of government—not by decree and not by force.

First, a word of background about my choice of the Tajikistan example. When I left government in 1981, I became involved in the Dartmouth Conference, which is the longest continuous bilateral dialogue between citizens of the Soviet Union and of the United States. Almost immediately, I became the cochair of a newly formed task force to probe Soviet-U.S. interactions in regional conflicts—places such as the Middle East, Angola, and Afghanistan where the superpowers competed through local proxies. Our purpose in this probing was to understand more deeply the central Soviet-U.S. relationship.

The Dartmouth Conference Regional Conflicts Task Force, as it was called, met every six months throughout the 1980s; it meets to this day. My Soviet cochair was Evgeny Primakov, who later became the Foreign Minister and then the Prime Minister of the new Russia in the 1990s. As we met, we began to understand that a succession of regular meetings made possible the transformation of relationships. From that experience I conceptualized a five-stage process of what I came to call "Sustained Dialogue."[6]

Sustained Dialogue is a public peace process that builds trust and consensus among citizens as a solution to violence. The five stages of the process are not rigid, and one should not expect a linear progression through the process, but instead an organic process that moves back and forth among different stages so that each party's concerns are addressed when needed. The stages are there, however, to measure progress and to focus the dialogues towards an achievable goal.

The first stage of any peace process is choosing to engage. All sides of the conflict must decide that an effort to achieve peace is preferable to the current situation. Then, individuals reflecting the experience and thinking of each side should be chosen—not high-ranking government officials, but respected community leaders who have access to both the leadership and also public opinion. This is important because the dialogue must truly represent the interests and concerns of the citizens involved in the conflict.

The second stage of the Sustained Dialogue is mapping the problems and relationships involved in the conflict. The participants must identify the main problems that affect relationships among them, and begin mapping all the significant relationships that are responsible for conflict. What, for example, are the causes of civil war? What are possible ways out? What are the interests of the main groups involved? This stage is important because the parameters of the dialogue are fleshed out; it surfaces the relationships that must be changed if an enduring peace is to be achieved.

After mapping the relationship, participants move on to the third stage: probing the dynamics of the relationship. At this stage, the dialogue moves past simply identifying the problem to genuine dialogue, in depth, on one or more specific aspects of the problem they have chosen to focus on first. They examine the problem from all angles, consider possible approaches to it, weigh the consequences of those approaches, and perhaps come to some judgment on one of them. If they wish, they can then move on to think about what actions they might take. All this may take several meetings.

The participants are now ready to move to the fourth stage: building scenarios. In this stage, the participants must devise practical steps to gradually transform their relationship. They should identify obstacles that could prevent them from moving in that direction, think of steps that can be taken in the political arena to remove those obstacles, and then identify actors capable of taking those steps. Lastly, they design a scenario of interactive steps that draw others into the action and are mutually reinforcing.

Finally, after agreeing to engage, mapping and probing the conflictual relationships, weighing possible approaches, and designing a process of interactive steps, the participants should be ready to act together towards the goal they now share. Of course, this is where realism and idealism meet, and it is very difficult for participants to move to this stage. Nevertheless, the Tajikistani Sustained Dialogue is an example of how relationships in conflict can be transformed into relationships of cooperation.

Let me turn now to how the participants in the Inter-Tajik Dialogue progressed through the five stages of Sustained Dialogue. In 1993, six members of the Dartmouth Conference Regional Conflicts Task Force—three Americans and three Russians—invited into their space individuals reflecting the views of the different factions of the civil war that had broken out in Tajikistan shortly after independence. At the peak of a vicious civil war, our Russian colleagues were able to identify nine Tajikistanis who were willing to risk dialogue at a time when there was no other communication between government and opposition. They sat down together in a Moscow conference room in March 1993, barely able to look at each other. By March 1994, they had played a role in precipitating decisions to join UN-mediated negotiations and had written a joint memorandum, "A Negotiating Process for Tajikistan." Three of them joined the teams that negotiated a peace treaty in 1997. Five participated in the National Reconciliation Commission that followed. On March 21, 2003, the Inter-Tajik Dialogue within the framework of the Dartmouth Conference, as the participants came to call themselves, met for the thirty-fifth time and celebrated its tenth anniversary.

In March 2000, members of the Dialogue created their own nongovernmental organization, the Public Committee for Democratic Processes in Tajikistan. Among their projects the Public Committee has launched sustained dialogues in seven regions of the country to deal with the critical subject, "State,

Religion, and Society." This topic has poignant meaning in a country with the only legitimate Islamic political party in Central Asia, a country in which Islamic elements formed a significant part of the United Tajik Opposition during the vicious civil war, a country now coping with Islamic extremists returning from the madrassas of Afghanistan and Pakistan. The Public Committee decided to use the process of Sustained Dialogue as the methodology for bringing nuclei of citizens together to address this challenge—defining the nexus between the practice of religious freedom and the need to shape and protect national identity where none existed before.

There are two central insights, each of wider application, that I have formulated from my experience working with Tajikistanis: the politics of inclusion and the politics of balance.

The Politics of Inclusion

First, religious freedom can make a significant contribution to national security by offering *inclusion* in political life to important elements of society that heretofore have been excluded. It can be a critical step in overcoming division and alienation. Even before the Soviet Union dissolved, a few senior Islamic clerics met to form Islamic parties for their own Soviet republics. In a meeting in 1989, the Islamic Renaissance Party (IRP) of Tajikistan was born. After independence, members and followers of the IRP joined with democrats and nationalists attempting to revive traditional Tajik culture in a coalition which won 30 percent of the vote for its candidate in the first post-Soviet presidential election. Having lost, they pressed the man elected president—a former Communist leader—for inclusion in the governing process. In the first full year of independence, they mounted demonstrations, gained a position in a coalition government, eventually forced the president to resign, and governed the country for four months at the end of 1992, before they were ousted by militias reflecting elements of former Communist power. They then went into armed opposition, and one of the bloodiest civil wars on former Soviet territory ensued.

The issue was inclusion—not just on the basis of religious demographics but on the basis of religious and political identities. When the war began, the opposition was fragmented. In December 1993, these factions formed the United Tajik Opposition. It included ideologies ranging across the political spectrum from moderate democrats to Islamic extremists. At that point, the issue was not explicitly religious freedom: the coalition functioned on the basis of an inclusive collaboration across diverse ideological boundaries.

Because the civil war was fought between the government and this ideologically diffuse opposition, the peace treaty was negotiated under United Nations mediation (1994–1997) between the government and that opposition. As a result, the Islamic Renaissance Party (IRP) became a legitimate political party in what the constitution defined, after considerable debate, as a "secular, democratic Tajikistan." Inclusion of the IRP was a critical step toward consolidation of national peace and security—a critical step, but not completion of that task.

The debate over that phrase—a "secular, democratic Tajikistan"—revealed a division within the Islamic elements themselves, a division that points up the delicate dynamic between religious freedom and national security. The Islamists who signed the peace treaty, negotiated the constitution, and became part of the new government had agreed to work within constitutional bounds. Extremist Islamic organizations charged them with "selling out" Islamic principles and aspirations. Some of them—for example, a group called Hizb ut-Tahrir (Liberation Party)—went underground with the intent of developing an Islamic caliphate across Central Asia. In such circumstances, religious beliefs can be manipulated by committed ideologues to inspire actions that threaten national security in its broadest sense—and, in the end, could threaten the full practice of religious freedom.

The Politics of Balance

My second point is that when a polity must deal with this threat of overthrow, limitations on the exercise of religious freedom must be discussed in a genuinely realistic (that is, *relationally* realistic) social-political context. At best, as in Tajikistan so far, these discussions take place in a collaborative way in a number of forums, each focusing on a particular facet of the problem.

Participants in the Inter-Tajik Dialogue have discussed this problem on a number of occasions. The Public Committee for Democratic Processes (the NGO that they created) began establishing its regional dialogue groups in 2001. Once, when I was leading a training session on "Freedom of Belief and National Security" among moderators of these dialogues, I was told of an elderly man in one of their dialogues who said: "We know who the extremists are. They live in our neighborhoods; they live on our streets; they even live in our homes. Our hope lies in bringing them into dialogue with us. We probably cannot talk with the hard-bitten leaders, but we can talk with the rank and file and perhaps draw them away from extremist leadership and practice." This insight is a vivid example of how participants can begin to imagine a desirable scenario towards which they can work.

In their regional dialogues, and in the dialogues among moderators, these Tajikistani citizens reveal important examples of how difficult it can be to find a religion-security balance in an environment where it has long been missing.

First, as citizens of a country barely twelve years old, cut loose suddenly and unexpectedly from more than two generations of obliterating totalitarian rule, they are now weighing two elements of their identity. In their words, they are trying to find a balance between their emerging national identity and their religious identity. They never experienced a national identity of their own. Most Westerners look at them as post-Soviets, and in some ways that is true. But deep beneath that surface, they never lost their Muslim faith and culture—and, after all, Islam is a way of life. Now they face a deep schism in their own religious worldview, a schism between what they call "political Islam" and "traditional Islam." They are torn between those who would use Islam to control secular power and those who would live a devout life in a constitutionally defined democratic secular state.

In one dialogue I conducted, they defined security in terms of protecting their constitutional order, which legitimizes freedom of religious faith and the existence of an Islamic party. They defined threats to their national security as threats to that constitutional order. To be sure, many Tajikistanis still see a constitution as merely a document, not as the embodiment of a way of life as most Americans do. Still, they recognize that it defines a polity that they want to preserve and develop. They recognize that the government, Islamic leaders, and citizens outside government are collectively responsible for making the hard choices that responsible freedom demands—defining and implementing practical measures to limit religious practices that could undermine their constitutional order, while at the same time maintaining conditions for a sustainable civil society characterized by respect for religious rights.

Alongside these regional dialogues, they are discussing a balance between, on the one hand, the government's formation of a religious council to provide a structure of governance for religious activities, and on the other hand the preservation of a meaningful role for citizens of faith. The Islamic clergy feels it needs the support of a structure in which they and government can work together. This would involve some sort of council including government officials and certain figures in the Islamic community. Senior Islamic clerics are deeply concerned by the deteriorating quality of education in Islamic schools and the deteriorating qualifications of Islamic clergy. Many newer clerics are returning from radical schools in Afghanistan and Pakistan and are opening "nonofficial" mosques and schools in many rural areas of Tajikistan. Often, according to Islamic participants in the Inter-Tajik Dialogue, these clerics are almost illiterate. So the senior clergy have raised the question among themselves of an Islamic council to set standards for the clergy and for Islamic schools.

In short, the clergy recognize that if holistic, sustainable national security is to be preserved, the practice of religious freedom must be subject to the same judicious and balanced governance as other freedoms. At the same time, senior government officials recognize that in their particular social context the disciplined practice of religion is essential to formation of a genuine national identity.

On the secular side, participants in the Dialogue, through their Public Committee for Democratic Practices, have recognized that they as citizens outside government must play an important role in preventing the growth of an extremist expression of Islam that threatens the constitutional order. On several occasions over the last two years, they have talked in depth about what causes young people to go into extremist organizations. Their answer: lack of hope to earn a living, lack of a voice in their own future in their communities, and lack of a larger purpose in life.

They are realistic in recognizing that leaders of extremist organizations are often educated ideologues, not poverty-stricken misfits. They are, at the same time, realistic in recognizing that many young people are drawn into extremist ranks because they have no hope of inclusion in the political or economic mainstream. Participants, then, must share a vision of a brighter future with these same young people, for people will only change conflictual relationships when they have hope that their lives afterward can be better than before.

Participants in the Dialogue see important roots of extremism in alienation and exclusion from the mainstream of life. Their response is not the response of realpolitik. Rather, their response is that the government alone cannot solve this problem. Solving it is the responsibility of citizens in and out of government in constructive dialogue—in other words, it is the responsibility of the whole body politic. Taking action, then, must be a relational activity, with both government and the citizenry working toward a desired goal.[7]

To be sure, the polity's ability to provide economic and political opportunities within the mainstream—that is, to draw potential extremists into the mainstream—is critical. But so is its own effort at a human level to engage citizens, in government and across spheres of civil society, in a continuous process of dialogue.

This suggests, in sum, that for religious freedom to be more than wishful thinking it must go hand in hand with the opportunity to experience practical participation in the larger society. This will happen only when we begin to view national security through a relational paradigm—one that takes advantage of the resources of the entire polity. The result will be a solution born of compromise and cooperation, which is the best defense against extremism. The nexus between religious freedom and national security must be shaped and reshaped through a continuous political process of dialogue, not by decree and not by force.

Notes

1. I would like to thank Dane Shelly, Research Associate at the Institute for Global Engagement, for his assistance in the preparation of this essay.

2. Richard Bauckham, *God and the Crisis of Freedom: Biblical and Contemporary Perspectives* (Louisville: Westminster John Knox Press, 2002), 9.

3. Bauckham, *God and the Crisis of Freedom*, 15.

4. Bauckham, *God and the Crisis of Freedom*, 15–16.

5. For a more complete history of the postindependence history of Tajikistan, see Randa M. Slim and Harold H. Saunders, "Managing Conflict in Divided Societies: Lessons from Tajikistan," *Negotiation Journal* 12, no. 1 (January 1996): 31–46.

6. For a full description of the process of Sustained Dialogue, see Harold H. Saunders, *A Public Peace Process: Sustained Dialogue to Transform Racial and Ethnic Conflicts* (New York: St. Martin's Press, 1999; Palgrave paperback 2001). Chapter 7 describes the experience of the Inter-Tajik Dialogue through its first five years in detail. For current writing please see the website of the International Institute for Sustained Dialogue, www.sustaineddialogue.org.

7. For an in-depth look at the cooperation between government and citizens in the Tajikistani dialogue, see Harold H. Saunders, "The Multilevel Peace Process in Tajikistan," in *Herding Cats: Multiparty Mediation in a Complex World*, ed. Chester A. Crocker, Fen Osler Hampson, and Pamela Aall (Washington, DC: United States Institute of Peace Press, 1999), chapter 8.

Conclusion: A Lively Experiment, A Most Flourishing Civil State

Robert A. Seiple

THERE HAVE BEEN TWO ENDURING REACTIONS to the atrocity we now casually call "9/11." First, there is surprise, a dangerously persistent attitude of bewilderment that has transcended the initial mind-numbing event. There is surprise that the first war of the twenty-first century is a religious war conducted not by countries with major ideological differences, but by nonstate actors resisting the perceived negative impact of modernity. There is surprise that these new antagonists, who are desperately seeking weapons of mass destruction, would come armed with scissors, box cutters, and a terribly focused rage. There is surprise that our first line of defense may now be police officers, firefighters, and air traffic controllers—perhaps even postal workers. The conventional defense establishment, with its wire diagrams and multibillion-dollar procurement budgets, could not prevent war waged by an asymmetric, flat, decentralized network of holy warriors. We were surprised by 9/11, and that surprise continues.

The second enduring reaction is that security has moved to the top of our hierarchy of values. We are aware of our vulnerability in a new way. Indeed, the security issue remains so prevalent today that any organization that cannot define its mission in the context of security risks irrelevancy. The single-issue human rights advocates, for example, are in trouble. Those who look at life through the lens of the moral imperative must get comfortable, quickly, with hard-nosed security specialists—and vice versa.

The real questions are these: can the human rights establishment and the security establishment exist comfortably together in a way that doesn't sacrifice relevance? Can these often disparate camps come together in a way that does not compromise rights out of fear? Can they work together in a way that does not replace values with false choices? The contributors to this volume have wrestled with these questions in what is perhaps the most complex yet urgent human rights context of our times—*religious* human rights. In this regard, they have shown that the challenge facing scholars and practitioners of international relations today is to create a common synergy between the moral imperative and realpolitik—that is, a mutual dependency and a positive nexus between religious freedom and security.

Often during my service in the U.S. State Department as the first-ever Ambassador-at-Large for International Religious Freedom (and even more often since leaving government in 2000 to found the Institute for Global Engagement, a think tank that works to cultivate sustainable environments for religious freedom for all faiths) I have been asked just what I mean by "religious freedom." By religious freedom, I specifically mean *soul freedom*: liberty of thought, conscience, and belief. Inherent in this definition is the assumption that for faith to be authentic, it has to be freely embraced. Notwithstanding all the contemporary hand-wringing over allegedly inevitable "civilization conflict" dividing the Judeo-Christian West from Islamic societies, this definition is widely shared among the children of Abraham. In the words of George Weigel, "The truth cannot be truly apprehended unless it is apprehended freely." Sheik Mohammed Sayed Tantawi, a respected Sunni Muslim leader from Al Azhar mosque in Cairo, says similarly, "If I force you to become a Muslim, I destroy Islam and I destroy myself. What you must have to come to the truth is freedom."[1]

Thomas Jefferson referred to religious liberty as the "First Freedom," demonstrating his own understanding that if the mind and heart are not free, nothing else really matters. Indeed, without religious freedom, none of the other rights such as freedom of the press, freedom of speech, or freedom of association will ever be credible or legitimate. Just as the true test of a government's commitment to liberal democracy is tolerance for opposition parties, the true test of commitment to civil society is religious freedom. This is the core of our being, a spiritual identity that works itself out in everyday activities. All of us who "work" this issue know people around the world who have demonstrated their willingness to die for this freedom.

We must also insist that religious liberty covers all faiths. The only sustainable objective of religious freedom promotion is a level playing field for all, a principled pluralism that eschews easy ecumenism and instead strives for justice and equal treatment. Martin Luther King provided a pragmatic echo to this thought when he stated succinctly, "If one is not free, no one is free." John Milton poetically pursued this point as well: "Though all the winds of doctrine were let loose to play upon the earth, so Truth be in the field, we do ingloriously, by licensing and prohibiting, to misdoubt her strength. Let her and Falsehood grapple: whoever knew Truth put to the worse in a free and open encounter?"[2]

In addition, in order to fully appreciate the positive nexus between religion and security, we need to ensure that we are not hamstrung by a pinched conception of the latter. Regrettably, in the fear-driven climate of today's war on terror, limited and short-sighted visions of security abound. Our aspiration should instead be to inclusive, holistic, and pre-emptive security—not just a missile shield for some, or the meticulous defense of national sovereignty at all costs, or the elitist security of a gated community.

In its most sustainable sense, security is generated through a successful fight against the causes of conflict. Poverty, illiteracy, loss of hope, despair—all conspire to create an environment of conflict. This is the "second front" in today's battle for an enduring security. We will certainly need to do more than simply eliminate today's terrorists, who are the symptoms and the outgrowth of much more complex and difficult environments. In the context of Afghanistan, for example, this inclusive vision of security is illustrated in the paradigmatic shift from mobilizing to win the war to winning the peace. As General Richard Meyers, Chairman of the Joint Chiefs of Staff, once remarked, U.S. forces have (too slowly) come to recognize the need to "adapt towards reconstruction." He was referring to a change of emphasis from the killing of a relative few to the creation of a positive environment for many. This is where the ultimate battle must be won if we are to achieve something more than simply a papered-over peace.

Saint Augustine's definition of peace, "the quietness of order," gets close to the heart of the matter. Inherent in such a definition is structured predictability that in turn depends on the presence of a critical mass of positive assumptions in civil society. This is the kind of peace and security that emerges from a values-based culture wherein freedom—especially the freedom of faith, the freedom of the soul—is protected.

Religion, Civil Society, and Security

What is it about a healthy civil society that can be mutually attractive to religion and security? Let me briefly summarize seven attractive elements of such a society. First, and perhaps most importantly, is *loyalty*.

Interestingly, this common-sense pragmatism appears very early in the religious history of the United States. The Rhode Island colonists, seeking to avoid the oppressive theocracy from which they fled, and a similar oppression from the Massachusetts Colony, forged the Rhode Island Charter from England in 1663:

They have ffreely declared, that it is a much on their hearts . . . to hold forth a livlie experiment, that a most flourishing civill state may stand and best bee maintained . . . with a full libertie in religious concernements; and that true pietye rightly grounded upon gospel principles, will give the best and greatest security to sovereignetye, and will lay in the hearts of men the strongest obligation to true loyalty.[3]

Religious freedom promotes security for the state through the captured loyalty of its citizens. Put simply, it is not hard to be loyal to a government that has our best interests at heart. For many of the American Founders, the nexus between religion and security was assumed. Loyalty continues to be a natural response of citizens to a government that promotes such religious freedom.

A second attraction is *shared values*, which are essential in creating civil society. I refer here to justice-oriented values, universal values, and natural law. It is such a contextual framework that allows for responsible political ideologies to take root. These are values that inform a government and shape how that government treats its people, especially its ethnic and religious minorities. This will say a great deal about how secure that country really is. Indeed, it is not too much to say that we can measure the extent to which a government truly embraces these shared values by how it deals with the issue of religious freedom. Religious freedom is a key marker on the continuum of human dignity and compassion.

Third is the attraction of *mutual accountability*. The security apparatus has to ensure that which contributes positively to its mission. Religious freedom, on the other hand, needs to hold security accountable to transcendent values. For this to work, it helps immeasurably if each is talking the same language, the language of practicality. Mutual accountability suggests much more than philosophical platitudes. Methodologies have to work—in faith-based terms, theology has to touch the ground.

Note how this works in the following example. In June 2002, the Institute for Global Engagement had a high-level government delegation from Laos visit the United States for fifteen days. The delegation was made up of members of the Lao National Front, the governing instrument in Laos that is responsible for the implementation of religious legislation. While they were with us, we exposed them to various governmental agencies, faith-based nongovernmental organizations, the entire spectrum of Lao-American groups, and a variety of cultural events. The underlying goal for the visit was to show the Lao that religion—practiced with integrity in an environment of synergy and accountability between security and religious freedom—poses no political threat to a government.

The highlight of the visit was a few hours spent on an Amish farm outside of Lancaster, Pennsylvania. After the farmer showed us various aspects of a working farm, he invited us into his home. He then began to talk to us about the Amish expression of worship. Worship was held in the home. Specifically, they met in the basement of that home. They were free to do so, a freedom that was protected by local, state, and federal authorities. You could almost see the wheels turn inside the Laotian officials' minds—a "house church" meeting "underground," servicing a minority faith, people who desire to be different. This "different" minority group was making a positive contribution to the society and the economy. They were doing so under the protection of a government, which was committed to the Amish's right to be different. Each was holding the other accountable for a relationship that was positive. Attractive societies specialize in such mutual accountability.

A fourth attraction of a values-based civil society is *responsible governance*, that is, a government system oriented toward ordered liberty rather than arbitrary paranoia. Such governments provoke a positive attitude about the need for religion unrestrained. Where there is no oppression, the potentially destabilizing "pushback" from religionists is eliminated.

This is, perhaps, common sense, but we always resist negative pressure. Psychologists call it "frustration aggression." Unfortunately, we see it far too often on today's world stage. Governments sometimes suppress what they neither understand nor control. This suppression is an unnatural restraint for individuals and they will inevitably resist it, either by overt or covert means. In China, for example, there has been suppression of the house church, because of its growth, and of the Falun Gong, because of its visibility. In both cases, those who are being oppressed resist—a natural reaction but one that can create a political problem. The irony of this is that, in the name of security, China has created a very insecure situation. China is failing to heed the lessons of history. As Lenin's first Commissar of Religion once noted, "Religion is like a nail. The harder you drive it, the deeper it goes."[4]

A fifth attraction is *moderation*. To be sure, we may not always know what "moderation" is—but we certainly know what it isn't. This is a value lost when governments overreach. In Uzbekistan, for example, the government of Islam Karimov has been threatened by a small terrorist group. On February 16, 1999, the threat was made dramatically real when this terrorist group bombed a government building in Tashkent, just a few minutes before Karimov was to be inside the building. In an instant, fear became legitimate—but the reaction to the bombing was extremely counterproductive. As detailed earlier in this volume, thousands of pious Muslims were thrown into jail, a classic overreach that had the effect of radicalizing moderate Muslims. Karimov's shortsighted crackdown ultimately prompted a report (March 2001) from the International Crisis

Group, commenting on security issues for the Central Asian countries, especially Uzbekistan: "Treat religious freedom as a security issue, not just a human
rights issue, and advocate unequivocally that regional security can only be assured if religious freedom is guaranteed and the legitimate activities of groups
and individuals are not suppressed."[5]

This report tapped some timeless truths, and echoed the Rhode Island
Charter of 1663. What was assumed by progressive visionaries of the seventeenth century is being recaptured in the pragmatics of the twenty-first century. In our contemporary context of escalating terrorism, it is tempting to
dismiss "moderation" as a pipe dream. But listen to Iran's President Khatami
in an extraordinary statement made to challenge the power of the hard-liners
in his country: "The best, most secure and legal option for this country is Islamic democracy, where both religion and freedoms are respected."[6]

This brings us to a sixth attractive characteristic of values-based civil societies: *respect*. Our mantra at the Institute for Global Engagement has been
for individuals to know their faith at its deepest and richest best, and
enough about their neighbor's faith in order to respect it. This respect is
more than a patronizingly thin form of "tolerance." Such tolerance is grace
applied to someone I don't especially care for, merely covering over that
which divides. Respect speaks to our common humanity and the celebration of the fact that each has been created in the image of God. This is not
universalism, but rather a profound understanding of divine intentionality.
Understanding our own faith and respecting our neighbor's is the single
greatest individual contribution that each of us can make to homeland security.

This is where, for instance, Osama bin Laden got it terribly wrong. He
adopted a truncated form of Islam and misunderstood the best of his faith. He
inappropriately applied the worst of his understandings, and he had absolutely no respect for the faith of others. Once this negative concoction is
placed into the hands of a religious zealot, bad things happen and security of
any kind is compromised. We remember the sad graffiti that appeared at
Ground Zero, "Oh God, deliver us from those who believe in You." Respect is
not a value for those with whom we are now at war.

A final attraction of a civil society is *diversity*, and the concomitant ability
to live with our deepest differences. Historically, religion has been one of those
deep differences. The seemingly inexhaustible array of identity conflicts
around the world suggests a troubling fact of human nature: we have real
problems living with those things that make us distinctively different, like religion or ethnicity. Writing in *Balkan Express*, Slavenka Draculic surveyed the
events in Europe over the last half of the twentieth century, and summarized
the situation with these sobering words: "History always repeats itself. . . .

Someone is always a Jew. Once the concept of otherness takes root, the unimaginable becomes possible."[7]

This is a key principle. It is why no one wants to be a minority in a hostile environment. Such an environment is destabilized by fear. The mantra of survival is to do it to "them" before "they" do it to you.

The effects of preferential treatment for some at the expense of others are always destabilizing. Religious freedom and security are immensely helped by a society that elevates diversity as a virtue. Still, there is cause to be careful. Our government officials said the right things about Islam, for example, immediately following the events of 9/11.[8] The question is, do we believe what we said? More importantly, do the Muslims believe us? Making diversity more than a slogan of political correctness is, in the final analysis, a security issue.

Let the People Go

This nexus can be contextualized by way of an historical example of what happens when religious freedom and security are *not* properly integrated—an example with particular salience to all of the Abrahamic faith traditions. I have already mentioned intranational identity conflicts, which have been so prevalent in recent years. My example, however, is not Rwanda, Bosnia, Kosovo, or the Spice Islands of Indonesia. Rather, it is the first biblically recorded identity conflict, a conflict that unfolds with all of its irony in the first several chapters of the book of Exodus, 3,500 years ago.

The patriarchal fathers—Abraham, Isaac, and Jacob—ultimately established themselves in the Promised Land, the land of Canaan on the eastern Mediterranean coast. Jacob, whose name would be changed to Israel, eventually had a dozen sons, one of whom, Joseph, managed to inspire a great deal of jealousy among his brethren. In fact, they got so fed up with him that they sold him into slavery, a terrible assault on his human rights and one that made him a refugee in Egypt. Joseph, in time, transcended the difficulties inherent in his situation, became something of an expert on food security, and rose to be indispensable to the pharaohs of Egypt, especially as they tried to deal with their episodic famines.

During one such famine, the regional severity was such that father Israel was compelled to send his sons into Egypt to see if food could be purchased from the surplus that was known to exist there. The ensuing negotiations brought the brothers face to face with Joseph, who made himself known to his brothers. A beautiful reconciliation was allowed to take place. Food was shared and, in due course, Joseph prevailed upon Pharaoh to allow his aging father and his brothers to come live in the land of Egypt. They did so, and they stayed for 430 years, assuming the role of an ethnic and religious minority living under the protection of Egypt. Indeed, it is important to recall that the nation of Israel was formed not in the Promised Land, but in the iron furnace of Egypt.

Over the centuries, the descendents of Israel prospered. Ultimately, there came an Egyptian Pharaoh who noted this prosperity, and began to fear it. This Pharaoh realized that the Hebrews were becoming more numerous, more visible, and more blessed. Fearing that his security was now in jeopardy, the Pharaoh launched three pre-emptive strikes against the ethnic and religious minority in his midst. First, he assigned and implemented oppressive work schedules for the Hebrews. Then he added impossible production schedules, demanding that the Hebrews make the same number of bricks each day with straw that would no longer be supplied by the Egyptian government. Finally, he violently oppressed the workforce, compromising its future by killing all of the Hebrew baby boys. At this point, we have a name for this horrific violation of human rights. It is called genocide.

The oppression of work, the beatings that took place when production schedules were not filled, the killing of innocents in the name of security—all represent what today would be labeled "gross violations" of every single international rights covenant, beginning with the Universal Declaration of Human Rights in 1948. To use the words of our own International Religious Freedom Act of 1998, this pharaonic oppression was "ongoing, systematic, and egregious." If this were happening today, we would designate Egypt a "Country of Particular Concern" more than worthy of stiff sanctions under the statute.

Pharaoh feared his security was in jeopardy. He essentially went to war with an internal minority group, negating any possibilities for a legitimate civil society that would have provided him with some of the security he desired. This is the painful irony, a classic overreach. As an Iraqi satirist once said, "The disease that is in us is from us."

The irony of the Exodus account deepens still further as one family's reaction to the imminent threat to a child named Moses was to set him afloat in a small basket in the bulrushes. Thus was the eventual leader of the Hebrews' liberation saved from the Pharaoh's order that all male babies be thrown into the Nile. Moses escaped the overreach caused by security concerns. Some eighty years later, chaos was visiting the land of Egypt, plagues that led to the destruction of this proud nation. Indeed it was Egyptian sons who were now being killed as the death angel passed over the land. To put it in present-day military terms, "hard power" lost out to "soft power," and the greatest military the world had ever seen was wiped out in the very same water whose bulrushes once protected a baby in a basket.

In this wrongheaded attempt to strengthen security, the seven critical elements of a healthy civil society were abused and attacked.

- Loyalty—it was, of course, impossible for the Egyptian regime to solicit support from slave labor; prisoners don't often vote for the incumbent.
- Shared values—this was a Pharaoh who "knew not Joseph," and thus there was very little in common and absolutely no corporate memory.
- Responsible governance—the Hebrews were made to live in a separate place (Goshen) and even Joseph wasn't allowed a seat at the Pharaoh's dinner table; a nonassimilating society is always potentially oppressive to minority groups.
- Moderation—this was abandoned out of immature fears and inability to see beyond the zero-sum game.
- Respect—human dignity is always the first casualty of an identity conflict, and in this case the result was escalating violence and genocidal strikes at the Hebrews.
- Diversity—the Pharaoh feared it so much that he tried to drown the babies of the "other" in his midst.

Again, "the disease that is in us is from us." It is not enough to say that Egypt was destroyed. More precisely, Egypt destroyed itself. Moses brings metaphor and reality together as he proclaims in his praise hymn (Exodus 15:5), "They sank into the depths like a stone." In short, the record of history is not kind to the overreaching oppressor.

A values-based civil society is the coin of the realm, and the two sides of that coin are religious freedom and security. Anything less than this is problematic at best and, at worst, capable of spawning chaotic violence of the most horrific kind.

What happened to that vulnerable baby floating in a basket in the bulrushes? The quick answer is this: he met an all-powerful God, a God who cemented a religious identity into a specific people-group. That people-group would now be a society that was values-based. When the Israelites left Egypt, they left with their religion and their security intact. Memories, realities, hopes—past, present, future—were now drawn together under a powerful mantra, "I am the Lord thy God who brought you out of the land of Egypt, out of the house of bondage."

This was a nation formed as "pilgrims in a foreign land" now realizing (with, I am sure, a deep sense of awe and mystery) that even with the Red Sea in front of them and a host of angry Egyptians behind them, they still had options. Their security and their freedom were one. Moses had led the persecuted, in faithful obedience, to a safe place. Exodus 15:19–20 captures it best:

When Pharaoh's horses, chariots and horsemen went into the sea, the Lord brought the waters of the sea back over them, but the Israelites walked through the sea on dry ground. Then Miriam . . . Aaron's sister, took a tambourine in her hand, and all of the women followed her with tambourines and dancing.

Morally Realistic, Realistically Moral

Security continues to be an issue for people of faith, but methodologies for obtaining it vary widely. Karl Barth had a simple but highly effective idea when he admonished those seeking to engage the world to go "with a Bible in one hand and a newspaper in the other." What did he mean? In my view, Barth's insight grew out of his appreciation of the necessary linkage between the moral imperative and realpolitik, that the world that we envision and the world that is must be better integrated. Today, the preeminent area of application is clear—the war for justice and the war against terrorism have to be integrated, and the touchstone of the effort must be religious freedom. The positive freedom "to" and the negative freedom "from" demand an understanding of each other, a nexus point of comprehension.

Jesus had something similar in mind when he employed two powerful metaphors for global engagement. He told his followers to be "gentle as a dove" and "shrewd as a snake" (Matthew 10:16). On the one hand, the need for sensitivity, humility, to have the skills of a good listener, cannot be overstated. But Jesus also made it very clear that we would need the streetwise common sense of the snake. It is not good enough to be one and not the other; to deny this is, as the theologians say, to go against the grain of the universe. Together, the dove and the snake are metaphors for concurrent methodologies—commonsensically wise and comprehensively relevant.

I conclude with one more historical illustration, a story that is more personal in nature. Before joining the State Department, I had the privilege of serving for many years as president of World Vision. In the early 1990s, World Vision, like many other humanitarian relief and development organizations, found itself in Somalia. Somalia was in the midst of a famine producing a whole host of starving children. The crisis was being exacerbated by a clash of Somali warlords, the worst possible congruence of natural and manmade catastrophes. Not unlike our previous historic example, a whole generation of children was about to be thrown into the proverbial Nile.

The humanitarian crisis was such that, ultimately, the United States deployed its military to the scene. As we at World Vision contemplated the possibility of an American military intervention, we hoped that the landing would take place at multiple points. Our work was concentrated in Baidoa, about 150 miles away from Mogadishu, the capital. We felt that if the U.S. military came ashore only in Mogadishu, a single point of entry, we would be highly vulnerable to all of the dangerous local elements that would inevitably push into our area of operation at Baidoa.

In the event, General Powell chose a single landing zone—Mogadishu. And, just as we expected, all of the "bad guys" promptly left Mogadishu and made their way to Baidoa. It would be more than two weeks before the U.S. military would bring ground security to the part of Somalia where we were working.

What to do? For starters, it was obvious that the humanitarians needed to find a way to work with those responsible for security, the military. This, of course, would bring together two seemingly disparate actors, one whose business was feeding hungry children, the other who dropped bombs for a living. But we did come together. I spent the greater part of a Saturday with aides to the Joint Chiefs devising a plan that turned out to be beautifully simple. Two or three times every day, on an unscheduled basis, we would have F-14 Tomcats fly over the town of Baidoa, at about 500 feet, with afterburners and full throttle. There may be no more fearful sight and deafening noise than this— certainly anyone thinking of "sinning" would recalibrate their intentions.

The plan worked. That daily show of considerable firepower kept the "bad guys" completely out of sight. The chickens didn't lay eggs for weeks, but our humanitarian work continued, and lives were saved.

What was going on here? On the one hand, we had a short-term need for security. This security not only helped provide conditions necessary to meet immediate needs, it also helped establish conditions under which work on longer-term security and stability could proceed. It was an instance of cooperation that, in those particular circumstances, served simultaneously to fight against a common enemy and support a common humanity. One bought the time necessary for the other to work on a more sustainable future. Realpolitik and the moral imperative came together.

This was done without replacing values with false choices. In the dusty town of Baidoa, Somalia, for the first time in a very long time, there was a substantial reduction in life's vulnerabilities. This vulnerability was replaced by hope—hope in the present, and greater expectation for a legitimate hope in the future.

The point is this: once we realized we had a mutually complementary "endgame," the nexus between us was not difficult to find. The nexus between religious freedom and security is also not as difficult to find as conventional wisdom often purports. Driving a wedge between religion and security is counterproductive. Instead, the second front of today's war for security—that is, the campaign for sustainable change and stable civil society—should be engaged in good faith by "realists" and "idealists" alike. While it will do no good, of course, to pretend that honest differences don't exist, the stakes are too high to indulge a spirit of partisanship that neglects the common ground that exists among all people, especially all children of Abraham. We must creatively and proactively seek that place where freedom *to* and freedom *from* become one, toward the end of a values-based civil society that is the true foundation for enduring security.

Notes

1. Sheik Mohammed Sayed Tantawi, quoted in Thomas Farr, "No Religion Can Flourish by Repression," *Times Colonist* (Victoria), 9 May 2003, A13.

2. John Milton, *Areopagitica,* 1643. This can be found at the Religious Freedom Page, University of Virginia, religiousfreedom.lib.virginia.edu (accessed 15 April 2004), which has archived many of the "sacred texts" of the history of religious freedom.

3. The Rhode Island Charter, 1663. Archived at the Avalon Project at Yale Law School: Documents in Law, History and Diplomacy, www.yale.edu/lawweb/avalon/ (accessed 15 April 2004).

4. The quote is attributed to USSR Commissar of Education Lunacharsky. See Bernard Pares, *Russia, Its Past and Present* (Denver, CO: Mentor Books, 1951).

5. International Crisis Group, "Central Asia: Islamist Mobilisation and Regional Security," March 1, 2001, www.crisisweb.org (accessed 15 April 2004).

6. President Khatami, quoted in "Iranian president makes bid for power," *The Montreal Gazette,* 29 August 2002, B1.

7. Slavenka Draculic, *Balkan Express* (New York: W. W. Norton & Co., 1993).

8. President Bush quickly emphasized that Islam, like all of the world's major religions, is peaceful. His words are inspiring: "These acts of violence against innocents violate the fundamental tenets of the Islamic faith. And it's important for my fellow Americans to understand that. The face of terror is not the true faith of Islam. That's not what Islam is all about. Islam is peace. These terrorists don't represent peace. They represent evil and war. When we think of Islam we think of a faith that brings comfort to a billion people around the world. Billions of people find comfort and solace and peace. And that's made brothers and sisters out of every race—out of every race." From a speech at the Islamic Center of Washington, D.C., on September 17, 2001, which can be found at www.whitehouse.gov/news/releases/2001/09/ (accessed 15 April 2004).

Index

About the Editors

Robert A. Seiple is founder and chairman of the board of the Institute for Global Engagement (IGE). IGE is a "think tank with legs" that works proactively to cultivate sustainable environments for religious freedom and educates emerging leaders in international affairs (www.globalengage.org). Prior to its foundation, he spent two years at the State Department as the first-ever U.S. Ambassador-at-Large for International Religious Freedom. He has spent his professional career in leadership positions, serving as: president of World Vision (the largest privately funded relief and development organization in the world) from 1987–1998, president of Eastern College and Eastern Baptist Theological Seminary (1983–1987), and director for athletics and the vice president for development at his alma mater, Brown University (1970–1983). His op-eds have appeared in numerous leading periodicals, and his books include *Ambassadors of Hope* (InterVarsity Press, 2004). He lectures widely and teaches classes in the Templeton Honors College at Eastern University.

Dennis R. Hoover is vice president for research and publications at the Institute for Global Engagement. He directs the Council on Faith & International Affairs (www.cfia.org) and is the editor of *The Brandywine Review of Faith & International Affairs*. Before joining the Institute, he was program associate at the Leonard E. Greenberg Center for the Study of Religion in Public Life at Trinity College in Hartford, Connecticut, where he was associate editor of the Center's journalism review magazine, *Religion in the*

News. He holds a doctorate in politics from Oxford University, and has taught political science courses at Eastern University, Trinity College, and Berry College. He has published in leading scholarly journals and magazines and has contributed chapters to several books, including *Sojourners in the Wilderness: The Christian Right in Comparative Perspective* (Lanham, MD: Rowman & Littlefield, 1997).